SAKHALIN

Japanese
1905-1945

MANCHURIA

(N)

KOREA

(S)

PEKING
+
TIENTSIN

SHANGHAI+

RYU KYU IS.
OKINAWA
In U.S.
occupation

THE
FAR EAST

Statute 0   100   200 Miles

CANTON
+

HONG KONG
(Br.)

MACAU
(Port.)

TAIWAN
(FORMOSA)

Areas held by Chinese Communists 15-8-45

Areas acknowledged as Communist by
KUOMINTANG Government

PHILIPPINES

116° 124° 132°

36°

28°

20°

116° 124°

CHINA
AND THE COLD WAR

CHINA
AND THE COLD WAR

A Study in International Politics

by

Michael Lindsay
(Lord Lindsay of Birker)

MELBOURNE UNIVERSITY PRESS

First published in 1955 by
Melbourne University Press, Carlton, N.3, Victoria;
printed and bound in Australia by
Wilke & Co. Ltd., 19-47 Jeffcott Street, Melbourne;
and registered in Australia for transmission by post
as a book

London & New York: Cambridge University Press

To friends in China

ACKNOWLEDGEMENTS

Acknowledgements are made to the following authors and publishers for permission to use extracts and quotations: George Orwell, *Shooting an Elephant and Other Essays* (Martin Secker & Warburg); George Orwell, *Nineteen Eighty-four* (Martin Secker & Warburg); Czeslaw Milosz, *The Captive Mind* (Martin Secker & Warburg); George F. Kennan, *American Diplomacy* (Martin Secker & Warburg); Maurice Dobb, *Soviet Economic Development since 1917* (Routledge & Kegan Paul); W. W. Rostow, *The Dynamics of Soviet Society* (W. W. Norton); E. H. Carr, *Twenty Years Crisis* (Macmillan); H. R. Trevor-Roper, *Last Days of Hitler* (Macmillan, London and New York); J. W. Wheeler-Bennett, *Munich—Prologue to Tragedy* (Macmillan, and Duell, Sloan & Pearce); Adrian Carton de Wiart, *Happy Odyssey* (Jonathan Cape); Louis Fischer, *The Soviets in World Affairs* (Jonathan Cape); Walter Görlitz, *The German General Staff* (Hollis & Carter); W. S. Churchill, *The Second World War* (Cassell, and Houghton Mifflin); Gustav Herling, *A World Apart* (Heinemann); Reginald Thompson, *Cry Korea* (Macdonald); Jacques Maritain, *The Range of Reason* (Geoffrey Bles); A. B. Ulam, *Titoism and the Cominform* (Harvard University Press); Anna Louise Strong, *Dawn out of China* (People's Publishing House); Philip Wylie, *Panic, Psychology and the Bomb* (Bulletin of Atomic Scientists); O. Lange, *Marxian Economics and Modern Economic Theory* (Review of Economic Studies).

CONTENTS

CONTENTS

INTRODUCTION

The origins of this book

In May, 1952, I joined with two of my colleagues at the Australian National University in drawing up a document which was taken to Peking by the Australian delegates to the Preliminary Conference for the Peking Peace Conference held in October of that year. The general theme of this document was that in Australia and other Western countries there was a very large body of influential opinion which would be ready to co-operate in any genuine attempt to work for peace. But the experience of people who had tried to co-operate with Communists in working for peace was not encouraging and had produced a very general suspicion that any movement or conference under Communist control would not be a genuine attempt to work for peace but only an attempt to use "peace" as an instrument for Stalinist propaganda. And the wording of the document proposing the Peking Conference and the past actions of some members of the Chinese sponsoring group intensified rather than allayed such suspicions. We therefore invited the sponsors of the conference to give a clear and unambiguous statement of their intentions to use the conference to discuss the conditions for peace and not simply as a means of propaganda, and assured them that such action would produce a widespread response.

It was originally intended to publish this document with a group of influential and representative signatures but, though the response in Australia was encouraging, the time available was too short to obtain enough signatures to warrant publication. So the document was sent to Peking as a private communication.

The only reply was a letter sent to me in June, 1952, by Mr. Rewi Alley, a New Zealander long resident in China who had been the main organizer of the Chinese Industrial Co-operatives and who is an enthusiastic supporter of the present regime. This letter dismissed any suspicions of Chinese sincerity in working for peace as entirely without foundation. To give a few illustrative quotations: "Can you, who knew something of the early struggle of the Chinese people to 'stand up' after centuries of exploitation and aggression, really imagine China as an aggressor?" "Today everyone talks of service for the motherland and adds, 'and the cause of world peace'. I have been away from home for a long time, but I ask you, do you Australians think every day in these terms of international goodwill?" Referring to internal conditions the letter says, "If only you could see it all as I have. It is China reborn in the old religious sense and strange as it may seem to you it is the Godless communist party which has led the way to this rebirth." And finally, "China needs all her old friends and a lot of new ones. But it needs not those who subjectively make mountains out of molehills."

A long reply to this letter was sent to Rewi Alley in July, 1952, but it was not acknowledged. Thinking that the letter might have been suppressed I eventually sent another copy through one of the Australian delegates who had been to the Peking Peace Conference. This second attempt produced a reply dated June, 1953, which admitted that the first copy of the letter had been received.

This second letter from Rewi Alley was a good illustration of the appropriateness of George Orwell's *Nineteen Eighty-four* for describing Communist thinking. His attitude had been perfectly described by Orwell's concept of *crimestop*—". . . the faculty of stopping short, as though by instinct, at the threshold of any dangerous thought. It includes the power of not grasping analogies, of failing to perceive logical errors, of misunderstanding the simplest arguments if they are inimical to [orthodox Communism], and of being bored and repelled by any train of thought which is capable of leading in a heretical direction."[1] Judging from the letter the only criticism which Rewi Alley had been able to understand was that the Chinese Communists refused to discuss peace except with people who already largely agreed with them. On every other point he had failed to understand my arguments and his replies were evasive, irrelevant, or question-begging. And some of the main arguments were not answered at all.

I wrote again in July, 1953, analysing the fallacies in Rewi Alley's second letter and ended by challenging him to substantiate his claim that the Chinese Communists were ready to discuss peace with anyone by trying to give a reasoned reply to my criticisms of Chinese foreign policy or, still better, by inducing someone in the Chinese Communist Party to do so. At the time of writing, June, 1954, this has produced no response.

Meanwhile, I had sent copies of my original letter to a number of people and these were passed on and recopied and seem to have reached a fairly large public. The *Nanyang Siang Pau* of Singapore asked for permission to publish a Chinese translation and has done so. A number of people suggested that the letter should be rewritten in a form suitable for publication and what follows is an attempt to do this.

Basically, what I have tried to do is to apply the standards of scientific method to a problem in international affairs. The original letter confined itself to an analysis of Chinese foreign policy and concluded that the evidence of Chinese behaviour was incompatible with the view that the Chinese Communists were acting with both good faith and good sense when they claimed to be working for peace. Numerous instances of Chinese Communist behaviour could only be explained either by the hypothesis that the Chinese Communist Party was not acting with good faith to promote peace or by the hypothesis that it was not acting rationally. In conclusion I urged Rewi Alley to combine his devotion to peace with some use of critical intelligence.

Writing at greater length it seemed unsatisfactory to leave the argument at this stage. A great deal of non-Communist opinion is inclined to accept the hypothesis of Communist bad faith without really considering the hypothesis of Communist irrationality. Whereas it seems to me that in many cases the hypothesis of Communist irrationality fits the facts better than the hypothesis of Communist bad faith. I have, therefore, gone on to discuss at some length the problem of Communist motivation and have tried to show that a great deal of Communist behaviour can be explained as the result of faith in the orthodox Marx-Leninist system. This in turn has obvious implications for the important practical problem of what non-Communist policy is most likely to promote peace. I have tried to draw some of these implications.

Finally, in criticizing Communist policy in terms of the standards of normal scientific method I am criticizing in terms of standards which Communists would not accept. A large part of my criticism is implied by a disagreement with orthodox Marx-Leninism about the nature of scientific knowledge. A proper discussion of this would mean writing a philosophical treatise which I have neither the qualifications nor the time to undertake. I have, however, added a short section entitled "The Standpoint of the Author" in which I have tried to summarize the basic assumptions and standards in terms of which I have judged Communist policies.

I have dedicated this book "To Friends in China" because much of it is the sort of thing I would like to say to the people in the Chinese Communist organisation whom I used to know, and the sort of thing I would try to say if I had the opportunity to revisit China and to take up again the arguments I used to enjoy in the intervals of work during the war. It is not likely that many people in China will ever read this book but if they do it may help them to understand how the recent policies of the Chinese Communist Party appear to non-Communist opinion. And all recent information from China seems to show that such understanding is completely lacking at present.

If there is to be any permanent peaceful settlement of Far Eastern problems the Chinese Communists will have to work with reasonable non-Communists—with people who would be able to influence non-Communist policy and who would be prepared to co-operate with Communists if the latter gave satisfactory evidence of their readiness to co-operate for peace, satisfactory by the standards of normal scientific procedure.

For the first part of the book which is based on the original letter I can say with considerable confidence that it does represent something like the views which such people would be likely to hold. Comments from a fairly representative sample of readers have said that it was a good statement of the non-Communist case. Apart from Rewi Alley's second letter the only critical comment I have received was that my position was too pro-Communist. For the latter parts I can only judge by the comments of a few friends but this smaller sample also encourages me to believe that parts at least of the argument represent more than my purely personal views.

Communists, as I argue later, tend to think in terms of a definite theoretical system which makes it hard for them to co-operate with people who do not share this system. And I think they really find it quite hard to understand the non-Communist position which is not based on any clearly formulated basic principles. This book is based on a fairly explicit formulation of basic principles which a considerable proportion of reasonable non-Communists accept, though they may not formulate them explicitly. If any Chinese Communists do read it, which seems more likely now than it did when the book was started, they may not agree with it but I hope that it may help to make the non-Communist position intelligible to them.

Some readers of my original letter objected that I had said

nothing of internal developments in China. I considered adding a section on this subject but found that it would need a completely different treatment from the rest of the book. In discussing international policy it was possible to base an analysis on a good deal of fairly well established factual evidence. The difficulty in giving any analysis of internal conditions in China is to establish the facts from wildly conflicting reports. For example, while the estimates of the numbers killed in the Thirty Years War differ within a range of about four to one, the estimates of the number of people executed in China in 1951 and 1952 vary over a range of about ten thousand to one. Again, to say whether the new regime has improved the living conditions of the peasants who form the great majority of the population one would need to know how much of his product the average peasant can now retain for his own use, how present taxes compare with rents before the land redistribution. On this basic question the figures even from Chinese official sources vary by more than two to one.

A careful study of the available evidence can narrow down this range of uncertainty. But a study of this kind would be quite out of keeping with the rest of the book and would make it of inordinate length. It therefore seemed best to confine the book to international problems. I believe, however, that a somewhat similar analysis could be applied to internal policies and would show that the real accomplishments of the new regime have been made in spite of and not because of its orthodox Communism. Even during the Yenan period it was noticeable that the Chinese Communists did a very good job when they used their common sense and a much less good job when they acted according to orthodox Communist theory or tried to follow Soviet practice. Similarly, in recent years there is very general agreement that the Communist government has done a very good job in technical fields, river control, improved transportation, stabilization of the currency and so on; that is, in fields in which Marx-Leninist theory is almost completely irrelevant. In fields of action where policy has been directly influenced by orthodox Communist doctrine the evidence tends to be conflicting or fairly definitely unfavourable. For the reasons just given I only suggest this hypothesis and do not try to establish it by a detailed analysis.

Australian National University
Canberra
June, 1954

1

Has Chinese Communism changed?

A GREAT deal of this analysis is strongly critical of Chinese Communist policy and I find that people often ask why I am now critical of an organisation about which I wrote favourably up to 1950. It seems to me that such questions show a disagreement about the nature of political judgment. They imply that the basic political decision is to choose sides, whereas I would maintain that the basic decision is to choose what standards of judgment to apply. I would maintain that the change in my position from one which was, on balance, strongly approving of the Chinese Communist Party to one which is, on balance, strongly critical has been the result of applying consistent standards of judgment to a changing Chinese Communist Party.

In so far as there has been a change in my standpoint it has only produced a change within the margin of uncertainty where the evidence admits of differing possible interpretations. Up to 1950 I was prepared to give the Chinese Communist Party the benefit of the doubt where their good intentions or good sense could be defended, because I had found that they had usually been in the right against their critics in the cases I could check by direct knowledge. The handling of relations with Britain was, however, quite clearly incompatible with the assurances I had been given in Peking in 1949 that the new regime wished for good relations with Britain and with what people called "democratic capitalist countries" and not merely with the British Communist Party. There is, I believe, an Indian proverb which says that if a man deceives you once he loses honour but if he deceives you twice you lose honour. Having worked for action from the British side to improve Sino-British relations, and having found that Chinese actions were in direct contradiction to the assurances given me by representatives of the Chinese government that they desired such an improvement, I have become less willing to give the Chinese Communist Party the benefit of the doubt in cases where their good intentions or rationality are doubtful.

In the period from 1938 to 1945 the record of the Chinese

1

Communist Party was one which could command general approval from independent judgment. The Chinese Communists were doing a very remarkable job in resisting Japanese militarism under conditions of extreme difficulty. Judging from the areas where I could make direct observations, they were very successful in carrying out a programme of economic, social and political reforms. Many of these reforms had long been generally accepted as necessary for China but had never been implemented by other regimes outside a few "model areas". For example, a student in the Far Eastern Area Programme at Harvard made a comparison between the pre-war Kuomintang land law and the land regulations of one war-time Communist region and found that where they differed the Communist regulations were slightly more favourable to the landlords. But the Communist regulations were enforced while the Kuomintang law was not. And the greater part of the war-time Communist programme was good by the empirical tests of gaining general popular approval and obviously improving the conditions of the people.*

Admittedly there was a strong element of "political tutelage" in the system but this was almost inevitable in a country where the masses had no political experience and were largely illiterate (see below, page 104). But the elements of democracy seemed to be stronger than in other Chinese regimes and there was evidence that Communist power rested on genuine popular support. Admittedly there were some extreme doctrinaires in the Chinese Communist Party but a high proportion of the leaders seemed to be quite unlike other Communists in treating their Marx-Leninism as a scientific hypothesis and not as a quasi-religious dogma. And in the early 1940's the Chinese Communist Party seemed to be developing towards the realization that it could only justify its claim to represent the masses if it accepted operational tests of what the masses really wanted, which implied free discussion and criticism and effective powers for freely elected non-Communist representatives.

In most of the war-time disputes with the Kuomintang the

---

* I realise that these statements will appear controversial to many readers, especially in America. Here I can only say that they are based on first-hand observation. My wife and I were living in the Communist areas from December, 1941, to November, 1945, and for the period of over two years when we were in Shansi-Chahar-Hopei we were travelling round a great deal. My wife had lived in the North China countryside as a girl and found it easy to make contact with peasant families in villages where we stayed and could also make a comparison with pre-war conditions.

Communists seemed to be in the right on the merits of the case, and in the complicated three-sided negotiations from 1944 to 1946 the Communists seemed to show greater good faith than either the Kuomintang or the Americans, though they were often very inept in handling their case.

Of course there were some serious defects in the system. At Yenan, for example, standards were in many ways lower than in the front line Shansi-Chahar-Hopei Region. I argued at the time that this was because Yenan organisations were much more under one-party control and did not get effective criticism from non-Communists. And one could see how standards might degenerate. (This is not just being wise after the event. A U.S. Army Intelligence Report of July, 1945, which was published in 1952, quotes me as saying, "If the Kuomintang doesn't reform it seems to me that there is a very big probability of China coming under exclusive Communist control which would be a pity in many ways as I feel that the real weakness of the democratic system here [in Communist controlled China] is that there is not enough real discussion which comes from having no real opposition party.")[1] But in 1945 standards were fairly high even at Yenan and the Communists would listen to fairly fundamental criticism. For example, I criticized particular failings in organisations at Yenan as the natural consequence of the Communist doctrine of democratic centralism.

On international affairs the judgment of the Chinese Communist Party was always seriously distorted by uncritical reverence for the Soviet Union. I remember, for example, making official protests when I was British Press Attache in 1940 over the line of the *Hsin Hua Jih Pao* (the Communist paper at Chungking) which combined frequent and vituperative attacks on the governments fighting Nazism and Fascism with very occasional expressions of mild disapproval for Hitler. But even here the Communists would listen to criticism. I remember many arguments in Shansi-Chahar-Hopei and at Yenan in which I maintained that the Comintern policy of considering the Social Democrats as worse enemies than the Nazis had been largely responsible for Hitler's rise to power and that Hitler would certainly have won the war if the British workers had been foolish enough to follow the leadership of the British Communist Party. I publicly criticized the propaganda for an immediate second front in 1942 and the slogan "Defeat Germany this year and Japan the next." However, at this period the Communists had no responsibility for foreign policy and only limited access to information. It was not unreasonable to hope that with responsibility and better information the Chinese Communist thinking would become less confused.

Thus, in the period from 1938 to 1945, the existence of defects did not alter the fact that the overall record of the Chinese Communist Party was such as to justify approval and support from people who were doing their best to make an objective judgment. And I have always been ready to defend this record against the attacks which have been made on it from Kuomintang and right-wing American sources, attacks which have largely depended on distortion or falsification of matters of fact.

However, since 1946 there seems to have been a progressive deterioration in the standards of the Chinese Communist Party and for the last few years the evidence seems to be quite incompatible with a rational belief in both the good faith and the good sense of the Chinese Communist leaders. The proclaimed objectives of peace and international goodwill are accompanied by policies which simply do not make sense as methods to obtain these objectives. Claims of enthusiastic and almost universal popular support for the new regime are accompanied by policies which only make sense as measures to enable an oppressive and unpopular government to retain its power. And the distinctive features of Chinese Communist administration seem to be giving way to an imitation of Soviet practice. Instead of basing policies on empirical, operational standards of what the masses really want, the Chinese Communist Party now seems more inclined to base its policy on what Stalinist theory says the masses ought to want.

There are two alternative hypotheses which can explain the evidence:

1. The Chinese Communist leaders are acting rationally but are not sincere in saying that they want peace and want to promote the well-being of the Chinese people. They are only making such claims as cover for some quite different objective such as the extension and consolidation of their power.

2. The Chinese Communist leaders are sincere in saying that they are working for peace and for the interests of the Chinese people but operate in a psychopathic state of emotional and intellectual confusion which makes them incapable of acting rationally to attain these objectives.

From my personal knowledge of some of the Chinese Com-

4

munist leaders I am inclined to believe that the truth is nearer the second hypothesis. But before making a tentative analysis of the motivation behind Chinese policy I would like to set out some of the evidence against the view of supporters of the Peking government who maintain that the Chinese Communist leaders are both sincere and rational.*

* As the terms "rational behaviour" and "functional rationality" are frequently used in the following argument it may be worth while giving definitions. Rational behaviour has been defined as follows: "A person has behaved rationally if he *would* have behaved in the same way if, with the same *factual* information, he had seen the full *logical* implications of his behaviour, whether he actually saw them or not. And if we define purposeful behaviour as trying (consciously or otherwise) to do or achieve something wanted, it follows that fully rational behaviour is a limiting case of purposeful behaviour." (Watkins, J. W. N., "Ideal Types and Historical Explanation," *The British Journal for the Philosophy of Science.* May, 1952. Page 40.) The only amendment I would suggest to this would be to substitute "available *factual* information" for "*factual* information", because a common form of irrational behaviour is to act without taking account of relevant factual information which could easily be obtained.

"Functional rationality" is used in a narrower sense to describe behaviour which would be rational if some definite objective is taken for granted, regardless of whether the attainment of this objective is rational in the wider sense of the above definition. For example, it is argued below that Communists may be acting with functional rationality for the indefinite extension of Communist power even though they may be acting irrationally in the wider sense because they are completely mistaken about the implications of an indefinite extension of Communist power.

2

International affairs

The hate campaign

FOR someone outside China it is easiest to judge Chinese policy on international affairs. And its most characteristic feature is its contradictions. For example, Rewi Alley apparently accepts the claims of the Peking Government to be working for international goodwill. But to someone outside China these claims appear completely fantastic. If one looks at almost any sample of Chinese publicity over the past few years one finds evidence of a campaign of abuse and misrepresentation to work up hatred for America and countries allied with America. The qualifications of goodwill towards the "American people" are rendered meaningless by the identification of the "people" with the small minorities ready to follow the Communist line. The leaders of the Kuomintang lobby in America make precisely similar qualifications in their campaign to work up popular hatred for China in which they identify the "Chinese people" with the small minority of Kuomintang supporters.

The official Chinese campaign to work up international hatred is no worse than what is being done on the other side by sections of the British and American press, but there is a vital difference. In the British Commonwealth and even in America there is public and influential criticism of these attempts to work up international hatred; from China there are no signs that anyone dares to point out the incompatibility between professions of desire for international goodwill and the practice of a publicity campaign to produce international hatred.

I am not trying to argue that there is an incompatibility between desire for international goodwill and criticism of America and American policy. Real disputes cannot be settled by pretending that they do not exist and, in the long run, frank criticism and plain speaking almost certainly help rather than hinder international understanding and goodwill. And the Chinese government has real grounds for criticizing American policy and for denouncing some powerful groups in America as

6

enemies of China. But the anti-American campaign goes far beyond the limits of frank criticism and plain speaking. One finds in Chinese publicity continual examples of statements designed to create hatred of America which are simply untrue and which the people making them must know to be untrue. Such deliberate attempts to work up international hatred by false or exaggerated statements are fundamentally different from honest criticism and are quite incompatible with a desire for international goodwill. As one illustration, consider a case about which I had strong personal feelings: the attacks on Dr. Leighton Stuart.* Dr. Stuart's whole life has been devoted to what he felt to be the service of China and the Chinese people and he did not belong to the irreconcilably anti-Communist group among American missionaries. In the period when I knew him from 1938 to 1941 he would help any Yenching student who wished to serve his country against the Japanese regardless of whether it was in the Kuomintang or in the Communist organisation. After the Kuomintang defeat he advised his former students that they could best serve their country by co-operating with the new regime. And after his return to America he opposed the extreme pro-Kuomintang group. The most the Chinese Communists could say against him within the limits of honest criticism would be that his friendship for China had sometimes been misguided and that his mistakes as ambassador had unintentionally harmed China. In fact, he has been denounced as an enemy of China motivated throughout his career by the objective of helping American imperialism to exploit the Chinese people and has been bracketed with General MacArthur as one of the two worst American enemies of the Chinese people. Such denunciation of a man whose sincere goodwill to China cannot reasonably be doubted really makes nonsense of any claims to desire goodwill between the Chinese and American people. An examination of any representative sample of Chinese publicity for the last few years would show similar though perhaps less striking cases of deliberate false statements, designed to rouse hatred against all Americans except the small minority of Communist supporters.

I have met people who tried to defend Chinese publicity with arguments on the following lines: the Chinese Communist Party

---

* Dr. J. Leighton Stuart was president of Yenching University, Peking, from 1918 to December, 1941, when he was imprisoned by the Japanese. He was appointed American ambassador to China in July, 1946, and remained until after the capture of Nanking by the Communists.

had decided that it was in the national interest to follow a pro-Soviet and not a pro-American alignment; but the Chinese people had a tradition of friendship and respect for America; therefore, in order to break down this tradition it has been necessary to use a violent publicity campaign which has had to include elements of exaggeration and falsehood. This argument depends on an implicit assumption of complete contempt for the intelligence of the masses which is quite incompatible with any claims to support a democratic system. The view that the masses are incapable of understanding the reasons for the policy decisions of a ruling elite and can only be induced to follow their rulers by lies and deception is a view which can be found in a whole series of ultra-reactionary writers from Plato to the theorists of modern fascism. The case for democracy rests on the assumption, for which there is strong evidence, that while the masses may be deficient in knowledge they are not deficient in intelligence and are capable of understanding the main issues in policy when they are not deliberately confused by propaganda. The resort of the Chinese leaders to falsehood and deception shows that either they do not believe in democracy or else that the case for a pro-Soviet and anti-American alignment is a bad one which the Chinese people could not be induced to accept by valid arguments. Chinese sources put the same general argument in a more euphemistic form by saying that the Chinese press is educational rather than informative. But what sort of education is it in which the teachers give their students information which they know to be false?

Quite apart from the question of democracy, this kind of publicity campaign greatly limits the ability of any government to work for peace. This applies on both sides of the Pacific. If there is to be any peaceful settlement in the Far East the Americans must be prepared to accept the fact that dealing with China means dealing with the Communists. But the ability of the U.S. Government to follow a realistic policy has been greatly weakened by the influence on public opinion of the hate campaign conducted by the extreme anti-Communist groups in America. It is equally true that no settlement is possible until the Chinese Government is prepared to accept the fact that dealing with America or the British Commonwealth means dealing with non-Communists. The ability of the Chinese Government to work for peace is greatly weakened by its insistence on maintaining a stereotyped propaganda picture of

8

America and the British Commonwealth, a belief that the leaders of every political party that is likely to obtain power by normal democratic procedures are irrevocably bent on war and that peace can only be obtained through an alleged "people's movement" led by the Communists and their associates. If the Chinese Government wants peace it must be ready to co-operate with the people who both want peace and are in a position to influence American and British policy. Such co-operation must involve the admission that Chinese publicity has been wrong in its sweeping denunciations as "war mongers" of everyone connected with American or British governments. The clearest illustration I have seen of this completely unrealistic Chinese position was Madame Sun Yat-sen's article *On Peaceful Co-existence*.[1] On the one hand she argues that peaceful co-existence is possible and that the great majority of the American and British people want peace. On the other hand, she denounces both Truman and Attlee as the willing tools of minority groups who want war, though even when the article was written it was clear that the only alternative governments which the British or American people were likely to choose would be still further to the right politically. That is, while talking of peaceful co-existence she uses arguments which imply that war is inevitable.

Sino-British relations

The Chinese handling of relations with England illustrates both the unrealistic attitude produced by Chinese publicity and also the contradiction between the proclaimed desire of the Chinese government for normal, peaceful international relations and actual Chinese policy. I certainly do not want to make a 100 per cent defence of British policy towards China which I have publicly and strongly criticized. In the period from 1945 to 1949 I think it was thoroughly discreditable and cowardly. China was treated as an American sphere of influence in which the British government never made a firm stand in favour of its proclaimed principles or even in defence of British interests. And the British government was not really prepared to defend its action, or rather inaction, but gave evasive or misleading replies to all public inquiries about its China policy. Also China has had good reasons for disliking many of the senior British officials with an "Old China Hand" mentality. My father was made absolutely furious by one interview at which a senior Foreign Office official held forth about his "twenty years experience of Orientals" which had convinced him that "not one of them could be trusted an inch." I can fully sympathize with a Chinese desire to make things unpleasant for this type of person.

However, there were also a lot of British officials who did not have the "Old China Hand" mentality and by 1949 there was a big change in British policy. There had been a growing good-will towards the New China extending far outside the circles in any way sympathetic to other Communist regimes. This goodwill was based on the belief that the Chinese Communist Party differed from other Communist parties in having genuine popular support and in actually improving the life of the Chinese masses. Pressure from this opinion was reinforced by British business interests in China which had had a bad time under Kuomintang rule and were quite ready to co-operate with a new regime that offered prospects of honest and competent administration. Judging from inside contacts as well as published material it was clear that, at the beginning of 1950, the British government was really trying to establish relations with China on a basis that would have satisfied Mao Tse-tung's slogans of "mutual advantage" and "equality of status." One can criticize British policy for acting too slowly and for not going far enough in demonstrating good faith and goodwill. But the British government was acting under strong criticism from right-wing Conservatives at home and from powerful groups in America for even recognising the Peking Government. It would have been very hard for them to go much further without some co-operation from the Chinese side. They could and would have done a great deal more if they had ever been able to say to their critics, "Our policy of working for better relations with China is producing results." But from the Chinese side there has never been any indication of readiness to co-operate. Chinese policy might almost be described as returning to the traditions of Ch'ien Lung.*

The pretexts on which the Chinese Government has so far refused to establish normal diplomatic relations with Britain are in themselves quite unreasonable. It was first alleged that Britain showed bad faith and unfriendliness by retaining a consulate in Formosa under the Kuomintang regime, by her actions over Chinese admission to the U.N., and by failing to

---

* The emperor Ch'ien Lung refused to receive an ambassador from King George III unless he agreed to perform a ceremony indicating acknowledgment of Chinese suzerainty.

hand over aircraft subject to a legal dispute in Hongkong. None of these arguments could be accepted at their face value. It has long been the normal practice for a consulate to deal with the de facto authorities in its area without prejudice to relations with the recognised government and this precedent had been accepted by the Chinese Communists. Foreign powers, including the Soviet Union, had retained consulates in Manchukuo under emperor P'u Yi and in Japanese occupied China under the Wang K'e-min and Wang Ching-wei puppet governments, and the Chinese Communist Party never suggested that this was un-friendly to China. The second point depends on taking a possible though very dubious interpretation of British action as an estab-lished matter of fact. British action in the U.N. during 1950 can be fully explained by the tactical decision that it was unwise to force a vote on the admission of the Peking Government until the support had been lined up to secure a favourable vote. By contrast, the Soviet tactics of forcing the issue on every possible occasion could be explained by a Soviet policy of preventing the Peking Government from obtaining the U.N. seat unless it could be presented as a concession extorted from a hostile U.N. by Soviet pressure. Governments which might have been ready to vote for China on the merits of the case would not give a favourable vote when it appeared to be yielding to Soviet threats. (This hypothesis about Soviet motives could not be definitely proved or disproved without access to Soviet archives but the case for doubting Soviet good faith is rather stronger than the Chinese case for doubting British good faith.) The third point about the aircraft at Hongkong was a demand that the British government should abandon its basic principles about the rule of law and overrule the courts by executive action.

More recently some Chinese spokesmen have tried to justify the refusal to establish normal diplomatic relations by the fighting between British and Chinese troops in Korea. But fighting which did not start before November, 1950, is an even more fantastic excuse for a Chinese policy decision which dates from January, 1950.

While making all these unreasonable claims the Chinese government has never given any indication of what it would accept as evidence of British good faith. If one argued with people concerned with British policy and said, "Even if the Chinese are being unreasonable, wouldn't it be worth giving way on the Formosa consulate issue instead of standing on our dignity about it?" the answer one got was, "Even if we met the present Chinese demands we would probably just be faced by a new series of even more unreasonable demands. There is no reason to believe that the Chinese government would be satisfied with anything short of a complete switch of British policy to the Communist line." There was little that could be said in reply to this argument because, so far as I know, the Chinese government has never given any indication of what it really wants.

Behind all these points of detail has been the underlying rejection of any objective standards. Almost every Chinese pronouncement on Sino-British relations has judged British actions by standards which are never applied to Chinese actions. It is claimed that any improvement in Sino-British relations requires Britain to give demonstrations of good will, good faith and independence from America. But while Chinese publicity is quick to denounce any alleged indications of British hostility, the British leaders are supposed to deduce Chinese goodwill from the fact that they are denounced in slightly less abusive terms than the Americans. And if either government needs to demonstrate its independence the need is stronger for the Chinese than the British. British policy has openly diverged from American on some important issues, and aspects of American policy are publicly criticized by influential groups in England; on the other side, the Chinese government has never publicly admitted the slightest disagreement with Soviet policy and has never permitted any criticism of the Soviet Union. It is hard to see how there can be any improvement in international relations in the Far East until the Chinese authorities are prepared to apply common standards of judgment to their own actions and those of other countries.

What has made the position almost hopeless has been the unwillingness of the Chinese authorities to join even in quite informal discussions of how to improve Sino-British relations with people in a position to explain or influence British policy. The clearest illustration was the visit to England in 1950 of a "friend-ship delegation" under Liu Ning-i. In itself the episode is not very important but it is worth describing because it provided such a very clear case of the difficulties in producing any improvement in Sino-British relations by action from the British side. The delegation received an extremely friendly welcome in Britain from all sorts of people and organisations who would not have been ready to welcome a delegation from any other

Communist country. The only people I found unwilling to join in receiving them were the right-wing Conservatives who had opposed the recognition of the Peking government. The delegates received invitations which would have enabled them to meet and talk with a large number of the people specially concerned with international affairs or Far Eastern problems. But they refused almost every invitation through which they could have met people in a position to explain or influence British policy, often with gross rudeness, and allowed themselves to be managed by the Britain-China Friendship Association, an organisation formed on the initiative of the British Communists and effectively controlled by them.

The Labour Party, at that time the government party, met with repeated rebuffs from the delegation. Arrangements for a visit to the Labour Party annual conference were cancelled on quite frivolous pretexts. (It was first alleged that it would be highly embarrassing for the delegates to attend any meeting at which they might hear opinions expressed on the Korean problem contrary to those of the Chinese government.) Later, arrangements were made for a meeting with the Parliamentary Labour Party Foreign Affairs Group. This Group had invited Liu Ning-i to address them on a previous visit to England so he knew they were ready to be friendly before the Chinese Communists had won the civil war. The delegation cancelled these arrangements at a few hours notice without a word of explanation or apology so that many Members of Parliament turned up to meet a delegation only to learn later that the afternoon had actually been spent in private conversations with the British Communist leaders. The one invitation that was accepted was to a lunch party with the Labour Party Executive (and it was almost unprecedented for such an unofficial delegation to be invited to a party including several cabinet ministers). But this meeting was only made the occasion for reading out a prepared speech denouncing the Labour Government in the set terms of Communist propaganda. And this speech was issued to the press without consulting the Labour Party and without mentioning the very effective reply it received from Dr. Dalton.

It would be interesting to see the Chinese reaction to similar behaviour from a British "friendship" delegation. Suppose that a British delegation in China were to refuse every invitation to meet representatives of the Chinese government or Chinese Communist Party except for one meeting with the Communist

Party Central Committee at which the British leader read out a speech denouncing the Chinese government for subservience to Soviet imperialism. It is unlikely that the Chinese leaders would show the same goodwill as the Labour Party Executive. In reply to Liu Ning-i's fairly insulting speech Dr. Hugh Dalton made a very courteous answer saying that, if the delegates really believed what Liu Ning-i had said, it showed that they had been completely misinformed about conditions in Britain and he hoped that they would stay longer or make another visit to find out for themselves what was the real position of the British government and the Labour Party.

Throughout their visit the delegation showed the most extreme suspicion of all non-Communist organisations. One episode which obtained considerable publicity was a ridiculous occasion when the delegates declared that they had been insulted by a request to sign the Lord Mayor of Manchester's visitors' book. I obtained the Manchester version of this episode from a reporter who had covered it and my wife obtained the Chinese version from one of the delegates. Putting the two together it was clear that there had been a misunderstanding. The delegates were expecting a formal civic reception like that which they had received in some other towns. What had actually been arranged was a private visit to the Lord Mayor. The Manchester representative of the Britain-China Friendship Association was apparently unwilling to tell the delegates that she had not arranged as elaborate a reception as they had received in some other towns. Instead of trying to clear up this misunderstanding the secretary of the Britain-China Friendship Association immediately issued a statement to the press denouncing the Manchester civic authorities. The delegates were left with the impression that they had been deliberately insulted and people in Manchester were left with the impression that the representatives of the New China were psychopathic types on the borderline of persecution mania, all in the name of promoting Sino-British friendship. The left-wing Labour magazine "Tribune" summed up the impression produced by this kind of behaviour by describing Liu Ning-i's group as "the worst mannered delegation ever to visit this country."

For a long time I was uncertain how far the delegates themselves were responsible for all this. It seemed possible that the trouble had been mainly caused by the British Communists and that the delegates had been placed in a false position from which they could only have escaped by an open break with the

Britain-China Friendship Association. However, when Australian delegates visited Peking in May, 1952, I was able to make certain that a summary of my criticisms and controversy with the Britain-China Friendship Association was placed in the hands of Liu Ning-i himself. His reaction showed that the British Communists had acted with at least full Chinese approval. Liu Ning-i professed himself very annoyed by my criticisms and said that he would write replying to them (which he has not done). He stated that he had made up his mind before coming to England as to the kind of people he wanted to meet there. This is exactly the point at issue. Liu Ning-i apparently accepted the accounts of British conditions given by Soviet propaganda and the British Communists and refused to make any attempt to test by his own direct observation whether these accounts were accurate. It was also very revealing of Dr. John Burton's position that he appeared to accept this explanation from Liu Ning-i as entirely satisfactory.

The arguments used by the management of the Britain-China Friendship Association showed that the Communist conditions for friendly Sino-British relations were such as no British government could possibly accept. It was argued that the British government had insulted the delegates by refusing to modify in their favour its declared policy over granting visas* and by failing to send representatives to their first public meeting on the new Chinese National Day (a meeting at which most of the speeches denounced the British government and supported the Soviet inspired "peace" movement). The British Broadcasting Corporation was alleged to have insulted the delegation by not

* The original visa application only mentioned the meeting on October 1 as the object of the visit to Britain and the delegates were, therefore, given a visa for one week. The application made in Peking for an extension of this period stated that the delegates wish to remain in Britain to work for the Sheffield Peace Congress, a purpose for which the British government had stated that it would not grant visas. When the delegation arrived in England Foreign Office officials made it clear that they would support an extension for the purposes of the Britain-China Friendship Association, but the B.C.F.A. management preferred to write to members of parliament and others urging them to bring pressure on the government to grant an extension. Shortly before the delegation left, one of the delegates told a friend who had managed to visit him that he believed that the extension of visas had only been secured through pressure from the British working class mobilised by the British Communist Party.

The B.C.F.A. management made it difficult for the public to make contact with the delegation. When in London they were housed at an obscure public house in Paddington in rooms which could be reached only through the bar counter.

immediately offering the opportunity for a talk on the Home Service. Other organisations were alleged to have insulted the delegation by not making their invitations sufficiently formal. In effect, it was claimed that the delegation should have had all the privileges and been treated with all the formality and protocol appropriate to an official, semi-diplomatic delegation but should still have been sponsored and managed, not by the official representatives of the British people, but by a subsidiary of the British Communist Party. Still more remarkable was the rejection of discussion. One member of the management committee argued that it would have been insulting to ask the delegates to join in any discussions at which their views might have been criticized and the president of the Association claimed that he could not understand how anyone could believe that discussions could be of any value except between plenipotentiaries of the British and Chinese governments.

The management of the Britain-China Friendship Association seemed to be subjectively quite sincere in expressing these views and the Chinese authorities have given no indication that they disagree with them. But it is obvious that they impose conditions for Sino-British friendship which no British government or non-Communist organisation could possibly accept. No British government could accept the claim that the British Communists were, in some sense, the "real" representatives of the British people and therefore entitled to act for Britain in handling relations with China. Almost no non-Communists would accept a situation in which Chinese representatives claimed the right to denounce British policy while refusing to listen to any criticisms of Chinese policy.

The episode has been discussed at some length because it is the clearest illustration of goodwill from the British side being rebuffed with hostility and suspicion from the Chinese side. In other cases British action has been much more open to criticism. It has been arguable that British good faith was not clear, that the Chinese had some reasonable grounds for suspicion, and that action from the British side could have produced a Chinese response for the improvement of Sino-British relations. But the record of the Liu Ning-i delegation provides an instance in which the maximum goodwill from the British side failed to produce the slightest response from the Chinese side. It shows that, until there is a marked change in the Chinese attitude, nothing that can be done from the British side could improve Sino-British relations.

At the end of 1952 the Chinese authorities still talked of wanting friendly relations with Britain but at the same time expressed their determination to channel contacts with Britain through the British Communists and organisations they control. And a desire for friendly Sino-British relations channelled through the British Communists is something like the desire of Henry Luce or Congressman Walter Judd for friendly Sino-American relations channelled through the Kuomintang.

There is still a strong body of British opinion which would like to improve Sino-British relations and to settle any Sino-British differences on their merits and which is strongly critical of American policy in the Far East. But such opinion must remain ineffective so long as the Chinese attitude offers no practical alternative to present British policy short of accepting the Communist line. So long as the Chinese authorities retain their policy of channelling contacts with Britain through the British Communists and rejecting all discussions in which the official Communist line would meet informed criticism it is certain that British non-Communists who hope for better Sino-British relations will be disillusioned as soon as their hopes are put to any practical test.

The Chinese policy towards Britain has already had serious consequences for peace and international goodwill. It is very likely that the establishment of normal diplomatic relations with Britain could have prevented the Chinese involvement in the Korean war. (This is assuming that Chinese intervention was the result of a genuine fear of American intentions produced by General MacArthur's advance towards the Chinese border, an assumption for which there is a fair amount of evidence.) The British authorities had grave misgivings about General MacArthur's policy, but when it came to changing that policy they could only offer their estimate that China might intervene against an American estimate that China would probably not intervene. The Chinese authorities may believe that they gave clear warnings of their intentions but, in fact, any warnings were rendered ambiguous by their context in a whole series of threats and denunciations of which a high proportion could not be taken seriously. According to people who had responsible positions connected with U.N. and with British policy, the total effect of Chinese pronouncements was to leave considerable doubt as to whether or not the possibility of Chinese intervention should be taken seriously.

The situation would have been completely different if there had been normal diplomatic relations and if the Chinese had been ready to co-operate with the British in restraining General MacArthur. If the British authorities had been able to discuss things with a Chinese ambassador in London and obtain from him precise statements of the limits beyond which U.N. military action in Korea would produce Chinese intervention it is almost certain that the British would have been able to keep U.N. action within such limits. Equally a British ambassador in Peking might have made it clear to the Chinese government that Britain would certainly not have tolerated an advance of the U.N. forces into China and might have persuaded the Chinese government to explore some of the offers made by the U.N. to work out some agreement which would safeguard Chinese interests and security. I am not arguing that responsibility rests solely with China. There is a great deal that is indefensible in the handling of both British and American policy at this period as is discussed later. But it is extremely likely that rather more common sense and rather less doctrinaire intransigence in Chinese policy would have been sufficient to prevent the immense losses caused by the continuation of the Korean war after 1950.

Quite apart from the Korean war, it is doubtful whether the handling of Chinese policy has helped Chinese interests. It is very likely that the Chinese government could have obtained the U.N. seat in 1950 if Chinese policy had been handled with a little common sense and elementary good manners. But again and again Chinese policy and Chinese publicity have done exactly what was required to strengthen the influence of the anti-Communist extremists, to discredit the influence of the people in British countries or America working for better relations with China and to raise suspicions about Chinese good faith. In England the results of Chinese policy could be seen very clearly. People in responsible positions who, at the beginning of 1950, were trying to work for better Sino-British relations had, by the end of 1951, become completely disillusioned and convinced that it was futile to make any further efforts from the British side because the Chinese did not seem to want any improvement in Sino-British relations. British business interests connected with China, which would have been quite ready to co-operate if the Chinese authorities had ever followed their declared policy of approving business relations which were to the mutual advantage of both parties, had been convinced by continued hostility and obstruction that the real Chinese policy was to squeeze out all foreign business.

What is the explanation for this Chinese policy? Why do the Chinese authorities talk about wanting normal trade relations and at the same time make conditions impossible for British firms trying to trade in China? Why do they go to considerable trouble and expense to arrange trading deals with unofficial British representatives which could have been equally well arranged by a few telephone calls in Shanghai? (The official Chinese claim that the difficulties in Sino-British trade have been caused entirely by the British embargo on strategic materials simply does not fit the facts. Even before the Korean war British firms in China were finding that the authorities were making it impossible for them to remain in business. In a number of cases where some British enterprise in China has been abandoned one of the first actions of the new Chinese government management has been to persuade the employees to accept "voluntary" wage reductions of up to 50 per cent. This is fairly strong evidence of conditions for foreign business being made impossible by exorbitant, officially backed wage demands. And most British businesses have had many other experiences of hostility and obstruction from the Chinese authorities.) More important, why do the Chinese authorities talk about wanting the peaceful settlement of international differences and go to considerable trouble to expound their desire for better Sino-British relations to unofficial British representatives sponsored by the Britain-China Friendship Association while at the same time they refuse to establish normal diplomatic relations with the British government or to co-operate with people able to influence or explain British policy?

One could only give a definite answer to such questions if one had access to Chinese government records and power to cross examine the responsible Chinese leaders. Failing this one can only speculate on the motives of the Chinese leaders and there are several hypotheses which could explain their behaviour. The official British view seems to be that the Chinese leadership is acting rationally but with bad faith. The refusal to establish diplomatic relations is explained by the intention to take over British business assets in China without compensation. It is argued that the Chinese government does not really want any improvement in Sino-British relations and that anything the Chinese leaders may say to the contrary is a purely propagandist device to embarrass the British government and weaken British-

American co-operation. The weakness of this hypothesis is that it does not provide an adequate rational motive for Chinese behaviour. Chinese policy has harmed Chinese as well as British interests and, if the Chinese government really wants to embarrass the British government and produce a split between Britain and America, it could probably work for these ends more effectively with normal diplomatic relations than without them.

Another hypothesis is that Chinese policy is determined by emotional rather than by rational considerations, that it reflects a resentment against British policy towards China in the past. Because at one time Britain took the lead in imposing extra-territoriality, foreign concessions and other restrictions on China's sovereignty and because many British officials still have an attitude of racial superiority, the Chinese authorities are determined to exact revenge for the past insults to China by trying to place the British government in a humiliating position and being hostile and insulting to British officials. What is really behind the unreasonable conditions for establishing normal diplomatic relations is an implied demand that the British government should express its contrition for British behaviour in the past. Because the leading British firms in China profited in the past from China's "semi-colonial" status the Chinese authorities are unwilling to conduct business through them even when it would be to the economic advantage of both parties. This attitude of sacrificing real advantages in the present and the future in order to pay off grudges from the past reflects a rather infantile state of mind. But it is a state of mind which exists in many countries which have emerged from a colonial or semi-colonial status and which also exists in China. In the past it was an attitude much more strongly represented in the Kuomintang than in the Chinese Communist Party. While Chiang Kai-shek in *China's Destiny*[2] placed the blame for everything wrong in China on the "unequal treaties", the Chinese Communist leaders would say that it was silly to waste time in raking up the past and that they would judge other countries according to their readiness to co-operate with China on terms of equality in the future. But it is quite possible that the Communist leadership has now become infected with the endemic hysterical, xenophobic nationalism and one can suggest explanations for the symptoms being even more marked in the Communist Party than in the Kuomintang. The Kuomintang, in spite of its Leninist constitution, was not a monolithic party, so the influence of the hysterical nationalists was counter-

20

balanced by the influence of more reasonable people. Also, while men like Chiang Kai-shek and Chen Li-fu may have had very strong anti-foreign feelings, the theoretical ideal type on which they tried to model their conduct was the Confucian scholar statesman who would lose face by any violent display of emotion or failure to observe the forms of good manners. The Communist super-ego, on the other hand, is not the scholar statesman but the theoretical proletarian, a figure rather like the type to which the less reputable advertising agents, newspaper owners and film producers of capitalist society address themselves, except that the proletarian's emotional life is centred on politics and not on sex.*
Communist theorists maintain that proletarian emotions should be allowed uninhibited expression and the Chinese Communist Party is sufficiently monolithic to make it difficult for any group to criticize the consequences of an emotionally charged Party line.

While this theory gives a possible explanation of the causes which have produced Chinese policy it does not show Chinese policy to be reasonable. It may well be true that the Chinese leaders are unwilling or unable to control an emotionally charged, xenophobic nationalism which their own propaganda has helped to work up. But until they do manage to control it China will not be able to work effectively for world peace. It will be very difficult to settle any dispute so long as Chinese representatives concentrate on declaiming that "The Chinese people can now stand up!" (a continually recurring theme in Chinese publicity). What is needed for peace is that the Chinese people should sit down and join in calm discussion of how conflicts of interest can be settled by compromise and disputed matters of fact by experimental investigation.

It may be true that British behaviour in the past has been an important factor in producing a hysterical nationalism in China. But what can the British people do about it now? On the British side most people would be ready to express regret for the policy typified by the Opium Wars and to admit that people with

---

* This does not imply any moral superiority in the proletarian as pictured by Communist theory. People are much more innocently employed when watching the most uncensored music hall show than when watching a public execution or participating in a mass trial. It would be possible to make out a very strong case for Aldous Huxley's view that "crowd delirium, as we may call it, is more immediately dangerous to social order, more dramatically a menace to that thin crust of decency, reasonableness and mutual tolerance which constitutes a civilization, than either drink or debauchery." (Huxley, Aldous, *The Devils of Loudun*. Chatto & Windus, London, 1952. Page 364.)

the "Old China Hand" mentality are pretty objectionable characters. But to say what British action would now be required to dispel the emotional resentment on the Chinese side is a problem for psychiatrists rather than for diplomatists. The British government could justifiably be criticized for continuing to employ in China some officials with the "Old China Hand" mentality but it cannot really be blamed for refusing to express contrition for the real harm done to China by British policy in the past by pleading guilty to quite unjustified Chinese accusations in the present. The retention of a consulate in Formosa was not an unfriendly action towards the Peking government, and to support China's claim for the U.N. seat in the way that would satisfy the Chinese authorities would almost certainly lessen the chances of China's obtaining the seat.

A very clear illustration was provided by the *Amethyst* case. British action was indefensible. It was asking for trouble to try to send a warship through the battle zone without obtaining, or even attempting to obtain, a safe conduct from one of the belligerents; especially since Communist history books had kept alive the memories of anti-Communist intervention by foreign warships in 1927 and 1930, and the British authorities had no excuse for not knowing this. British action, and subsequent excuses by government spokesmen, such as Lord Alexander's speech, showed that some people in the Foreign Office had failed to realise that the China of 1949 was different from the China of the warlord period in the 1920's. It would have been hard for the British government to avoid a public admission of error if the Chinese authorities had stated their real case; that the local commander was entirely justified in opening fire on a warship entering the battle zone without a safe conduct and refusing to stop. In fact, the "Old China Hands" in the Foreign Office were able to maintain their indefensible position because the Chinese authorities took up an equally indefensible position. The most conciliatory people on the British side were not prepared to express contrition for their real mistakes by pleading guilty to false charges of trying to intervene on the Kuomintang side and unprovoked attack on Communist shore positions. If the *Amethyst* had not managed to escape the dispute might have dragged on for years, and most disputes do not have similar short-cut solutions.

There is still another complicating factor which may partly explain Chinese behaviour, namely a reluctance to admit that the implications of Communist theory may not fit the facts. In 1950 the general British goodwill towards China was based on a belief, which Chinese policy at the time seemed to justify, that there were very important differences between Chinese Communism and Soviet Communism, that the Chinese Communist Party was unique in basing its power on popular support and not on terrorism. But even in the early 1940's when the practical differences between Chinese and Soviet Communism were most marked, the Chinese Communists were reluctant to generalize from their experience. In private conversations some Chinese Communist leaders would talk of doing better than the Russians and learning from Soviet mistakes but public statements never criticized Soviet practice in the light of Chinese experience. By 1949 the Chinese Communist Party was committed to a completely pro-Soviet line. Although, at that time, the absence of terrorism in Communist China was in striking contrast not only to other Communist countries but also to the Kuomintang regime in China the Chinese Communists were not willing to discuss the view that ability to govern without resort to terrorism was evidence of real popular support. In this situation the establishment of contacts with informed British non-Communist opinion would have presented the Chinese Communists with an awkward problem. A point of view, which judged popular support for a Communist regime by empirical tests and which was ready to give approval to the Chinese Communist Party so long as it governed without terrorism while remaining strongly hostile to Stalinism, would simply not have fitted into the theoretical picture of the world in which the Chinese Communists believed. Thus the development of friendly Sino-British relations would have been a continual challenge to the whole system of orthodox Communist doctrine. And there is abundant evidence for the generalisation that any group of people with a strong faith in some doctrinal system are inclined to avoid experience which would challenge the basis of their thinking. Again, according to Communist doctrine the British Communists should be the real leaders of the British masses in their struggle against capitalism and imperialism. To admit that the British Communist Party was a small minority group deeply distrusted by the great majority of even the working class would be to admit that Communist theory does not fit the facts. Thus actual Chinese policy has been such as to allow the Chinese Communists to retain their faith in Communist theory, at the expense of a retreat from the empirically real world into a world of fantasy and delusion. This sort of retreat from reality is by no means confined to the Chinese Communist Party. An even more striking illustration is the tendency of some people in America to think in terms of an imaginary world in which Chiang Kai-shek has been a faithful champion of Jeffersonian democracy, who would have defeated the Communists if he had had rather more military supplies from America. But anyone who operates in terms of a world of theory that does not fit empirical reality is a danger to world peace. Such a person may be subjectively quite sincere in wanting peace but the actions which would promote peace in his imaginary world are likely to have the opposite result in the empirical world.

To sum up, Chinese foreign policy, especially in relations with Britain, has not made sense as a policy directed to peace and the lessening of international tension. The hypothesis which seems to give the best explanation of Chinese behaviour is that the Chinese leaders may be subjectively sincere in wanting peace and in wanting Sino-British friendship but that they operate in a state of emotional and mental confusion in which various widespread influences that tend to make human behaviour irrational are strengthened by a faith in the Communist dogmatic system. And no action from outside China which does not somehow produce a change in this Chinese attitude is likely to produce more than a limited and temporary improvement in international relations.

The pro-Soviet line

Probably the most important single factor in producing suspicions of a genuine Chinese desire for peace has been the completely uncritical Chinese support for the Soviet Union. There is very strong evidence that the Communist Party of the Soviet Union under Stalin degenerated into an organisation with imperialist ambitions of dominating and exploiting other countries. This is far too large a subject to set out in detail here and a vast amount of published material exists. A certain proportion of the allegations against the Soviet Union is almost certainly exaggerated or definitely false but there remains a great deal that is well established by any normal standards of evidence which supporters of the Soviet Union have failed to refute. I can only say that I have made some study of Soviet behaviour in Eastern Europe and, especially in the case of Germany and Austria, I

24

have been able to check published material by first hand accounts from people who could make direct observations. The result has led me to feel about the Soviet organisation in much the same way as I felt about the Japanese militarists in China and to regard the Soviet secret police organisation as quite as objectionable as the Japanese gendarmerie and special service.

A large part of the opposition to the Soviet Union is the product of the similarity between the Soviet system and the Nazi system. Obviously the similarity is not complete. An important difference between the C.P.S.U. and the N.S.D.A.P. is the absence of an element of sexual perversion in the Russian organisation. The Nazis, in many cases, took a positive delight in cruelty and terror for their own sake; the Soviet leaders are only completely unscrupulous in using cruelty and terror as a means to extend and enforce their power. Stalin resembled Himmler more than Hitler. Hitler obviously derived an intense emotional thrill from imagining scenes of large scale bloodshed and destruction. Both Himmler and Stalin were merely indifferent to cruelty but had no scruples whatever about eliminating any number of human beings who, according to their theories, were actual or potential obstacles to the realisation of their ideals. And Marx-Leninism is far more respectable as an intellectual system than National Socialist doctrine. But these points of difference do not destroy the similarity between two totalitarian groups trying to extend their power.

In this situation the Chinese Communist Party has greatly discredited itself by its completely uncritical support for the Soviet Union. It is impossible to put much faith in the Chinese denunciations of imperialism so long as they are combined with unrestrained praise for the enslavement and exploitation of East European nations by Soviet imperialism. People with some knowledge of China realize that the Chinese leaders are not in the same position as the Communist leaders of Eastern Europe. They could take a stand against the Soviet ruling caste in the interests of world peace or of the Chinese people without risking the fate of Kostov or Gomulka. Why then do they not do so? One obvious explanation is that they wish to follow the same policies as the Soviet leaders, but in the Far East—to use the slogans of anti-imperialism and national liberation as a cover for consolidating their control over the Chinese people and for extending Chinese power over neighbouring peoples. Because this hypothesis seems to explain Chinese behaviour it is widely believed and inevitably rouses suspicions of Chinese good faith in wanting peace.

Here again, there is an alternative explanation of Chinese behaviour; this time in terms of philosophic dispute about empiricism. The Chinese Communists consider empiricism to be a fallacious and old fashioned way of thinking. Many non-Communists consider it to be the essential constituent of scientific method. There is an article by Herbert Dingle, professor of the History and Philosophy of Science at London, which gives a very good summary of the modern non-Communist view of scientific method.[3] He refers to "the scientific revolution inaugurated by Galileo and established by Newton . . . the essence of that revolution was the substitution of the examination of experience for speculation about the external world." He later goes on "We can no longer say, The World is like this, or The World is like that. We can only say, our experience up to the present is best represented by a world of this character; I do not know what model will best represent the world of tomorrow but I do know that it will co-ordinate a greater range of experience than the world of today." Not many people formulate the assumptions of scientific thinking so explicitly but a very high proportion of non-totalitarians do in practice accept the principle that it is reasonable to believe the hypothesis which gives the most complete co-ordination of experience.

For anyone who thinks in this way it is reasonable to believe that the Soviet Union under Stalin became an imperialist power. If you want to use Marxian terminology, the analysis of the Soviet Union given by the Yugoslav theorists such as Milovan Djilas has the characteristics of a scientific hypothesis. The theory that Communism in the Soviet Union has degenerated into "bureaucratic centralism" under which a new "ruling caste" uses imperialist expansion and the exploitation of subject peoples to alleviate the contradictions and conflicts caused by its policies at home is a theory which explains and co-ordinates a mass of evidence which orthodox Stalinism has to evade or explain away by all sorts of special hypotheses. The same general analysis has been given in non-Marxian terms by other writers and can even claim the credit for successful prediction. As far back as 1920 Bertrand Russell wrote, "This is what I believe to be likely to happen in Russia: the establishment of a bureaucratic aristocracy, concentrating authority in its own hands, and creating a regime just as oppressive and cruel as that of capitalism."[4]

As against this empirical approach the Chinese Communists seem to believe that they know the essential nature of the Soviet system from which they can deduce that all evidence which seems to indicate Soviet imperialism must either be false or capable of being explained away. I remember one discussion in 1949 in which I had been giving some accounts of Russian behaviour in Berlin. A theorist of the Chinese Communist Party replied, "But, Mr. Lindsay, if you had read Marx, Engels and Lenin you would know that these stories cannot be true as it is theoretically impossible for the representatives of a socialist power to behave in such a way." And it is worth noting that almost all the arguments with which the Chinese Communists defend the Soviet Union are theoretical deductions from abstract general principles. As an illustration it is worth examining Liu Shao-ch'i's *Internationalism and Nationalism* which devotes a chapter to an attempted refutation of the charges by the Yugoslav theorists and others that the Soviet Union is an imperialist power. Liu Shao-ch'i first argues at considerable length that Communists would be betraying their principles if they ever used their power for aggression or for the oppression and exploitation of other peoples. The crucial point in his argument is the following passage: " the Communists must be the most determined, most reliable and most capable leaders of the movement for the liberation and independence of all oppressed nations . . . They cannot pursue a policy of aggression against any other nation or a policy of oppressing the national minorities within their own country.

"Thus we can understand that there is not the slightest basis for such demagogic propaganda and malicious slander of the imperialists as . . . 'The Soviet Union is guilty of Red imperialism' . . . 'The Soviet Union pursues an expansionist policy' etc."[5]. Liu Shao-ch'i jumps from what Communists should do if they are true to their principles to an assertion about what particular Communists actually do. As a reply to the Titoist case this argument is entirely beside the point because the whole question at issue is whether or not the C.P.S.U. is true to Communist principles.

The dispute could be summed up in two syllogisms. Liu Shao-ch'i argues, "Communists who are true to Communist principles cannot oppress or exploit subject peoples; the leaders of the Soviet Union have always been true to Communist principles; therefore, the leaders of the Soviet Union have never oppressed or exploited subject peoples." The Titoist theorists would deny the minor premise and argue, "Communists who are true to Communist principles cannot oppress or exploit subject peoples; the leaders of the Soviet Union have oppressed and exploited subject peoples; therefore, the leaders of the Soviet Union have not been true to Communist principles." Someone who did not believe in any form of Communism might argue, "If Communism is so defined as to be incompatible with the oppression and exploitation of subject peoples, then the empirical evidence about Soviet behaviour proves that the Soviet Union is not Communist on this definition." All these arguments are logically consistent and the whole dispute really depends on questions of fact about Soviet behaviour. While the critics of the Soviet Union support their assertions with numerous instances of actual Soviet behaviour, Liu Shao-ch'i, in the course of a lengthy argument, only produces one instance to support his views and this is irrelevant because it is taken from the period immediately after the 1917 revolution and the Titoists at least do not claim that the Soviet Union was an imperialist power under Lenin's leadership but only that it became one under Stalin's leadership.

Liu Shao-ch'i's argument has been examined at some length because he is one of the leading theorists of the Chinese Communist Party and should have been able to produce rational arguments in support of the Chinese Communist position. The tendency to ignore empirical evidence and to rely on purely abstract reasoning is even more marked in the more popular arguments used to defend the pro-Soviet line. One widely used argument is the following, "Imperialism is the highest stage of capitalism; the Soviet Union is not capitalist; therefore, the Soviet Union cannot be imperialist." This particular argument can be refuted by well established empirical evidence from fairly ancient history without bringing in the controversial subject of Soviet behaviour at all. Thirteenth century Mongolia was certainly not a capitalist society; but Genghiz Khan and his successors established an empire extending from China to Russia in which a Mongol ruling group conquered and exploited subject populations. Apparently no one in present day China dares to use this kind of obvious argument which might lead to the conclusion that non-capitalist imperialism can be even more unpleasant for subject populations than capitalist imperialism.

Thus, given that the Chinese Communists really reject empiricism and really believe in some form of what Professor K. R.

Popper calls "essentialism",[6] it is quite possible that they are subjectively sincere in denouncing imperialism while giving uncritical support to the Soviet Union. But such subjective sincerity has little relevance for the actual problems of peace. Non-Communists are interested in the world of empirical experience and not in the world of Communist theory. Whatever may be the right name for the experiences of East European peoples in relation to Russia they are experiences which China's neighbours do not want to share in relation to China. The Chinese leaders can only persuade non-Communists that there is nothing in Chinese intentions or Chinese policy which should give them cause for alarm or justify military preparations for defence if they are ready to give assurances that China will not try to act in the same sort of way as the Soviet Union. It will be very hard for them to give such assurances in any convincing form so long as they continue to maintain that there cannot have been any Soviet actions which could give other countries reasonable grounds for alarm or for military preparations for defence against Soviet attack. The essential conditions for peace are not only subjective sincerity but also a readiness to allow deductions from Communist doctrine to be tested by the evidence of empirical observation. And, unfortunately, the readiness to modify theory in the light of experience, which made the Chinese Communist Party unique in the period between 1937 and 1946, seems to have become progressively weaker since then.

Is China aggressive?

The existence of a fear of Chinese aggression is a matter of empirical fact which can easily be verified by a study of the serious press in America and the British Commonwealth or by discussions with people responsible for British and American policy. If the Chinese leaders both wanted peace and were acting rationally (defining rationally in terms of scientific method), they would take account of this fear and try to remove it even if they believe it to be unjustified. But this is just what they consistently refuse to do. They never seem to ask themselves, "Why are peace loving people in other countries suspicious of our good faith in wanting peace?" or "What should we do to make clear our good faith and to remove these suspicions which are endangering peace?" Instead of this they seem to act on the assumption that their good faith is so obvious that any doubts about it merely show the bad faith of the doubters; and in consequence they never seem ready to modify or even to explain those aspects of Chinese policy which have caused suspicion.

The Chinese leaders have not even been willing to give an unambiguous denial of aggressive intentions. Chinese claims that war can be avoided and all disputes settled peacefully often make an explicit exception for "national liberation struggles" which Communist governments should support. And other Chinese pronouncements claim that any Communist Party in a non-Communist country may be the leaders of a struggle for national liberation. Even Mr. Harry Pollitt has been acclaimed as the leader of the British people in their struggle for liberation from American imperialism. None of China's non-Communist neighbours can really feel secure so long as the Chinese leaders say in effect, "We are against war and aggression, but of course support for a national liberation movement is not aggression and we claim the right to consider any Communist movement in a non-Communist country as a national liberation movement." This sort of evasiveness does not make sense as part of a rational policy for peace. It could be explained by the hypothesis that the Chinese government has aggressive intentions and also wants to maintain the claim of Party infallibility which would be destroyed if aggression followed an unambitious repudiation of aggression. But, here again, Chinese Communist behaviour can be explained as the result of a type of irrationality to which Communists are specially prone. "They will never utter a word but hem and haw when a clear explanation or avowal would be helpful, and it is impossible for them to keep their traps shut when discretion would be the better part, not only of valor, but of strategy and tactics as well."[7] This was written about the French Communist Party in the 1920's but it would apply to the Chinese Communist Party in the 1950's.

The problem is not entirely theoretical. Within the last few years a Chinese army has conquered Tibet, the power of Viet Minh in Indo-China has depended largely on active support from China, the Malayan Communist Party has received at least moral support, and Chinese troops have been fighting in Korea. In some ways the invasion of Tibet was the most interesting case. It could be argued that the invasion of Tibet was merely the re-establishment of sovereign rights over a dependent territory, rights which had never been renounced but had only fallen into abeyance during a period of Chinese weakness. From this legal standpoint there was nothing wrong with Chinese action. But can the Chinese government justify its actions in terms of a principle which it does not accept? If any state is justified in using force to establish its sovereign rights over territory to which it has a legal claim then China was justified in invading Tibet even though the population was not Chinese and had enjoyed practical independence for about fifty years; equally, France and Britain were justified in restoring their control over Indo-China and Malaya. And the Chinese government does not accept the application of the principle of legitimacy in these latter cases.

In terms of the principles which the Chinese government does profess to accept the invasion of Tibet was hard to justify. There was no evidence of any spontaneous Tibetan popular demand for Chinese intervention or even of any large scale active opposition to the old government. There may be a considerable amount of truth in Chinese claims to have freed the Tibetan people from a conservative and superstitious native government. But similar claims have been made by most colonial powers and have often been at least partially true. India under direct British rule was certainly much better administered than China under the later Ch'ing emperors or the warlord period of the Republic and there are several instances which indicate that the masses may enjoy greater personal security and better material conditions under colonial administration than under native governments. And reports of famine in Tibet indicate that so far the new Chinese administration has not even managed to produce better material conditions. But it is doubtful whether the Chinese Communists would accept the principle that ability to provide better administration is a justification for conquest, even though the Russians have used this sort of argument to justify the Tsarist conquests in Central Asia. Most progressive non-Communist opinion would be inclined to accept the principle that good government is no substitute for self government.

Thus, if one denies the right of the Chinese government to benefit by a legal principle which it does not accept, the conquest of Tibet can only be explained as an example of old fashioned nationalism with the operative motives of strategic security and national prestige.

In Indo-China the Chinese claims to be supporting a national liberation movement have more empirical justification. Viet-Minh is a powerful organisation under local leadership. But

31

even here it seems likely that such popular support as Viet Minh enjoys is in spite of and not because of its Communist leadership. In Malaya the Chinese Communist case is much weaker. The Communist organisation fighting the government is a small group largely composed of immigrant Chinese and the available evidence about popular opinion indicates that though the people may not much like British rule only a small minority would really like to exchange British rule for Communist rule.

Looking at this general record of Chinese Communist statements and actions one can only say that the experience which would justify a fear of Chinese imperialism on the Soviet pattern is inconclusive. The people who argue that Chinese expansion is a real danger to world peace can point to some Chinese statements and Chinese actions which seem to support their view that the long term policy of the Chinese government is to extend Chinese power, mainly by the use of minority Communist groups dependent on Chinese support. As against this, Chinese behaviour can be explained in terms of a desire for security and a genuine fear of aggression against China combined with a large element of emotional and intellectual confusion related to an irrational faith in Communist doctrine. Both of these hypotheses are compatible with the available evidence. The hypothesis which is not compatible with the evidence is that the Chinese leaders both want peace and act rationally in ways that are likely to promote it.

The faults are certainly not all on the Chinese side. If the Chinese Communists have discredited themselves by uncritical support for the Soviet Union it is also true that many people in America and British countries have discredited their claims to support liberty and democracy by turning a blind eye to the activities of Chiang Kai-shek's secret police and similar behaviour by other anti-Communist governments. A great deal of American and British policy should be criticized for failing to take account of the empirical fact that Chinese public opinion has been genuinely afraid of aggression from America. But two blacks do not make a white. It is no defence of Chinese policy to show that it has been no worse than the less defensible aspects of British or American policy

3

Korea

THE truce agreement of July, 1953, in Korea left almost every point of dispute unsettled. The only point of agreement really recorded was that neither side considered it worth while to go on with the fighting. The basic point which still remains in dispute is what the war was about to begin with. Was it, as the U.N. claims, collective security against North Korean aggression? Or was it, as the Communists claim, an act of aggression against North Korea instigated and supported by the United States? I have read a good deal of what has been published by Chinese and other Communist sources on this question and it seems to me extremely unconvincing.

The following three points seem to be established beyond reasonable doubt: 1. In June, 1950, North Korea had an army which was much stronger and better equipped than South Korea. 2. In the period after 25 June, 1950, the North Korean government used this army in an attempt to conquer South Korea, an attempt which nearly succeeded and which certainly would have succeeded but for U.N. intervention. 3. The North Korean government refused to accept the U.N. request of 26 June to remain on the frontier pending an investigation of the events of 25 June.

Whatever happened on 25 June the North Korean leaders used it as a pretext for an attempt to conquer South Korea. And, in the ordinary meaning of words, an attempt to conquer and annex a neighbouring territory by military force is an act of aggression. There is strong evidence that the conquest of South Korea was an operation that had been planned for at least some months before. For instance, the North Korean forces which occupied Seoul a few days after the fighting started brought with them police and political officers specially trained for taking over the city with prepared lists of opponents to be arrested.[1]

If the North Korean government had accepted the request to remain along the frontier pending investigation, the whole basis for U.N. intervention would have disappeared and the *status quo ante bellum* would have been restored in a few days. And the fighting in the first few weeks of the war showed that the North Korean army had such a marked superiority that it could have repelled with ease any South Korean attacks. Thus on either 25 June or 26 June the North Korean leaders faced a clear cut choice between peace and war and deliberately chose war. They chose to gamble on the chance of being able to conquer South Korea before U.N. intervention became effective and did not make any overtures for peace until they faced military defeat.

What happened on 25 June is a matter of dispute. I think the weight of evidence is in favour of the U.N. view that the war was started by a North Korean attack. But even if the Communists could prove their claim that the fighting started with a South Korean attack it would not justify a verdict for the North Korean government of "not guilty of aggression." It would only justify a verdict of "guilty with mitigating circumstances of provocation." (Consider the analogous case between individuals. A plea of self defence will only secure an acquittal if it can be shown that the force used was no greater than was necessary for self defence. Proof that the weaker party had struck the first blow in a fight in which the weaker party could certainly have been killed except for police intervention would not secure the acquittal of the stronger party. It could only reduce a charge of "attempted murder" to "attempted manslaughter.")

I have not seen any Communist arguments which answer this basic case against the North Korean government. Consider, for example, Vyshinski's speech to the U.N. in October, 1952. He argues at considerable length on events up to and including 25 June, 1950, but says nothing about the North Korean refusal to accept the U.N. request of 26 June to remain on the frontier pending investigation and nothing to justify the subsequent North Korean attempt to conquer South Korea.

All the complications in detail are only relevant to this question of whether North Korean war guilt had mitigating circumstances of provocation. Leaving aside the disputed events of 25 June, the South Korean leaders had certainly been making provocative statements and would probably have been ready to invade North Korea if they had had a suitable opportunity. But the United States had refused to supply them with the types of armament which would have been necessary for a successful invasion. Then there are the allegations of some more or less complicated plot on the non-Communist side to start the war. (I. F. Stone's *Hidden History of the Korean War* is a good example.[2]) But the point on which both Stone and Vyshinski are completely evasive is that any such plot depended entirely on North Korean co-operation. Suppose, for the sake of argument, that Syngman Rhee, General MacArthur, John Foster Dulles and others had actually been engaged in a plot to start a war in Korea as Stone alleges. The plot would have ended in a fiasco highly discreditable to those concerned in it if only the North Korean army had stayed on the defensive and not tried to conquer South Korea. To show that Kim Il-sung may have been co-operating with General MacArthur to start the war would not prove him to be innocent.

The arguments about legal defects in the U.N. proceedings ignore the fact that the North Korean army was rapidly overrunning South Korea and would have succeeded in conquering it completely if rapid action had not been taken to stop them. Even if it were true that the original U.N. action condemning North Korea as an aggressor was taken on inadequate evidence or without proper formalities, this would not justify subsequent North Korean action. Whether or not the original condemnation of North Korea as the aggressor was justified, the North Korean government did not try to show that the accusation was false but, within the next few days, acted so as to make it clearly true. The people who try to justify North Korea on these grounds appeal implicitly to a principle which is obviously ridiculous if stated explicitly, namely, that anyone who is accused of some crime without adequate evidence or proper formalities should not be blamed if he immediately proceeds to commit the crime of which he had been accused.

Finally there are the arguments, which are found in Sir John Pratt's writings, which try to justify North Korean and subsequent Chinese action by implicit appeal to a principle which might be called "anticipatory self-defence." It is alleged that the North Koreans were justified in trying to conquer South Korea because they were afraid that they would be attacked by American forces based on South Korea; that Chinese intervention in Korea was justified by a Chinese fear that General MacArthur might not stop at the Korean border. But this principle of anticipatory self-defence is one which would make a general war quite certain. If every government claimed the right to take the offensive merely to anticipate a hypothetical future attack of which it was afraid the international situation would become unstable and any increase of international tension would precipitate a general war.

And it is worth noting that the people who use the "anticipatory self-defence" argument, both Communists and non-Communists, always assume that the right of anticipatory self-defence only holds for their own side.

In my opinion a major defect in U.N. policy has been the failure to press for a war crimes trial over Korea. A proposal for an investigation of war guilt would have been the obvious reply to the first North Korean peace overtures after their defeat following the U.N. landing at Inchon. The U.N. objective of enforcing collective security would have been satisfied by the punishment of those responsible for aggression while if the North Korean leaders had refused to submit to the investigation of their actions by some international tribunal it would have provided fairly clear evidence that they, at least, did not believe in the Communist propaganda which asserted their innocence. Even now it is hard to see how there can be any real settlement in Korea, as opposed to an unstable truce, until the rights and wrongs of war guilt have been clearly established. If there were a full investigation of war guilt the probable result would not be a completely clear cut black and white but it is fairly certain that it would reveal a very uneven distribution of responsibility for the war. The North Korean leaders would almost certainly be convicted of planning and waging an aggressive war and it is quite probable that the Soviet leaders would be clearly implicated. (It is unlikely that the North Korean government would have embarked on the original offensive without fairly definite assurances of Soviet approval.) On the other side the South Korean leaders would almost certainly be revealed as having behaved in a very provocative way, in words if not in deeds, and as not being the aggressors from want of opportunity rather than from want of intention. It is possible that some individuals in the American organisation might be implicated as accessories before the fact in that they knew of North Korean intentions but deliberately withheld their knowledge from the American government because they hoped that a war would start in Korea. Some well informed Americans have told me that intelligence reports warning that a North Korean attack was imminent failed to reach Washington. But these sort of charges which might perhaps be proved against the South Korean leaders and individuals in the American organisation could not do more than provide some extenuating circumstances for North Korean war guilt.

In psychological warfare it is a fatal mistake to try to defend the indefensible and the U.N. has weakened its case and made Communist allegations more plausible by failing to admit the limited degree of guilt and responsibility on its side. But such admissions would refute and not confirm the basic Communist case. America's allies should certainly criticize the American government for failing to hold the type of inquiry which could clear up the rumours and allegations spread by Mr. I. F. Stone and others. But it is practically certain that such an inquiry would provide strong additional evidence of North Korean war guilt.

By committing itself to unconditional support for the North Korean government from the very beginning of the war the Chinese government was giving approval to aggression. It was, by implication, maintaining the principle that it did not consider invasion and conquest to be aggression so long as the invaders were Communists. And this principle is quite incompatible with world peace. Equally, on the original decision to resist the North Korean attack, the U.N. under American leadership acted in support of collective security in a way which the League of Nations under British and French leadership failed to do in the 1930's. And if the U.N. had reacted to aggression with the same hesitancy as the League of Nations the result might have been equally disastrous. Instead of a local war in Korea there might, by now, have been a general world war.

Later the issues became much more confused. The U.S.A. discredited its position very early when it used the North Korean aggression as a pretext for reversing its policy over Formosa. (This was a good example of the "anticipatory self-defence" argument.) Later the whole U.N. position was badly discredited by the failure to formulate definite war aims and by the failure to restrain General MacArthur. It seems quite likely that the Chinese involvement in Korea was mainly the result of confusion and not of considered policy on either side. Even the responsible Chinese leaders seem to have been confused by their own propaganda and to have believed that America was really likely to invade China and had got themselves into a position where they could neither form an accurate view of the outside world nor convey intelligible warnings of their intentions to it. Subjectively, they may really believe that Chinese intervention in Korea was an action in self-defence against a hostile army advancing towards the Chinese border in spite of Chinese warnings that this would be considered a *causus belli*. On the U.N.

side there was a failure to make proper allowance for the empirical fact that, rightly or wrongly, Chinese opinion was really afraid of an American attack. In these circumstances General MacArthur was a highly provocative figure because he was the man whom Kuomintang supporters in America had frequently suggested as the commander of a joint U.S.-Kuomintang army to fight the Communists in the Chinese civil war.* And the handling of the situation by the U.N. did seem to suggest that General MacArthur was largely out of control. The only point at which he seems definitely to have disobeyed a U.N. directive was in allowing South Korean officials to function North of the 38th parallel. But the U.N. was never willing to state a clear formulation of its war aims in Korea and the impression one obtained even in England was that this was because no one was prepared to bell the cat, to give a clear directive on war aims and insist that General MacArthur should obey it. The British authorities certainly had the most serious misgivings about the offensive towards the Chinese border which finally produced Chinese intervention. The U.N. could be strongly blamed for not formulating definite war aims. The American government could be strongly blamed for not failing to make clear that General MacArthur would only be allowed to hold his command so long as he loyally followed the orders of his superiors, and there were several opportunities for doing this. The British government could be strongly blamed for not translating its entirely justified fears about the results of leaving decision largely in General MacArthur's hands into some definite protest or action.

This sort of confused situation can only be settled peacefully when both sides are willing to admit their mistakes. But here one comes up against the basic difference between Communist and non-Communist countries. In the British Commonwealth and America the indefensible aspects of U.S. and U.N. policy have been subject to active and influential criticism; in Communist countries there are no signs of any criticism of the indefensible aspects of Communist policy. Very powerful forces on the non-Communist side have long been ready to say in effect, "While we consider that the original U.N. intervention in Korea

---

* It is hard to give definite evidence about the state of public opinion in a totalitarian country. But official publicity in China had been stressing the risk of an American attack even before the Korean war started and the limited evidence from people who were in China during the period suggests that this official publicity was largely believed even by educated Chinese opinion.

was justified, the whole situation has now got into a complete mess. Let's get together and try to find some way out which both sides can accept." If the Chinese authorities had ever been willing to co-operate with such people it is fairly certain that the war in Korea could have been stopped in 1951.

The handling of the truce negotiations has not been very creditable for either side. The material published in Peking certainly confirms the view that the U.N. made a very bad mistake in leave the conduct of negotiations in the hands of American army officers.[3] The original decision to use military negotiators was understandable because most people expected that the arranging of a truce would be a technical problem which would be settled in a matter of weeks. As soon as it became clear that arranging a truce involved much more than technical military problems the U.N. should have replaced the American army representatives by a competent team of negotiators and the failure to do so illustrates the disastrous results of subordinating rational action directed to tangible objectives to intangible considerations of prestige.[4] But in the course of the negotiations any unreasonableness and intransigence from the American side has almost always been matched by an even more complete unreasonableness and intransigence from the Chinese side. Even though the truce was finally reached through Chinese concessions the Chinese press and publicity has done its best to misrepresent the situation to avoid any admission that the Chinese concessions were only the abandonment of an indefensible position.

Voluntary repatriation

Writing to Rewi Alley in July, 1952, I said, "If P'eng Te-huai proposed any scheme which could give an objective investigation of the disputed matter of fact—which prisoners really wish to become political refugees rather than return to their own country —he could get a settlement," and the agreement of June, 1953, confirmed this. For more than a year the Korean war went on simply because the Communists would not allow a disputed matter of fact to be settled by the scientific procedure of properly controlled experiment. On the one hand they claimed that any prisoners who said that they did not wish to return to their own countries had only done so under duress and coercion, that "voluntary repatriation" was merely a cover for "forcible detention." On the other hand they refused to allow these claims to be tested by any procedure which would have allowed the prisoners to express their wishes in circumstances which would guarantee freedom from coercion. Some of the schemes proposed from the U.N. may not have offered satisfactory guarantees, but the Communist negotiators did not press for satisfactory guarantees but opposed any form of experimental test. And the scheme they finally accepted was almost identical with the Indian proposals they had rejected six months before. If the Communists believed their own claims they should have welcomed any procedure which would have allowed the prisoners freedom to express their wishes. The result, if Communist claims were true, would have been to secure the return of almost all prisoners and greatly to discredit America in world opinion. The actual Communist attitude was only rational on the assumption that they believed their claims to be false. The hypotheses which would provide a rational motivation for Chinese behaviour are that the Chinese authorities considered a continuation of the war to be a lesser evil than the admission that the "People's Government" had made itself so unpopular with the Chinese people that a considerable proportion of a sample from the Chinese army might prefer the uncomfortable existence of political refugees to returning to their own country. Or alternatively, the Chinese authorities did not really want to end the war and used the prisoners issue as a pretext. Here again, the hypothesis which is clearly incompatible with the evidence is that the Chinese authorities both wanted peace and were acting rationally to get it.

Apart from this question of fact the prisoners issue raised questions of principle which are worth discussing because they show that some differences of opinion relevant to world peace cut right across the division between Communist and non-Communist. The legal position seems to depend on whether articles 7 and 118 of the Geneva Convention are interpreted strictly or in the light of the Convention as a whole whose objective is to safeguard the rights of individual prisoners and not the rights of governments. And when the Convention was drawn up there seem to have been differences of opinion as to whether the principle of voluntary repatriation should be explicitly included. Most of the people who argue against voluntary repatriation do so from what might be called the authoritarian standpoint. They assume that the maintenance of discipline in armies and of the authority of governments over their citizens are in themselves desirable and necessary for the order of society and, therefore, that anything which tends to weaken them is bad. As against this authoritarian standpoint is the standpoint which wishes to allow the individual freedom of choice and to put responsibility on the conscience of the individual. (It is interesting that the same general issue came up in a recent controversy in England about military law—how far "superior orders" should be a valid defence against war crimes charges.)

If one asks, "Which standpoint is most likely to promote world peace?" it is clear that the authoritarian standpoint is a bad one. The unquestioned acceptance of army discipline and governmental authority means that any aggressive group which manages in some way to obtain control of a government will meet with no affective internal resistance. This showed very clearly in recent history. The German and Japanese officers' corps accepted the authoritarian view and in consequence carried out orders which they knew to be criminal and went on fighting when they knew it to be against the interests of their country. Similarly, loyalty to established authority made a high proportion of French officers support the Vichy government and even fight for the Germans until Admiral Darlan gave them an excuse for changing sides. Judging from such cases, it is highly desirable in the interests of world peace that army discipline and governmental authority should break down under any government which tries to pursue a criminal aggressive policy. In so far as the principle of voluntary repatriation means that any government, which tries to fight a war of which its people disapprove, is likely to face large scale surrenders and desertions in its army, it is a principle which every lover of peace should support.

It is likely that the humanitarian motives behind the U.N. stand on voluntary repatriation were strongly reinforced by considerations of creating a precedent which might prove very important in any general war between Russia and America. World War II showed that citizens of totalitarian countries were prepared to fight against their own governments in very large numbers and the Americans are probably reckoning that any future war would produce very large scale desertions from Communist armies provided that the principle of voluntary repatriation enabled them to offer security to such deserters. But even if the Americans have been partly or even mainly motivated by self-interest this does not show them to be wrong. The fact that America and her allies support the principle of voluntary repatriation shows

41

that they feel confident that in any general war only very small numbers of their soldiers would want to join the Communist side and that they really believe their claims that a considerable proportion of the population in Communist controlled countries would like to oppose their governments. Conversely, the Communist opposition to voluntary repatriation showed that the Communist leaders are not confident of the loyalty of the masses in Communist controlled countries and that they do not really believe their own claims about popular opinion in non-Communist countries sympathizing with the Soviet Union. On the question of principle about the desirability of encouraging individual citizens to escape from the authority of their government the Communists are aligned, not with progressive non-Communist opinion, but with the authoritarian right-wing non-Communist standpoint.

Finally, it is worth pointing out that the Soviet Union under Lenin supported the principle of voluntary repatriation. A whole series of treaties in the first years of the Soviet Union show this quite clearly. For example, a treaty with Hungary signed on 28 July, 1921, says, "Repatriation ought not to be enforced; it is left to the free choice of the prisoner to return to his homeland, in agreement with the present treaty, or to remain in the country in which he resides at present, with the agreement of the government of that country."[5]

Germ warfare

The germ warfare issue is another case where the Chinese authorities have refused to allow a disputed matter of fact to be decided by investigation. If they believe their allegations to be true they should have had every reason to support the type of investigation most likely to establish the facts beyond reasonable doubt. An investigating commission with adequate powers to operate on both sides of the front and composed of such scientific and legal experts as would be generally trusted to put professional standards above political loyalties could have given a verdict that would be generally accepted by world opinion. But while the Americans have always professed themselves willing to permit this type of investigation the Communists have always refused it on various pretexts, pretexts which illustrate the evasiveness that inevitably produces suspicions of Communist good faith. Chinese spokesmen have sometimes argued that an investigating commission would enable the Americans to find out how far germ warfare had been successful. This line of argument would imply that the Chinese authorities would not permit any investigation likely to publish an accurate report. More often it has been argued that suggested investigating agencies were not impartial. For example, at a meeting of the executive committee of the World Peace Council in March, 1952, Kuo Mo-jo "declared that the governments of China and (North) Korea did not consider the International Red Cross Committee sufficiently free of political influence to be capable of instituting an unbiased inquiry into the field. This objection was later extended to the World Health Organisation as a specialised agency of the United Nations. However, the two governments were entirely desirous of inviting an international group of impartial and independent scientists to proceed to China and to investigate personally the facts on which the allegations were based. They might or might not be connected with organisations working for peace, but they would naturally be persons known for their devotion to humanitarian causes."[6]

There are a number of obvious comments on this statement. Firstly, while criticizing the Red Cross and the World Health Organisation the Chinese authorities did not try to suggest some alternative plan for getting an investigating commission which would be acceptable to both sides and which, therefore, would be able to operate on both sides of the front. Secondly, in asking the World Peace Council to appoint an investigating commission the Chinese authorities illustrate their refusal to accept any objective standards. Any standards which rule out the Red Cross and the W.H.O. as "not sufficiently free of political influence to be capable of instituting an unbiased inquiry" would quite certainly rule out the World Peace Council which, unlike the Red Cross and W.H.O., has openly taken sides on many questions of world politics and which many people consider, with some reason, to be little more than a Soviet propaganda agency. Thirdly, Kuo Mo-jo would almost certainly maintain that the only organisations really working for peace were those which accepted Communist leadership and that the interests of humanity were bound up with those of world Communism and the Soviet Union. It is, therefore, very probable that the last sentence quoted could be translated from Communist euphemism into plain English and would then read, "Members of the commission might or might not be avowed Communists or Fellow Travellers, but they would

naturally be known for their strong pro-Communist sympathies."
In fact, the British member of the International Scientific Commission was the President of the Communist controlled Britain-China Friendship Association.

Thus, the Communists have always refused to allow their claims to be investigated except by a commission which was appointed by a strongly pro-Communist organisation, whose members, at least in some cases, were strongly pro-Communist in their sympathies, and which could only operate on the Communist side of the front. (This applies to the committee from the International Democratic Lawyers as well as to the International Scientific Commission.) If the Chinese authorities really believe their own claims this behaviour was just silly and irrational. It would, however, be entirely rational if they did not really believe their own claims and knew that an objective investigation would discredit them. Conversely, in expressing their readiness to allow a full investigation the Americans were taking a tremendous risk if they actually had been using germ warfare. They were acting quite rationally if they knew that an objective investigation would prove them to be innocent. The Americans did not insist on the Red Cross or W.H.O. as the only organisations they would accept and it is, at any rate, very doubtful whether the Communist objections to these organisations were justified. A non-Communist scientific or legal expert who accepted the philosophical assumptions of scientific method might start with an inclination to trust the Americans rather than the Communists but would certainly feel obliged to change his opinions in accordance with the evidence. And the Communists would have full opportunities for presenting evidence to any commission which operated on both sides of the front. The notorious Red Cross report whitewashing the Nazi concentration camps was not the result of refusing to accept evidence but of undertaking an investigation at all under conditions in which it was not possible to establish the truth because the presentation of evidence was entirely controlled by one party, the German government. But the International Scientific Commission undertook an investigation under the same conditions in which the presentation of evidence was entirely controlled by one party, the Communists.

In fact, the report of the International Scientific Commission does not seriously investigate one hypothesis for which there is a fairly strong *prima facie* case, namely, that the evidence of germ warfare was planted by some Communist secret service organisation. If the Americans were going to risk incurring the odium of world opinion through using germ warfare it seems improbable that they would use it so ineffectively, using methods that most experts say are obsolete and often under conditions when these methods were unlikely to produce results, such as dropping insects under severe winter conditions. (It is said that even Chinese opinion was impressed by this point and that a joke current in Peking was, "Isn't America wonderful? Even the insects have skis and arctic clothing.") On the other hand, a Communist secret service organisation faking evidence to support germ warfare charges would have every reason to use methods which were unlikely to produce more than small scale casualties. And this hypothesis would fully explain the Communist unwillingness to allow an objective investigation in which both sides could present evidence and argue a case. The International Scientific Commission may have ruled out this hypothesis on the evidence of the confessions they report from American airmen. But the value as evidence of confessions from prisoners under Communist control has been rendered very doubtful by a whole series of confessions at trials in Communist countries. Here again, the evidence could only be properly investigated by a commission entrusted with adequate powers by both sides which could have examined the prisoners under conditions which ruled out duress. The Communists claim that the prisoners repudiated their confessions under duress after repatriation. However, the American case was greatly strengthened by the evidence of other repatriated prisoners of attempts to force them to make confessions.

It seems likely that there never will be a proper investigation of the germ warfare charges so that some element of uncertainty will always remain. However, so long as the Americans profess themselves ready to allow the type of investigation which could best establish the facts while the Communists refuse to allow it, there must be a strong presumption that the Americans are speaking the truth while the Communists are not.

Such a presumption is strengthened by eyewitness accounts which show that the Chinese Communists have no scruples about faking evidence. For example, after an American air raid in Korea which killed a few American prisoners the Chinese "lugged some dynamite into the camp, exploded it, and took numerous photographs of the resulting craters. When the prisoners pointed out that such pictures, however impressive, would be considerably less than truthful, the Chinese were indignant. 'We no lie,' one of them said. 'We make facts. You see the facts being made.'"[7]

This sort of behaviour is explicable in terms of Stalinist philosophy. It is possible that a Chinese Communist representative speaking frankly might be prepared to admit that, by empirical standards, official Chinese claims were often not true. But he would go on to maintain that it was wrong to judge true and false by empirical standards, that "truth is that which serves the interests of the masses," and that, by this correct standard, official Chinese claims were true.

4

Communist philosophy

The two standards of truth

A COMMON feature of most totalitarian philosophies is the rejection of the view that the truth or falsity of a statement about matters of fact can be tested by empirical observation and experiment. The difference in standards of truth shows most clearly in the writing of history. Judged by normal scientific standards a great deal of Soviet and recent Chinese official history is a deliberate falsification of the facts. For example, the accounts of Chinese history in the 1920's based on original source material agree that a number of Comintern representatives played an important part, that Chinese Communist policy was largely determined by Comintern directives and that Mao Tse-tung's line of reliance on the peasantry as a revolutionary force was at one time condemned not only by the Chinese but also by the Soviet Communist leadership. (Benjamin Schwartz's *Chinese Communism and the Rise of Mao*[1] is a good illustration of a study with detailed references to original sources.) In Hu Ch'iao-mu's official history of the Chinese Communist Party all this has completely disappeared.[2] The Communist defeat is ascribed entirely to the mistakes of Ch'en Tu-hsiu and other Chinese leaders since condemned by the Party who are presented as ignoring invariably correct and wise general advice from Moscow. There is no mention of Mao's unorthodoxy or of the activitities in China of any Comintern agents. If truth is judged by correspondence with the evidence, Hu Ch'iao-mu's history shows a marked degeneration in Chinese Communist standards as compared with the history of the Party given to Anna Louise Strong at Yenan in 1946.[3]

Defenders of Stalinist history often argue that all historical writing involves some selection and interpretation and that someone like Hu Ch'iao-mu is not doing anything essentially different from non-totalitarian historians. This, like many Stalinist arguments, depends on the assumption that the world must be describable in terms of sharply defined classes. Though it may

47

be impossible to make a sharp distinction between interpreting history from a particular viewpoint and falsifying history to fit a preconceived view this does not mean that the distinction is an unreal one. And in sections of Hu Ch'iao-mu's history falsification predominates over interpretation.

The issue shows still more clearly in the falsification of documents. The text of, say, Mao Tse-tung's *New Democracy* is not something which can vary with the standpoint of the observer. It is a definite number of characters in a definite order. If one looks at successive editions one finds that the text remains unchanged up to 1948; but in the 1952 edition of Mao's *Selected Works* there are considerable alterations in passages which would show, in their original form, that Mao had not been infallible in his interpretation of the international situation. (It is interesting that while the Chinese text was only falsified after 1948 the English translation prepared by the Eighteenth Group Army office in Chungking in 1944 left out a number of passages giving the international Communist line in the period of the Nazi-Soviet pact. The result caused considerable embarrassment to Mr. Earl Browder who produced an American edition on the basis of a manuscript which he was told was a complete official translation and was then accused of falsifying the text by people who had read a Chinese edition.)

The falsification of history goes much further in Soviet practice and it can also be found in non-Communist totalitarian systems. Chiang Kai-shek's *China's Destiny* is a good example and it is interesting that he agrees with Hu Ch'iao-mu in leaving out all reference to the Comintern agents who operated in China during the first period of Kuomintang-Communist co-operation. Wang Chung-hui's official translation of *China's Destiny* is also a good example of falsification of texts. The passages which show that Chiang was opposed to liberal democracy as well as to Communism are all distorted, often by the insertion of qualifying phrases which have no basis at all in the Chinese text.[4]

The official Chinese line on germ warfare, the origins of the Korean war and many of the other points I have discussed shows just the same sort of attitude to empirical evidence as is exemplified in the official falsification of more remote periods of history. The rewriting of history thus provides additional evidence for the hypothesis that Chinese behaviour in the international field is not the result of a deliberate policy of aggression but follows naturally from the assumptions of Stalinist philosophy which may quite well be combined with a subjectively sincere desire for peace and international goodwill.

But the choice between alternative standards of truth is directly relevant to the problems of peace. Disputes between people who accept objectivity and who judge truth by empirical standards can be settled peacefully. When they disagree on matters of fact they can still reach agreement about the sort of evidence which would settle the dispute and can co-operate in trying to obtain such evidence. In effect, they agree on allowing their dispute to be settled by impersonal standards. If they are faced with a real conflict of interest they can normally reach a compromise which will leave both parties better off than if they had resorted to war. But a stable compromise can only be reached when the interests and bargaining strength of both sides are judged by objective standards and when there is some security that agreements once reached will be observed. The basic principle of compromise could be summed up by the English proverb, "Half a loaf is better than no bread." A secure half loaf is preferable to fighting for the whole with the risk of being left with nothing or destroying most of the bread in the fight. But the motive for compromise disappears if the half loaf is no more secure than the whole. If one is dealing with people who cannot be trusted to keep agreements it will never be worth while to make any concessions which might weaken one's future bargaining strength because a concession cannot secure anything more than a slight postponement of fresh demands. It is much more reasonable to fight for even the slightest chance of getting the whole loaf rather than face the certainty of losing everything by stages at each of which it is harder to resist fresh demands.

When one party to a dispute holds totalitarian views the chances of a peaceful settlement become very small. The Chinese Communists ought to know this from their experience in dealing with Chiang Kai-shek. As far as I could judge from the people I knew at Yenan in the autumn of 1945, Mao Tse-tung really wanted to reach a compromise which would spare the Chinese people the horrors of civil war and managed to secure acceptance for a policy of compromise against criticism from some sections of the Party. And the record of Chinese Communist policy up to the summer of 1946 shows a real willingness to make concessions in order to secure a peaceful settlement. For example, the evacuation of areas south of the Yangtze after October, 1945, and the Military Agreement of February, 1946, showed that the Communists were prepared to make important sacrifices of military strength in order to obtain an agreement.* But no possible Communist policy could have secured a peaceful settlement because of the totalitarian rejection of objectivity by Chiang Kai-shek and his associates. One factor in producing the civil war was the inability of the Kuomintang leadership to make an objective judgment of their real bargaining strength. Because the Kuomintang leaders believed that they could win a complete victory in a civil war in a matter of months they were never prepared to accept a compromise that had some relation to their real strength. And they were never prepared to judge both sides by objective standards. The Communists were asked, in effect, to abandon the security given by the possession of a private army in return for nothing but promises by Chiang Kai-shek that they would enjoy the security guaranteed by a democratic constitution. But Chiang Kai-shek's past record had made it quite unreasonable to put much trust in his promises. In the years before 1946 he had promised to introduce constitutional government, to guarantee civil liberties, to make reforms in administration and so on and these promises had always been evaded or broken. And subsequent developments showed that the guarantees in the 1946 constitution were valueless. The ordinary citizen never had any security against the arbitrary exercise of power by the Kuomintang authorities. Even though the constitution had provisions for emergency powers whose use could have been justified by the civil war, the Kuomintang often preferred to act in ways that were flagrantly illegal. Even in Shanghai, where the Kuomintang government was concerned to keep up appearances, the garrison commander refused to allow the courts to investigate the legality of his actions.

Behind a façade of high sounding phrases about democracy and legality, Chiang Kai-shek continued, in effect, to demand submission to his authority as leader of China; and as soon as developments in the spring of 1946 had made it clear that the Kuomintang was not really prepared to abandon one-party rule or to curb the powers of the secret police the Communists were acting quite reasonably in refusing to make any further concessions which would have weakened the security they enjoyed through the possession of military power.

* For a period after the Japanese surrender the Communists held a strip of territory from the Yangtze Valley to Hangchow Bay.

Chiang Kai-shek provides a very good illustration of the practical uselessness of subjective sincerity. Many quite honest and competent observers were impressed by his sincerity in proclaiming his desire to serve the Chinese people, to introduce reforms, and to establish democracy and the rule of law. Where they often went wrong was in failing to realize that someone who holds a totalitarian philosophy can combine sincerity with dishonesty. Because Chiang Kai-shek's mind operated in a world in which principles were not invalidated by lack of correspondence with empirical fact, and concepts such as democracy or the rule of law were not defined by operational standards, it was quite possible for him to be completely sincere in proclaiming his principles and intentions and, at the same time, to act in ways which, by empirical standards, were quite incompatible with these claims. He seems to have had a real faith in his mission as leader of China and to have had really benevolent intentions to the Chinese people, in so far as they fitted into this theoretical scheme by submitting to his authority. He was never willing to face the incompatibility between this demand for submission to his personal authority and any operational definition of democracy or the rule of law.

While the totalitarianism of the Kuomintang ruling group made it impossible for any Communist policy to secure a peaceful settlement and the establishment of a reforming democratic government in China, it has been argued that Communist totalitarianism made it equally impossible for any Kuomintang policy to secure a peaceful settlement. The general record of Stalinist parties certainly makes doubtful the possibility of reaching a peaceful compromise with them. In all the countries of Eastern Europe the ruling Communist groups, like Chiang Kai-shek and his associates, have refused to accept any position except one in which everyone else makes an unqualified submission to their authority. All promises of free elections and civil liberties or of freedom for other parties inside a coalition government have been broken as soon as the Communists have felt strong enough to break their promises with impunity. In China for the crucial period in 1945 and 1946 the answer is doubtful because Communist claims were never put to any empirical test. In my opinion the basic mistake in American policy was the failure to make any empirical test of the Communist claims to stand for the interests of the Chinese people and to be ready to accept the position of a political party in a democratic system which could obtain power only by competing for popular support as expressed in free elections. And Soviet behaviour provided a very favourable opportunity for making such a test. Suppose that the Americans had used whatever degree of pressure was necessary to force Chiang Kai-shek honestly to observe the agreements reached under General Marshall's mediation, to accept a coalition government and ensure civil liberties. Suppose then that the Americans had offered to support this new government in protesting against the Soviet looting of Manchuria under the pretext of "war booty" and against the behaviour of some Soviet army units towards the civilian population. The Chinese Communists would then have faced a clear cut choice between loyalty to the Chinese people and loyalty to the Soviet Union. It is probable that a high proportion of the Communist leadership would have given first priority to loyalty to China and that Chinese Communism would have gone Titoist in 1946. In this situation the divergences between Chinese Communism and Stalinism would almost certainly have increased instead of diminishing. Although China might very likely by now have a predominantly Communist government owing its power to free elections it would not be a Stalinist government and both the international situation and the internal situation would be more favourable for peace and for the interests of the Chinese people. Alternatively, if the Chinese Communists had come out of a coalition government on this issue and had fought the civil war as a purely pro-Soviet party their chances of victory would have been much smaller, especially against a government rendered much more honest and competent by the previous elimination of the extreme right-wing elements in the Kuomintang.

All this is largely speculative, but if one turns to the present situation one can say with some assurance that, in so far as they consistently accept a totalitarian philosophy, the Chinese Communist leaders are taking up a position which is incompatible with the peaceful settlement of disputes. Communist totalitarianism is more sophisticated and more of a logically coherent system than Kuomintang totalitarianism but it does imply the same demand for submission. So long as the Chinese Communist leaders say, in effect, "Truth is what we consider to be in the interests of the masses" there is no way in which any dispute can be settled peacefully except by other people accepting the Communist view. On this definition of truth it is theoretically impossible to change the Communist view by any process of rational persuasion. To point out that Communist statements or their implications do not correspond with observable evidence is to rely on empiricism, which the Communists denounce as a fallacious way of thinking. To argue that Communist policies are unlikely to produce the results claimed for them is, by Communist standards, merely to reveal that one judges events from a viewpoint opposed to that of the masses, because the Communist party represents the masses, and the masses are always right. And if no process of rational persuasion can change the Communist view the only possible basis for agreement is acceptance of the Communist view.

In the short run the impossibility of reaching agreement does not necessarily imply war. The objective of a great deal of diplomacy is not to settle disputes but to postpone or evade any real settlement. And, quite often, if some issue is evaded for long enough it ceases to be of practical importance and is no longer a threat to peace. However, in other cases, this kind of diplomacy only lessens the immediate risk of war by making war more likely in the future. Some issue which could have been settled as soon as it arose with only a little courage and goodwill on both sides becomes, through postponement, so involved and acquires such far-reaching implications that any settlement becomes extremely difficult. And disputes may arise in which it is not possible to evade or postpone a settlement.

In the long run an almost essential condition for peace is that the Communists should abandon their claims of Party infallibility and become ready to allow disputes to be judged by objective standards and questions of fact to be decided by experimental tests. Up to a point non-Communists may be willing, for the sake of peace, to accept Communist claims even when they believe them to be false. But beyond certain limits many non-Communists would be prepared to fight rather than submit to Communist authority, and so long as the Communists maintain their belief in Party infallibility with its implied claim for submission it is almost certain that sooner or later these limits will be reached.

The doctrine of Party infallibility is not usually stated in an explicit and unambiguous form but it appears as an implicit assumption in a great many statements of the Communist position. Consider, for example, the following description of Chinese Communist practice: "there is a great deal of inner party discussion, criticism and self-criticism. This goes on continually and covers everything from the smallest details of personal behaviour to the largest questions of national policy, which the rank and file may have little say in formulating but which *are invariably discussed until they are unanimously accepted.*"[5] (My italics.) (This particular passage was written by a foreign supporter of the regime but its substantial correctness can be confirmed from Chinese official documents which make the same assumption that discussion must end with acceptance of the Party Line.) It is assumed that on very complex issues of national policy the higher Party authorities can make decisions which are not only correct but so obviously correct that discussion can only lead to their unanimous acceptance. For someone who thinks in terms of the philosophical assumptions behind scientific method this assumption seems to ascribe superhuman wisdom to the Communist Party leadership. Even in the comparatively simple field of natural science controversies may go on for years before one view becomes generally accepted. A good illustration was the chemical formula of penicillin. For several years there was a bitter controversy, at first between several and finally between two rival views and one rival view only secured acceptance when evidence became available from another branch of science. Most questions of national policy are vastly more complicated. The number of relevant variables is much greater and it is not usually possible to make experiments to obtain evidence. By any scientific standards, policy decisions can seldom be made with any high degree of certainty. The choice within a range of possible alternatives must nearly always be made on the basis of imperfect knowledge of factors which are often incapable of precise measurement. It is only after the event, and perhaps not even then, that it becomes possible to say whether or not the alternative actually chosen was the best. Under these conditions it is extremely unlikely that discussion will produce unanimous agreement and this is true whether or not the policy actually chosen finally turns out to be correct. Claims of unanimous agreement only prove that there is lack of freedom in the discussion and, in fact, the Party Line only secures unanimous acceptance in an environment where conformity is enforced by social pressure or definite penal sanctions.

Another variant of the claim of Party infallibility can be found in the Chinese publications about the anti-3 movement* and ideo-

---

* The anti-3 and anti-5 movements were campaigns conducted by the Chinese Communist Party against certain alleged defects in the working of

logical reform in the universities. Part of the campaign was directed against fairly obvious failings such as wasteful organisation, excessive preoccupation with salaries and status, uncritical following of foreign text books, and so on. But as soon as it got beyond this common sense level it was clear that the object of the campaign was to secure complete submission to Communist Party authority from the intelligentsia. Beliefs were not denounced because they were untrue, by non-totalitarian standards, because they were illogical or incompatible with empirical evidence. The criticism was almost always that certain views reflected "bourgeois ideology"; and "objectivity" was one of the standards denounced for this reason. What was required is shown by an article on ideological reform at Nankai university which praises some professors for "accepting in all modesty the opinions of the masses."[6] And it is taken for granted that the "opinions of the masses" are identical with the Party Line. Instead of Mao Tse-tung's old slogan "Seek the truth by reference to fact" the Chinese Communist Party now seems to operate on the slogan "Seek the truth by reference to class."[7]

A claim that the only standard of truth is the ideology of the working class and that this ideology is represented by the Communist Party is equivalent to a claim of Party infallibility. By these standards no evidence and no argument could ever show that the Party Line was wrong.

Not only does this claim of infallibility make it impossible to reach agreement in any dispute between Communists and non-Communists in which the Party Line fails to satisfy scientific standards of correctness; it also makes agreement very difficult even in cases where the Communist position happens to be, by scientific standards, largely right. The more the Chinese leaders become accustomed to operating in an environment in which everything they say is always accepted, the less capable they become of stating a case in a way that is likely to convince people accustomed to using critical judgment in an environment of free discussion. There have already been a number of disputes in which the Chinese Communist Party actually had quite a strong case but either failed to set out the evidence on which its case was based or else discredited itself by combining its valid arguments with claims that were wildly exaggerated or demonstrably false.

various organisations in China including universities, private business and government institutions.

"Doublethink"

The rejection of empirical standards gives a curious air of unreality to many Chinese pronouncements. In the intellectual atmosphere of modern China many things seem to be generally accepted as self-evident which, by empirical standards, appear to be highly controversial if not clearly untrue. One is continually reminded of the Hans Andersen story of *The Emperor's Clothes.* (The emperor is offered at a very high price some wonderful clothes which have the singular property of being invisible and intangible to anyone who is stupid or disloyal. No one dares to admit that they cannot see the clothes until they are worn in a state procession when a child calls out that the emperor has nothing on. In the story everyone then becomes ready to admit the evidence of their senses and people realize that they have been tricked. But if Hans Andersen had been writing today the story might have ended with the child being taken away for "brain-washing" and the emperor continuing to wear his invisible, intangible clothes.)

If the emperor had insisted on wearing his new clothes out of doors in severe winter weather he would probably have died of exposure however efficient his police and education departments had been in eradicating the "disloyalty" and "stupidity" of those who were unable to see the new clothes. Similarly, if the Chinese Communist Party were entirely consistent in claiming infallibility and in substituting "Seek the truth by reference to class" for "Seek the truth by reference to fact" its power would soon collapse through inability to correct its mistakes.

When mistakes have no practical consequences the claim of infallibility can be maintained simply by denying the facts. Hu Ch'iao-mu's falsified history is now the official text book from which everyone has to study the history of the Chinese Communist Party; Mao Tse-tung's argument in 1940 that a Chinese alliance with Britain and America could not be directed against Japan has simply disappeared from recent editions of his works; and so on.*

In many cases, however, mistakes cannot be denied without disastrous practical consequences and the thinking of people in

---

* It is interesting that the revisers of Mao's *Selected Works* failed to spot one passage which reveals complete ignorance of the European situation by referring, in September, 1939, to ". . . the parts of Western Poland occupied by the German army or the parts of Western Germany occupied by the French army." (*Mao Tse-tung Hsuan Chi*. Peking, 1952. Vol. II, Page 564.)

totalitarian organisations cannot be explained except in terms of something like the concept which George Orwell defines as "doublethink." "Doublethink means the power of holding two contradictory beliefs in one's mind at the same time, and accepting both of them . . . the essential act of the Party is to use conscious deception while retaining the firmness of purpose that goes with complete honesty. To tell deliberate lies while genuinely believing in them, to forget any fact that has become inconvenient, and then, when it becomes necessary again, to draw it back from oblivion for just so long as it is needed, to deny the existence of objective reality and all the while to take account of the reality one denies—all this is indispensably necessary . . . For the secret of rulership is to combine a belief in one's own infallibility with the power to learn from past mistakes."*

For internal policy the most common device for combining a belief in Party infallibility with the ability to correct mistakes is the fiction that mistakes are always caused by individual Communists who have misinterpreted the Party Line. And, to the non-Communist observer, it often appears that Party directives are deliberately made ambiguous so that lower officials can be blamed if anything goes wrong. For instance, cadres were ordered to push the collectivization of agriculture but to do it without using compulsion. When the policy produced a fall in agricultural production the Party could denounce "deviation of rash advance" without admitting that there had been anything wrong with its original directives. The cadres who were criticized were not allowed to make the obvious defence, that to produce rapid progress in collectivization without using compulsion was, in most cases, an impossible task.

* Orwell, George, *Nineteen Eighty-four* (Secker & Warburg, London, 1950). Pp. 215-6.

It is unlikely that *Nineteen Eighty-four* will prove any more accurate as a prediction of what will actually happen than similar books, such as H. G. Wells' *When the Sleeper Wakes* or Jack London's *The Iron Heel*. All three were extrapolations of trends which existed when they were written but which in the real world, were very unlikely to continue unmodified as imagined in the book. However, the more theoretical parts of Orwell's book, such as the chapters from *The Theory and Practice of Oligarchical Collectivism* or the dialogue towards the end between O'Brien and Smith, could be paraphrased as an entirely serious discussion of the question, "What would a totalitarian system have to be like in order to be completely and permanently successful?" In natural science the consideration of practically unrealizable, theoretical limiting cases often has great practical value. Similarly, it is useful to consider existing totalitarian systems in terms of approximation to a pure totalitarianism which, fortunately, is never likely to exist.

If one looks at the Chinese press one finds a great deal about mistakes and their correction. But if one examines this material at all closely one finds that any criticism beyond the most superficial level is usually part of some campaign decided on by the higher Party authorities and that the much vaunted "Communist self-criticism" almost always stops short before admitting any defects in the official Party Line or implicating any high ranking Communist official. To the non-Communist observer it often appears that the mistakes which are admitted are the natural result of some defect in Communist policy or organisation, but criticism published in China never seems to carry its analysis to the point where such conclusions might possibly emerge. For instance, one finds frequent cases in which local officials are publicly criticized for arbitrary behaviour towards the population under their control and in which the Party claims credit for intervening to remedy the grievances of the people. The conclusion which is never hinted at is that this type of mistake is almost certain to recur continually in a system without the rule of law; that intervention by the higher Party authorities after the event to remedy those grievances which have been brought to their attention is a very poor substitute for giving the Chinese people what Engels called "the first condition of all freedom; that all functionaries should be responsible for all their official acts to every citizen, before the ordinary courts and according to the common law."*

Up to a point this device of combining a claim of Party infallibility with a readiness to admit that individual Communists may make mistakes works fairly well. On technical questions and points of detail the readiness of the Chinese Communist Party to modify its action in the light of experience compares quite favourably with the behaviour of some British official organisations which make no theoretical claims to infallibility but have a traditional dislike of admitting mistakes. But the more serious mistakes in Chinese Communist policy are seldom corrected until their results have become so serious that the higher Party authorities can no longer ignore them, and the refusal to generalise from particular mistakes to a possible cause in defective Party policy means that certain types of mistake recur

* From letter to Bebel in March, 1875, in which Engels criticized the Gotha Programme for failing to include this "first condition of all freedom". (*Marx Engels Selected Works*. Foreign Languages Publishing House, Moscow. 1949. Vol. II. Page 38.)

again and again because their underlying cause is never corrected.

In international affairs it is seldom possible to maintain that a correct Party Line has been misinterpreted by individual Communists. The relevant decisions are normally in the form of official Party pronouncements or actions by people who are too high up in the Party to be repudiated or criticized without a major purge. As a result the essential practical flexibility is secured by evasiveness or by operating with unresolved contradictions. Chinese foreign policy shows a whole series of fairly clear "doublethink" positions, some of which have been discussed above.

This "doublethink" is slightly less dangerous to world peace than an uncompromising and consistent claim of infallibility would be because it does make it possible for the Party to compromise. When a situation arises in which the Party Line would produce disastrous practical results, such as a major war, the Party Line can be modified. But it still remains impossible to end any dispute by a settlement in which Communists and non-Communists reach agreement, as opposed to a compromise which both sides accept only because they prefer it to fighting. The use of "doublethink" makes it very difficult for the Communists even to begin the process of discussion and exchange of views which might lead to agreement. A "doublethink" position is fairly easy to maintain in an environment in which no one calls attention to the contradictions in it or calls for their resolution. It would be hard to maintain in an environment of free discussion. And it is noticeable that Chinese Communist representatives tend to avoid such an environment.

For instance, when Wu Hsiu-ch'uan went to New York he and his staff refused almost every invitation for informal discussions with British representatives. This is quite understandable when one reads his set speech. Its argument depend very largely on the introduction of controversial statements as unsupported assertions or implicit assumptions. In any informal discussion the Chinese representatives would almost certainly have been asked to give some evidence for the controversial statements in Wu Hsiu-ch'uan's speech and this would have placed them in a very embarrassing position even though their non-Communist questioners might have been entirely friendly. So long as the Chinese authorities take up this sort of position which makes it impossible for Chinese representatives to have frank discussions with informed non-Communists the peaceful settlement of any dispute is bound to be extremely difficult.

So long as the non-Communist world is faced by an official Chinese position in which there are glaring contradictions between different official statements or between official statements and the observable facts about Chinese Communist behaviour, the real motives behind Chinese Communist policy can only be a matter for speculation. And this complete uncertainty about what the Chinese Communists really want inevitably produces suspicions which are a very serious obstacle to any lessening of international tension.

There are a large number of questions about which it would be very interesting to cross examine some responsible representative of the Chinese government in order to clear up some of the uncertainties about Chinese objectives. To give only a few illustrations from points which have been discussed here: How can the official Chinese claims to be working for international goodwill be reconciled with some aspects of the "hate America" campaign? How can the official claims of desire to promote international cultural relations be reconciled with the denunciations of those Chinese professors who have tried to maintain foreign contacts?[8] How can the official claims to want foreign trade under conditions of "mutual advantage" and "equality of status" be reconciled with the actual treatment of British firms in China? What are the real reasons for the Chinese refusal to establish diplomatic relations with the U.K.? The reactions to such questions would clarify the real objectives of the Chinese authorities in general international contacts.

Again, how can the official claims that the Soviet Union is incapable of aggression be reconciled with the changes in the map of Europe between 1938 and 1946?—changes which show that every European country bordering on the Soviet Union, including several with which the Soviet government had non-aggression pacts, has suffered total or partial annexation by the Soviet Union. How can Mao Tse-tung's slogan "If you have not investigated you have no right to speak" be reconciled with the numerous cases in which the Chinese authorities have given immediate and unqualified support to some Soviet statement which they have had no opportunity of verifying? Why are the denunciations of rearmament and continuing Nazi influence in West Germany not applied to the earlier rearmament and close Communist-Nazi collaboration in East Germany? And how can the denunciations of the East German workers for their revolt of June, 1953, be reconciled with the claim to support liberation movements and the working class? Why did the Chinese Communists never protest against Russian behaviour in Manchuria and why do they continue to allow the Soviet Union a military base with extraterritorial status in Chinese territory? The reaction to such questions would clarify the problem of whether or not the Chinese government's support of the Soviet Union is so unqualified and so uncritical that Chinese policy is in practice indistinguishable from that of a satellite under effective Soviet control.

Yet again why did the Chinese government give unqualified support to the North Korean attempt to unify Korea by military force? What were the real motives behind Chinese intervention in Korea? Why did the Chinese government reject the Indian proposals at the end of 1952 when they were ready to accept almost identical terms for a truce six months later? The reaction to such questions would clarify the real motives behind Chinese actions in Korea.

It would be easy to extend both the list of subjects and the numbers of relevant questions on each subject.

In fact, such questions never seem to be discussed. It is yet another element of "doublethink" in the Chinese position that the Chinese authorities claim to be ready to discuss any problems related to peace and at the same time avoid discussions with any people who would be likely to press the really relevant questions. It is interesting that this particular criticism of the Chinese position was the one argument which Rewi Alley showed that he had understood. He tried to refute it by citing his experience of free discussions with foreign visitors to Peking. But these foreign visitors have been a highly biased sample of non-Communist opinion. Nearly all of them have been sponsored by some organisation largely under Communist influence, such as the Britain-China Friendship Association or its equivalent in other countries. At least in the case of British visitors, the published reports of their discussions show that they have almost all been either avowed Communists or Fellow Travellers or else people of general goodwill but without the necessary background knowledge to press the really interesting questions.

An interesting piece of evidence is the Chinese reaction to Dr. John Burton who visited Peking in May, 1952, as a member of an Australian delegation to the preliminary conference for the

Peking Peace Conference. Dr. Burton's standpoint was in many ways quite close to the Communist position. For instance, he largely accepted the official Chinese view on the origin of the Korean war and the refusal to establish diplomatic relations with the U.K.; he saw nothing objectionable in the Communist falsification of the historical record or in the abject repudiations of academic standards published by men who used to be scholars of international reputation. But he did have the ability and the knowledge to make an effective presentation of his views. The result was, in Rewi Alley's words, "that Burton was the 'enfant terrible' of the conference . . . He challenged all the basic beliefs." It is a fairly clear indication of the normal standards of discussion at Peking that the presentation of a viewpoint differing from the Communist position as little as Dr. Burton's should appear as a unique and outstanding challenge to accepted beliefs.

A contrast to the friendly reception of Dr. Burton was the treatment of Mr. John Clews who visited Peking in 1950 as the U.K. delegate to a conference of the International Union of Students. Mr. Clews' position was more nearly typical of non-Communist opinion. He was in favour of co-operation with Communists in international organisations in so far as the Communists were prepared to co-operate for the ostensible objectives of the organisation, but he was not prepared to allow such co-operation to be perverted to serve purely Communist objectives. Like Dr. Burton he had both the ability and the knowledge to make an effective presentation of his views, but he encountered at Peking strong hostility and a complete refusal to join in discussions of international questions.

These two instances indicate that the range of difference from the official Communist position within which the Chinese Communists are now prepared to join in discussions is a fairly narrow one which would exclude the great majority of well informed non-Communists.

It is true that the opportunities for pressing discussion have not been fully used. A good example was the visit of some British members of parliament to Peking in 1952.[9] Although, as members of parliament, they had a semi-official status the British Foreign Office seems to have made no attempt to give them any background information on recent Sino-British relations and the British representative at Peking seems to have expounded his conclusions about the motives of the Chinese government without giving any of the evidence on which these conclusions were based and without explaining the British case in reply to the official Chinese arguments which the visitors were sure to hear. As a result the most obvious questions remained unasked. For instance, when Kuo Mo-jo justified the refusal to establish diplomatic relations by the fighting between British and Chinese troops in Korea he was not asked to explain how fighting which only started in November, 1950, could be the cause of a Chinese policy decision dating from the previous January. The Peking Peace Conference was another opportunity for pressing discussion. It would have been possible for the Australian government to have secured the sending of an Australian delegation with a considerable proportion of people both able and willing to raise the questions relevant for peace. In fact both the Australian government and the Australian Communist Party tried to discourage the participation of such people.

Such failures on the non-Communist side to press the issue leaves some uncertainty about how far the Chinese authorities would go in avoiding any effective informal discussions of international problems. However, the behaviour of Chinese representatives abroad, the selection of foreign visitors who have been welcomed in Peking, and the treatment of the occasional foreign visitors who have been willing and able to make an effective statement of the non-Communist case, all make it appear unlikely that any efforts from the non-Communist side to secure frank discussions would meet with a willing Chinese response.

(Since this passage was written there has been some change in Chinese policy. Chou En-lai has had a number of discussions with members of non-Communist governments and the invitation to the British Labour Party delegation has made possible a visit by people in responsible positions with enough knowledge of international affairs to ask the relevant questions. On the most optimistic interpretation this may represent a reaction against McCarthyism in China and a swing back towards the more reasonable attitude of the early 1940's. On the most pessimistic interpretation it may be purely a tactical manoeuvre to prevent or delay the formation of a non-Communist Asian defence agreement. The information about developments within the Chinese Communist Party is so inadequate that any attempt of an outside observer to decide between these possibilities must be almost pure speculation. The challenging of Communist "doublethink" positions remains relevant as an important source of experimental evidence on this problem.)

Quite apart from this question of readiness to join in discussions the distinction between Communist and non-Communist cannot be presented in clear cut black and white. Contradictions which inevitably produce suspicions and thus hinder any lessening of international tension are certainly not confined to the Communist side. But though non-Communist contradictions raise real problems they are different problems from those raised by Communist contradictions. To a very large extent democratic systems do not even claim to operate in terms of a single unified policy. When Communists express suspicions of Western good faith because government policy statements are contradicted by opinions expressed in the press they are simply showing complete ignorance of the working of a democratic system. (And some Soviet leaders have argued in this way at international conferences.) But when this tolerance of conflicting opinions appears inside a single government it does afford real grounds for suspicion. American government operates with sufficient publicity to show that actual policy is often only the resultant of an internal struggle between different groups with incompatible policies and objectives. Even America's allies often find this situation disconcerting. One could cite Mr. Attlee's question as to whether President Eisenhower or Senator McCarthy really controlled American policy. The most reasonable and peace loving Chinese Communist representative would have real reasons for misgiving about the influence of the extremist pro-Kuomintang China Lobby. It would be quite reasonable for the Chinese government to regard official statements of American government intentions with considerable suspicion unless they were accompanied by evidence that the American government was both willing and able to uphold its announced policy against opposing pressure groups and to enforce discipline against officials or military commanders who tried to nullify it. British policy preserves more of a façade of unity but even here there are indications of conflicts at the top and of officials trying to nullify policies with which they disagree.

For both America and the British Commonwealth there is strong evidence that many people in responsible positions are so distrustful of any general principles that they do not seriously try to behave consistently, or so inhibited by conventional diplomatic training that they may subordinate functionally rational behaviour to blind adherence to convention or precedent.

All this means that there are serious defects in the British and

American systems which are a potential danger to world peace and which do produce contradictions. But, except among minority totalitarian groups, these contradictions are seldom the result of clear "doublethink" positions.

The Communist system, on the other hand, claims to operate in terms of a single, unified, and consistent policy, developed by detailed consideration in terms of a single theoretical system. This claim may not always be realised in practice but the instances of disunity and struggle between rival groups are not sufficient to explain the contradictions in the Communist position. The Communist organisation takes very elaborate precautions to ensure that all Communist statements and actions are subordinated to the official Party Line. It is very unlikely that any Communist official or any newspaper in a Communist controlled country would make statements which did not have the approval of the Communist leadership. It is fairly certain that the higher Communist authorities would have no hesitations in taking strong action against any officials or local organisations which were acting in ways of which they really disapproved. The great emphasis on theory and correct doctrine makes it unlikely that any important contradictions in the Communist position come from something like the woolly-mindedness and opportunism which is often found in non-Communist systems even among people in responsible positions. All this means that the contradictions in the Communist position cannot normally be explained except as the result of deliberate decisions by the Communist leadership; and why should they make such decisions? This question raises the basic problem of the motivation behind the Communist system, a problem which applies to other Communist parties just as much as to the Chinese.

5

An analysis of Communism

What is the ultimate Communist objective?

ONE possible hypothesis about Communist motivation is that the basic objective behind Communist policy is simply a drive for power. While other motivations, such as serving the people, may be important in some sections of the Communist organisation and may even have been predominant in pre-Stalinist Communism, for the present Communist leadership they are subordinate to the ultimate objective of an indefinite extension of the power of the Party or are used as rationalizations for this objective. Given this ultimate objective the "doublethink" elements in Communism can be explained as functionally rational. They both serve to confuse and thereby weaken the opposition to the expansion of Communist power and also to secure the support of the masses under Communist control who would be less willing to follow a leadership which explicitly stated its objective as the indefinite extension of its power.

This hypothesis about Communist motivation is largely accepted by many people in responsible positions in non-Communist countries. It is stated quite explicitly by some political leaders and in important sections of the British and American press, even of the left-wing press.* Other people are reluctant to state it explicitly, not so much because they disbelieve it as because they do not like to face something which they suspect to be true but which has such very far reaching and unpleasant implications. The wide extent to which this view of Communism is believed is a matter of fact about which the evidence from published material can be confirmed from the evidence of private conversations with people in responsible

* A good illustration is the following quotation, "The Chinese Communists . . . wish to extend their power beyond their own border as far and as fast as their growing strength permits." This is from an editorial by Harland Cleveland in *The Reporter* of 1st September, 1953. *The Reporter* is well to the left of centre in American politics and has consistently attacked the pro-Kuomintang China Lobby. This particular editorial was a criticism of the American government for its uncompromising opposition to Chinese admission to the U.N.

positions. The facts do not support the Communist theory that expressions of a fear of Communist aggression are always rationalizations or camouflage for some other reason for opposition to Communism.

This hypothesis about the motivation behind Communist "doublethink" provides a logical justification for a great deal of non-Communist policy, such as rearmament and "bargaining from strength." If the Communist leaders are irrevocably determined to extend their power by every possible means, but are also realistic enough not to start a war which they would probably lose, then the only rational policy for non-Communists is to build up their armed strength and to make it clear that any attempt to expand Communist power will be resisted by force. So long as an organisation with great military strength remains committed to a policy of extending its power by every possible means there can be no hope of permanent peace. This implies that only after the elimination of Communist power will it be possible for the world to relax its preparations for war. And this in turn implies that the choice between a policy of "containment" and a definite anti-Communist crusade is purely a question of expediency.

The hypothesis also provides a logical justification for hostility towards peace movements, even those which are not Communist inspired. If the Communists are really determined to extend their power by every possible means, then Communist claims to want peace cannot mean anything more than a preference for getting the fruits of victory without fighting for them. Anything they say about "peaceful co-existence" or the possibility of settling all disputes by negotiation cannot be anything more than devices to confuse and weaken the opposition to Communist expansion. If nothing can deter Communist aggression except a clear demonstration that it will be resisted by a prepared and determined non-Communist world, then even non-Communist peace movements may be a danger to world peace. If they incline the Communist leadership to believe that aggression will not be met by united and determined resistance they will increase the risk of a Communist attempt at expansion which will start a general war.

This general view of the Communist problem seems to lie behind a great deal of American policy and is largely though less completely accepted in other non-Communist countries. Given the initial assumption about Communist motivation, it is an entirely rational view. The only point at which this theory and the policies based on it can justifiably be criticized is that the basic assumption about Communist motivation has not been fully established.

There is nothing inherently impossible about the existence of an organisation determined to achieve world domination. The megalomaniac conquerer and the completely ruthless and unscrupulous fanatic are types that have appeared again and again in human history. There does seem to be a real, though not a sharp distinction between expansion from motives of economic advantage or strategic security and conquest for its own sake. In the first case peaceful compromise is possible, in the second it is not.

Genghiz Khan at the outset of his career was entirely frank about his motives. "The greatest joy a man can know is to conquer his enemies and drive them before him; to ride their horses and take away their possessions; to see the faces of those who were dear to them bedewed with tears, and to clasp their wives and daughters in his arms."[1] Later he started to use rationalizations about his mission to bring order to the world, and more modern societies dominated by the drive for power have usually rationalized their motives in terms of pseudoscientific theories. But such rationalizations do not make these societies any less dangerous to the rest of the world. The Mongol Empire under Genghiz Khan and his successors was a system with which "peaceful co-existence" was impossible. It was equally impossible with Germany under Hitler, as both Chamberlain and Stalin found by experience. And there have been many other examples of societies which offered their neighbours no choice except armed resistance or submission to enslavement. The question is whether or not Communist power should be placed in this class? And this question is quite fundamental for forming a judgment about Communism, not only in China but also in the rest of the world.

The arguments that Communist power should be placed in this class usually depend on the assumption that the Communist leaders are operating with functional rationality, that is, that they are acting in the way most likely to produce the results they intend. Consider, for instance, the evidence of Communist organisation. The Communist system of organisation with centralised authority and strict discipline was developed by Lenin for the express purpose of seizing power. In the environment of Tsarist Russia where the government could only be changed by force the use of this type of organisation could be explained as a preliminary step towards setting up a new regime in which government would be dependent on popular support. But why do Communists use the same system of organisation in countries whose institutions allow opposition parties the opportunity to win popular support by legal activities and where the government can be changed without the use of force? Why do Communist parties continue to maintain Leninist organisation in countries where their power has been established? Not only in China but also in almost every other country the rise to power of a government under Communist control has been followed, not by the relaxation but by the tightening of Leninist centralisation and discipline. The only country in which a Communist government has deliberately worked for the decentralization of authority is Yugoslavia. This continued use of Leninist organisation can be very simply explained as functionally rational by the hypothesis that the real objective of Stalinist Communist parties is to maintain and expand their power without regard for popular support. To explain it as a functionally rational part of a policy to maintain or establish regimes serving the interests of the masses and having majority support involves a large number of very dubious and controversial assumptions both about political theory and also about matters of fact.

Again, most instances of Communist evasiveness and "double-think" can be explained as functionally rational parts of a plan to extend Communist power. For instance, if the Communist parties of Eastern Europe had announced in 1945 the policies they actually carried out as soon as their power was firmly established, it is extremely unlikely that they would have obtained power, except as purely puppet regimes maintained by the Soviet army. The system of evasiveness and "doublethink" has enabled the C.P.S.U. to establish effective control over Eastern Europe and to put through a policy of *Gleichschaltung* with the Soviet Union without ever provoking united and determined opposition from those who were opposed to such developments. (And there is strong evidence that this opposition would have included a majority of the population in every country.) The Communists have been able to gain all the advantages of deceiving their opponents by false promises without incurring all the discredit that would have been caused by the open repudiation of unambiguous promises. The power of the C.P.S.U. in the Soviet Union itself has depended to a considerable extent on the same sort of process. Even in China it would have been harder for the Communist Party to gain power if it had advocated before 1949 the policies it has actually followed since 1950.

On the other hand, Communist evasiveness and "doublethink" would be very difficult if not impossible to explain as functionally rational parts of any plan to secure "peaceful co-existence" and the settlement of disputes by negotiation instead of war. The handling of Communist policy, including the Communist led "peace" movement, in such a way as inevitably to rouse suspicion and hostility among those who judge Communism by empirical standards from the evidence of Communist behaviour, simply does not make sense as part of a functionally rational policy with peace as its objective.

This is not intended as an exhaustive analysis of Communist policy. It would be easy to cite further evidence such as the readiness of Communist Parties to collaborate with extreme right-wing political organisations or police state regimes, as in Germany or South America. I only wish to make the following point: if it is assumed that Communist leadership is acting rationally, then there are important aspects of Communist behaviour which can be very simply explained by the hypothesis that the basic objective of Communism is to extend indefinitely the power of the Party, but which are hard if not impossible to explain on the hypothesis that the objectives of Communism are peace and democracy. Applying the basic principle of scientific method, that the best hypothesis is that which gives the simplest and most complete co-ordination of experience, it follows that a view of Communism as a conspiracy for world power is more reasonable than a view which accepts at their face value Communist claims to be working for peace and democracy and ignores or tries to explain away the evidence inconsistent with such claims.

Are Communists acting rationally?

Though the view of Communism as a conspiracy for world power is more reasonable than the view which uncritically accepts Communist good faith, it is still not a really satisfactory theory. It is unsatisfactory by the same standards of scientific method because there is a great deal of evidence which it fails to explain and co-ordinate.

One serious objection to the theory of Communism as simply a conspiracy for world power is that it fails to explain the evidence about the motivation of individual Communists. No Communists admit that they are motivated by a simple desire for power; they always claim that the Party seeks power only as a means to altruistic objectives. And these claims by people in the Party, which are made with every appearance of sincerity, are supported by the evidence of people who have left the Party and are now bitterly opposed to it in describing their motivation when they were Party members. In very many cases Communists act with great individual self sacrifice in a way which can easily be explained as motivated by altruistic devotion to a cause but which is hard to explain as motivated by a desire for power.

Some people argue that the conspiracy for world power only exists in the higher ranks of the Party while the ordinary Party members and Fellow Travellers are dupes of the higher leadership and usually unaware of the real objectives of the organisation to which they belong. But this subsidiary theory creates as many difficulties as it solves. It implies an almost super-human skill in deception and propaganda among the higher ranks of the Communist organisation and it is interesting that people who believe in the "conspiracy for world power" theory of Communism do tend to accept this implication. The arguments used in America to justify the opposition to top level talks with Soviet leaders, and the arguments used in Australia against participation in the Peking Peace Conference, nearly all depended on the assumption that any non-Communist who takes part in discussions with Communists is bound to get the worst of it. It is assumed that, although the Communists have a bad case and the non-Communists a good one, yet any conference would be bound to produce results favourable for Communist propaganda; that, while the contradictions in the Communist position discredit the Communist claims to want peace, yet the Communists would certainly be successful in any debate in which they would face a challenge to explain these contradictions.

This theory of almost super-human Communist skill in propaganda is not only inherently improbable but also conflicts with the evidence from the actual record of Communist propaganda. During a year as adviser to the New China News Agency at Yenan I was much more impressed by the incompetence than by the skill of Chinese Communist publicity. It was fairly effective in rousing enthusiasm among people who were already pro-Communist but it was extremely inept in presenting a case to a critical or potentially hostile public. On many points in dispute with the Kuomintang or with the Americans the Communists actually had a very strong case and had everything to gain by presenting this case to world opinion. But it was extremely difficult to persuade anyone that non-Communist foreign opinion, which would not be influenced by unsupported claims and abusive denunciations, might be influenced by the statement of a reasoned case supported by detailed and verifiable evidence. Many people at Yenan seemed to accept a doctrinaire Marxist theory of publicity according to which all opinions, except those of the Communist elite, were entirely the product of class situation and not at all of rational judgment, so that publicity could not do more than make people hold more strongly beliefs which were already determined by non-rational causes. And there is no evidence that other Communist Parties are more skilled in propaganda than the Chinese. Where Communist propaganda has been successful under competitive conditions it has usually been opposed by an even less skilful anti-Communist propaganda which has consistently failed to attack its weak points.

There are other equally serious objections to this theory. For instance, all sorts of difficulties arise in trying to draw the line, which the theory demands, between conspirators and dupes in the Communist organisation. It is not obviously absurd to argue that the ordinary Fellow Traveller or even the ordinary Party Member may be the dupes of conspirators in the Kremlin. But the arguments which try to show that the leaders of the Chinese Communist Party are only dupes or puppets of Moscow have all the characteristics of arguments trying to defend an untenable theory against the clear weight of the evidence.

It would be possible to continue the list of objections but it is more to the point to show that most of the difficulties disappear if one gives up the assumption that the Communist leadership is acting rationally. This assumption implies that, whatever they may say to the contrary, Communists are really acting in terms of policies determined by the standards of empirical scientific method. By giving up this assumption it becomes possible to accept the simple and obvious explanation of Communist motivation, that most Communists really believe in the system they profess to believe in—a system which rejects empiricism and the

72

standards of normal scientific method and is, therefore, by these standards, irrational.

In terms of this system of beliefs most Communist behaviour is logically consistent. The drive for Communist power is always thought of as a means to an end, the classless society in which the state with its means of coercion will wither away and mankind will live in freedom without injustice or exploitation. The aspects of Party policy which would, prima facie, be condemned for dishonesty or for causing unnecessary suffering and injustice are justified by Communist theory as unavoidable steps to the realization of the new society in which the permanent gains of humanity will many times repay the sacrifices incurred in winning them. And in justice to the more altruistic type of Communist one must admit that they are as ready to sacrifice their own lives as to sacrifice other people's for the cause in which they believe.

Except for people who hold some form of "essentialist" philosophy the question of whether or not Communist faith constitutes a religion is really a question of definition. If religion is defined so as to include a belief in the supernatural, then Communism is not a religion. If religion is defined as an emotionally charged faith in a system of beliefs which claims to give a satisfying account of the nature of the world and man's place and duties in it, then Communism is a religion. The obvious analogy is with systems such as Confucianism which, like Communism, have many of the features normally associated with religion but without a belief in the supernatural. And it is interesting that Confucianism includes something very like the Communist doctrine of the withering away of the state.*

There is no reason to suppose that Communism is any more free from hypocrisy than other systems of faith. There are many indications that the second generation Soviet Communist leadership is more cynical and less altruistic than the first generation Chinese Communist leadership. The attitude of a large proportion of the Soviet ruling group to the ideal society of Communist theory in which privilege and arbitrary power will have withered away could probably be summed up by Saki's aphorism, "It is one of the consolations of middle-aged reformers that the good they inculcate must live after them if it is to live at all." But it is unlikely that any of the Soviet leaders would explicitly repudiate

---

* For an interesting discussion of this point see pages 29-38 in P. A. M. Linebarger's *The Political Doctrines of Sun Yat-sen.* Johns Hopkins Press. Baltimore, 1937.

the ideals of Communism. Even those who practise a completely cynical pursuit of power would be unlikely to admit, like the Party leader in Orwell's story, "The Party seeks power entirely for its own sake. We are not interested in the good of others; we are interested solely in power . . . One does not establish a dictatorship in order to safeguard a revolution; one makes the revolution in order to establish the dictatorship."[2] And there is a great deal of empirical evidence that a system of faith may provide a powerful motivation even when its nominal leaders have largely abandoned its ideals in practice.

This theory that a faith in Marx-Leninism is a basic motivation for Communist behaviour does provide a more complete co-ordination and explanation than either the theory of Communism as a conspiracy for world power or the theory which assumes that Communists are acting in good faith for peace and democracy in terms of standards which non-Communists would accept as rational. People who have had contacts with Communists, in particular with the Chinese Communists, find it hard to reconcile their experience with the theory that Communists are a group simply seeking to extend their power. On the other hand there is very wide agreement that most Communists are fanatics, convinced of the absolute rightness of their cause and intellectually rigid. Judging from my personal experience it seems to me very unlikely that the Chinese Communists whom I knew and respected in the period from 1938 to 1945 should have degenerated into power seeking megalomaniacs. On the other hand it seems quite possible that the people whom I respected should have lost power relative to the doctrinaires in the Party, whom I also knew and distrusted.* It seems quite possible that China should have suffered from a process similar to the growth of McCarthyism in America but in a form made much more severe by certain features of Communism. The McCarthyist attitude is much more dangerous when it appears as an interpretation of an official orthodoxy which everyone accepts than in the form of comparatively unsystematic prejudices in a society with no official orthodoxy. And the tradition of preserving the unity of the Party at all costs must make it much more difficult for reasonable people to oppose doctrinaires who have once managed to commit the Party to official support of their views.

* I do not mention names, as expressions of approval in a book critical of Communist policy might create difficulties for the people mentioned.

To people concerned with world peace, Communism motivated by a faith in orthodox Marx-Leninism presents nearly as serious a problem as Communism motivated by a desire for world power. When Liu Shao-ch'i said, "The Party has no particular interests of its own other than the people's interests. The maximum good for the greatest number is the highest criterion of truth and consequently of all the activities of our Party members,"[3] it is extremely probable that he fully believed what he said and that most Party members would agree with him. If the Party acted with functional rationality in terms of this motivation it would not be a danger except to the representatives of vested interests opposed to the interests of the people. But in other sections of the same work Liu Shao-ch'i argues that the Party must strictly follow democratic centralism in organisation and Marx-Leninism in theory, and concludes by maintaining that the Party must "increase its rigidity ideologically, politically, and organisationally."[4] It is clear that he believes that by following such methods the Party will in fact be best able to serve the interests of the people and promote "the maximum good for the greatest number." But to anyone who does not accept the orthodox Marx-Leninist faith this belief must seem extremely doubtful.

When judged by the standards of scientific method there are fundamental contradictions in the position of people who hold the orthodox Marx-Leninist faith. In principle they are working for objectives which would command general approval. Few non-Communists would maintain that it was wrong for an organisation to devote itself to serve the interests of the people, or even that "the maximum good for the greatest number" was a bad principle. It is the basic assumption of non-Marxist Welfare Economics and, as such, has been criticised for being indefinite but not for being wrong. Many non-Communists would agree that the ideal Communist society in which the state has withered away would be a good form of society, if it could be realised. On the other hand, their faith in the orthodox Marx-Leninist system leads Communists to work for these objectives through policies that are almost certain to produce totally different results. And it is easy to see some of the aspects of orthodox Marx-Leninism which lead to this Communist failure to act with functional rationality.

"Democratic Dictatorship"

One result of a faith in orthodox Marx-Leninism is to produce a blindness to the possibility that a Communist Party may abuse its power. The orthodox theory explains exploitation and injustice as the result of power based on the ownership of property and considers every political party to represent some particular class interest. In terms of this theoretical system the destruction of power based on property and the concentration of power in the hands of the party representing the class interests of the majority of the population must result in the ending of all large scale injustice and exploitation. Because the Communist Party represents the interests of the masses there can be no danger in allowing the Communist Party to exercise almost unrestricted power. The dictatorship of the Communist Party is a democratic dictatorship because it represents the majority of the population and the only possible threat to democracy is a revival of power based on property.

In fact there have been many societies in which power based on ownership of property has been much less important than power based on position in the apparatus of government. In such societies the ruling group which owes its power to control of the apparatus of government has usually oppressed and exploited the mass of the population quite as badly as feudal or capitalist ruling classes whose power has depended on ownership of property. Ancient Egypt or Inca Peru were examples of societies in which private property had very little importance. The situation in the Ottoman Empire was summed up as follows by an English traveller in the 1830's: "In the Ottoman dominions there is scarcely any hereditary influence except that belonging to the family of the Sultan; and wealth, too, is a highly volatile blessing, not easily transmitted to the descendants of the owner. From these causes it results that the people standing in the places of nobles and gentry, are official personages."[5] An American writer describes nineteenth century Chinese society in very similar terms: "Notwithstanding the fact that Chinese society is so homogeneous when considered as distinct from the sovereign, inequalities of many kinds are constantly met with, some growing out of birth or property, others out of occupation or merit, but most of them derived from official rank."[6] Though feudal power based on landownership did exist in Imperial China it was only important at the local level and the only way to large

76

scale power or really large scale wealth was through position in the imperial bureaucracy. The old Chinese system has special interest for comparison with modern totalitarian states because the power of the ruling group depended very largely on their success in indoctrinating the population with a single official ideology. The system was so stable until the nineteenth century because everyone with enough education to provide leadership or run the administration was a fully indoctrinated believer in Confucianism.

The example of such societies seems to show that private property is not the only possible basis for the power of an oppressive and exploiting ruling class. Though most Communist governments have gone very far in restricting power based on property this does not rule out the possibility that a Communist Party may degenerate into a new ruling group basing its power on control of the apparatus of government. And there is a lot of evidence which indicates that Communist power does tend to degenerate in this way. The available evidence about the Soviet Union and the East European satellite states indicates that the differences in real income between privileged and unprivileged groups have become at least as great as in many capitalist societies and people from the Western democracies who come in contact with the Soviet organisation are frequently surprised by incidents which reveal extremely sharp class distinctions. To give one illustration, when a party of Soviet astronomers visited America the Americans were surprised to find that the regular astronomers refused to eat at the same table with one of their party who was only a technician. And accounts of conditions in Eastern Europe indicate that the masses find the new Communist ruling groups quite as oppressive as the former ruling classes.

Such degeneration of Communist power into the establishment of a new ruling group oppressing and exploiting the masses is a natural result of faith in a system of theory which implies that such degeneration is impossible. There is no need to suppose that Communist leaders have deliberately or explicitly tried to make themselves into a new bureaucratic aristocracy or to set up the type of social structure which the Yugoslav theorists call "bureaucratic centralism." In fact there is a good deal of evidence that many Communist leaders have disliked the results of this process and have tried to remedy them. Even Lenin in the last years of his life seems to have had misgivings about the trend of developments in Russia and there have been frequent denunciations of the evils of bureaucracy in most Communist ruled countries.

But remedies based on a wrong diagnosis are very unlikely to be effective. If Lenin was expressing his real opinions when he wrote *The State and Revolution* he seems to have believed in 1917 that very soon after the revolution society would be able to function without any permanent ruling group. If so, it is natural that he should have failed to consider the problem of how to ensure popular control of a managerial ruling group. By the time that it had become clear from Soviet experience that the type of organisation envisaged in *The State and Revolution* would not work—that industrial management was not so simple that the economic system could be controlled by a succession of workers' representatives with no qualifications except literacy and elementary arithmetic—Lenin was a sick man preoccupied with urgent immediate problems, and it is again understandable that he failed to undertake a reconsideration of his theories in the light of new experience. Other Communists with less excuse than Lenin have continued to deny the existence of a problem of how to ensure popular control of a managerial ruling group. For instance, Christopher Caudwell, in a book published in 1938, still thought in terms of *The State and Revolution* and claimed that "This world (of Communism), with its replaceable officials not specially trained for the task, is the opposite of the old Fabian dream or nightmare, the class Utopia in which the ruling class now takes the form of a permanent, intellectually trained bureaucracy, wielding the powers of the state for the 'good' of the proletariat."[7] For anyone not blinded by a faith in Marx-Leninism Caudwell's "Fabian nightmare" was even then a fairly good description of the reality of Soviet administration.

The Communists would be the first people to denounce a view which ascribed the evils of capitalism to the moral failings of individual capitalists and tried to remedy them by punishing bad capitalists whose badness was explained by the lingering influence of feudal ideas. But the official Communist attempts to restrain the evils of bureaucracy, such as the "anti-3 anti-5" campaign in China, are exactly analogous to this. The officials against whom action is taken are denounced for their individual moral failings which are ascribed to the remnants of bourgeois ideology. There is never any admission that a system in which a closely organised group enjoys a monopoly of power may be inherently liable to corruption by power, or that certain features of Communist organisation may make it likely that the people who come to the top after Communist power has been established will be those distinguished by lack of scruples and skill in intrigue rather than by desire to serve the interests of the people.

Like Confucianism, orthodox Communism tries to find the answer to the question of how to ensure that government serves the people through some scheme of indoctrination and selection imposed from above which will produce virtuous officials. Such schemes are not entirely futile. A good emperor could raise the standards of government in China. A bureaucracy periodically purged from above may even be more efficient than one in which promotion depends on avoiding positive mistakes and is, therefore, the reward of lack of initiative rather than of competence (though some reports from China indicate that one result of the "anti-3 anti-5" campaign was to produce a general reluctance to accept responsibility). However, in the long run, a system which tries to secure virtuous officials by action from above is almost certain to be less effective than a system which recognises that officials are not likely to be specially virtuous and which, therefore, employs devices to make it possible for the common people to protect themselves against officials who act against their interests. Such devices are the rule of law, the decentralization of authority, free elections, and freedom of criticism and discussion which compels the government to act so as to secure support from a public sufficiently well informed to judge its actions. These devices are not fool proof but government is more likely to serve the interests of the people in systems which include them than in systems which do not.

It is worth noting that any Communists who escape from official orthodoxy enough to ask the question, "How can we be sure that the Communist Party does really represent the interests of the masses?" naturally move towards what orthodox theory would denounce as bourgeois democracy. This can be seen not only in Yugoslavia after 1948 but also in China between 1937 and 1946. Articles in the *Chieh Fang Jih Pao* at Yenan in the early 1940's argued that the Communists could best serve the masses by remaining in a position in which they could only implement policies for which they could secure the support of freely elected non-Communist representatives and went so far as to say, "Only when a party is functionally separate from the government can it be fitted into a system of democracy . . ."[8]

It is also worth noting that modern Marx-Leninist orthodoxy is much more doctrinaire than Marx himself. Marx based his theory largely on a study of mid-nineteenth century British capitalism, a system in which the dependence of power on property was exceptionally great. But there are also passages in his works which discuss "Oriental Societies." K. A. Wittfogel described the results of bringing these passages to the attention of Chinese students who were supporters of the Chinese Communist Party. One "showed a firm determination not to engage in the study of ideas whose very mention disturbed him deeply," another ended by denouncing Marx as a "Western imperialist."[9] Again, Milovan Djilas supports his criticisms of the Soviet system by references to passages in Marx, Engels and Lenin which argue that socialist society after the revolution will be threatened not only by the dispossessed bourgeoisie but also by its own bureaucracy.[10]

Democratic Centralism

On the one hand parts of orthodox Marx-Leninist doctrine make Communists blind to the danger that Communist power may degenerate into a new ruling group quite as oppressive as those which it replaces. On the other hand, principles of organisation, also held as articles of faith, make such degeneration more likely and make it harder for Communists to behave with functional rationality in other ways.

The principle of democratic centralism is laid down in article 21 of the Constitution of the Chinese Communist Party. "Every Party member may carry on within the Party and in Party meetings free and practical discussion to express his or her views on Party policy and on various issues before decisions are reached. However, when a decision is reached, it must be abided by and carried out unconditionally."[11]

The principle is related to a real problem: the correct balance between acting with speed and decision, and acting on the basis of a properly considered judgment. Too little investigation and discussion may produce a decision which is wrong, or at least not the best alternative; too much investigation and discussion may mean missing opportunities, or at least losses from delay. On a common sense view the correct balance must vary with circumstances. Democratic centralism as practised in the Communist system puts the balance very far on the side of quick and decisive action, and this may have been quite reasonable when Lenin originally made democratic centralism part of Communist organisation. The Bolsheviks faced an armed struggle for power with the Tsarist regime and in a military struggle quickness and decision are of extreme importance. But the principle has remained unchanged when Communist Parties have come to power and face problems of social and economic policy where quickness and decision are relatively much less important and where the cutting short of discussion and investigation may have serious and cumulative bad effects.

One could see the bad results of democratic centralism even on the small scale of Communist organisation at Yenan. It quite often happened that the application of some Central Committee directive had results which were neither foreseen nor desired. When these defects were brought to the attention of the leadership by someone outside the Party, such as myself or even some visiting foreign journalist, action would be taken to correct them. But people in the Party were inhibited by democratic centralism from making any criticism of the directive even though their work was hindered by it. To give one small illustration: it was decided that the standard time at Yenan should be Yenan Local Time on the grounds that this was "keeping close to the masses." The decision was very inconvenient to organisations in regular communication with the outside world such as the New China News Agency or the Army Communications Department. But no one in the Party organisation would criticize the decision except in private conversation. As a non-Party adviser to both departments I had no hesitation about writing a strong letter of complaint to Mao Tse-tung and I still have his letter of reply which thanks me for my action and explains that someone had been instructed to investigate which standard time would be most convenient and that, as a result, the decision had been changed from Yenan Local Time to West China Standard Time. If someone outside the Party had not felt free to criticize a Party decision the original wrong decision would not have been corrected.

The general effect of democratic centralism on organisations completely under Party control was that mistakes were not corrected until their results had become so serious that the leadership could no longer ignore them. During the war it was noticeable that organisations in Shansi-Chahar-Hopei where there were a fair number of able non-Communists in responsible positions tended to be more efficient than their equivalents at Yenan under purely Communist control. This was not just my personal impression. It was confirmed by other people who came to Yenan both from Shansi-Chahar-Hopei and other front line base areas which also had more non-Communist participation.

It is extremely likely that many of the major mistakes in Chinese Communist policy, some of which have eventually been admitted by the party, have been the result of democratic centralism combined with the loss in influence and power of independent action by non-Communists.

Yet another important long term result of democratic centralism is to favour the rise to power of unscrupulous intriguers by making it very hard to reverse a Party decision even if it has been obtained by some dishonest manoeuvre.

Democratic centralism is also related to the faith in Party infallibility and to some very dubious theories about the nature of scientific knowledge. Orthodox Marx-Leninist theory explicitly claims that scientific theories can give absolutely certain knowledge. An interesting example is the passage in the official *Short History of the Communist Party in the Soviet Union* in which Stalin quotes with approval a passage from Engels' *Anti-Duhring* in which Engels maintains that the Copernican theory was for a long time only a very probable hypothesis but became absolutely certain when Leverrier used it to predict the existence of the planet Neptune.* The point is that Stalin supports his view that scientific theories give absolutely certain knowledge with an instance which had been disproved nearly twenty years before when the crucial experiments had confirmed Einstein's theory and had shown Leverrier's work to be based on a theory which was incorrect but which, in most cases, gives results which are very near the correct values.

The usual Communist defence of democratic centralism is based on this view of scientific knowledge. It is assumed that it is often possible, from the data known at some particular time, to work out a theory or policy whose correctness will be absolutely certain. To anyone who thinks in terms of the normal

---

* The passage in Engels is slightly confused as Leverrier did not base his calculations on the theories of Copernicus, who believed that the planets moved with exact circular motion, but on the theories of Kepler and Newton. However, the general sense is clear.

procedures of natural science this assumption must appear quite fantastic. There may be fields of science in which some theory is so well established that it is very unlikely that any fresh discoveries could lead to its complete abandonment. But in the highly complex fields of economic and social policy and international relations it is nearly always necessary to act on the basis of data which are obviously incomplete and which are compatible with several alternative hypotheses. A policy decision can seldom be based on more than a weighing of possible alternatives and any new data may alter the balance. The cutting short of discussion and investigation is extremely likely to lead to persistence in error, and science since the time of Galileo and Newton has developed on the assumption that all theories are potentially liable to modification or replacement in the light of new evidence and that it is never possible to say that any theory represents final and absolutely certain truth.

It is possible that this sort of fundamental philosophical confusion has had an even more important influence on Communism than Marx-Leninism in the ordinary sense. A recent analysis of some of Stalin's writings gives instances to show that he did assume that the world could be completely described in terms of a classifying logic and that he attached an almost magical importance to words because he thought of all definitions as "true" and not as conventional.[12]

A great deal of orthodox Communist thinking might, indeed, be described as pre-Newtonian and has a curious similarity to the arguments which were used to oppose the development of natural science from a metaphysical standpoint. Both are based on what Professor Popper calls an "essentialist" philosophy. Many orthodox Communist arguments depend on the assumption that the world can be completely described in terms of sharply divided classes. They are valid on the assumption that the world can be completely described by statements of the form: "X is either A or B" or "X either is or is not caused by Y." They can be seen to be fallacious if it is allowed that certain aspects of the world can only be described by statements of the form, "X is in a range of which A and B are limiting cases" or "X is a function of several variables of which Y is only one." For instance, some defenders of Communism have used the following argument: societies either do or do not restrict freedom; both Communist ruled and democratic capitalist countries restrict freedom; therefore, there is no essential difference between them. The fallacy

83

is obvious if one recognises that restriction of freedom is a matter of degree and that certain undesirable social consequences are a function of restrictions on freedom which makes them become rapidly more important when restrictions on freedom get into a certain range.

A further source of confusion in orthodox Communist thinking is the view that the truth or falsity of any statement should be judged by its consequences in the future and not by standards of logic or relation to evidence at the time when it is made. Liu Shao-ch'i in a passage quoted above says "the maximum good for the greatest number is the highest criterion of truth" and Communists continually defend the making of statements which, by non-Communist standards, are simply false on the ground that they serve the interests of the masses. This argument has been used to justify Lysenko's theories in biology, as the basis of Soviet statistics, to denounce objectivity as a "bourgeois" error, to justify the highly distorted picture of the world given in the Communist press, and so on. The obvious question is "How can it be known whether or not the making of any particular statement does serve the interests of the masses"? On a common sense view the answer would be that action to promote the maximum good for the greatest number is more likely to be effective when it is based on a view of the world as near to empirical truth as possible and that the making of statements incompatible with empirical evidence or logical consistency can only be justified as part of a policy of deliberate deception. But Communists do not accept this common sense answer and are very reluctant to admit that they do indulge in deliberate deception of their followers as well as of their opponents. This theory about the nature of truth leads in practice to "doublethink" positions and, if one pursues the argument, Communists are usually driven to a variant of the claim that the Party is infallible: the Communist Party represents the masses; therefore, all statements made by the Party are in the interests of the masses; therefore, all statements made by the Party are true.

The practical consequences of Marx-Leninism

All this may seem rather theoretical but the Communists would be the first people to maintain that correct action is only possible on the basis of correct theory and these aspects of Marx-Leninism do have very direct practical implications.

The totalitarian organisation of Communist controlled societies is a logical result of the Communist theory about the nature of scientific knowledge. If it is believed that the Communist elite is in possession of a system of perfectly certain and final truths then it is quite logical to organise society so as to secure the universal acceptance of these truths. It may be preferable to secure their acceptance by persuasion, but when persuasion is ineffective it is quite justifiable to use whatever degree of pressure or force that may be necessary. This is, in fact, the present attitude of the Chinese Communist Party as described by some of its supporters. As against this, the view of the nature of scientific knowledge that underlies the development of natural science implies that a society which has secured the universal acceptance of any single system of ideology has thereby cut itself off from certain possibilities of progress and rendered certain problems insoluble.

Again, the principle of democratic centralism makes it certain that an orthodox Communist government will only correct its mistakes after an unnecessarily long delay. And the recognition and diagnosis of mistakes will be made more difficult by the theoretical rejection of objectivity. All published reports in countries under Communist rule show a very marked bias towards emphasizing all evidence presenting the working of official policies in a favourable light and minimizing or suppressing all unfavourable evidence. The bias may be less in reports not intended for the public but statements by people who have worked in Communist organisations and also indirect evidence indicates that it still exists. So even if the Communist leaders want to correct mistakes it is likely that they will seldom learn just how bad their mistakes have been.

The orthodox Marx-Leninist tendency to think in terms of a simple two-valued class logic leads to a neglect of feed-back effects which may cause some mistaken policy to produce cumulative and perhaps irreversible results. In fact, Communist arguments tend to assume that all mistakes are reversible, that after a mistake has been remedied the development of society will quickly return to very nearly the same line as it would have followed if the mistake had not been made. In terms of an analysis not tied down to the categories of orthodox Marx-Leninist thinking this assumption is extremely dubious. An obvious and important illustration is the Communist attitude to the use of terrorism and police state methods. Orthodox Communist arguments assume that terrorism is an instrument which can be used to suppress groups in society opposed to the new order and discarded without leaving any permanent ill effects when this opposition is no longer dangerous. It is often admitted that terrorism may go too far and inflict serious injustice on innocent members of the community but this is usually excused with the argument that the interests of a few individuals are comparatively unimportant compared with the long term interests of the community. In fact the use of terrorism and police state methods involves very serious risks of starting a cumulative and irreversible process of social degeneration. On the one hand, the injustices involved in suppressing one irreconcilable opposition by terrorism and police state methods may create a new irreconcilable opposition which can only be controlled by the continued use of terrorism. On the other hand, the secret police organisation may acquire a very strong vested interest in the continuance of conditions which will justify the continuance of its powers. A government which once starts to use terrorism and police state methods may find it very hard to stop and may produce a social tension lasting, perhaps, for generations. Cromwell's policy in Ireland influenced Anglo-Irish relations 250 years later and French society still shows the effects of left-wing terrorism in 1792 and right-wing terrorism in 1871 although the terrorism was mild by present day standards and only lasted for comparatively short periods.

There may be circumstances in which the risks of using police state methods may be worth taking. If the German Social Democrats had been less scrupulous about the methods they were prepared to use against the irreconcilable enemies of the Weimar constitution the Weimar Republic would almost certainly have survived with far reaching and highly beneficial results both for Germany and the rest of the world. The use of emergency powers in Britain in 1940, such as the famous Regulation 18b, involved serious cases of injustice but did manage to eliminate the danger of a Nazi fifth column without producing serious long term effects. But the limited use of police state methods by people who are aware of the dangers involved is very different from the widespread use by people who seem to be quite unaware of the dangers. A good analogy would be the use of drugs such as morphine. In special circumstances they have a useful place in medicine but a doctor who used them freely without realising the dangers of addiction would be a serious

menace to his patients. And most Communists simply refuse to
think about the possibility of social addiction to police state
methods. In Peking in the summer of 1949 there was general
agreement that the Communists were ruling without terrorism
but passages in Mao Tse-tung's speech *On People's Democratic
Dictatorship* seemed to envisage a possible resort to terrorism.
I wrote a fairly long memorandum in which I tried to set out
the case for believing that resort to terrorism involved serious
dangers and tried to get comments on it from friends in the
Communist Party. But people simply refused to discuss the
question.

In fact, a generation after the revolution Soviet society shows
little indication of being able to overcome the addiction to police
state methods. For a short period after Stalin's death there were
signs of an attempt to make some change but these practically
disappeared in a few months. Quite apart from the citizens of
the Soviet Union it is a matter of vital concern to the rest of the
world that one of the most powerful organisations in the Soviet
Union should have a strong vested interest in the continuance of
international tension. The secret police organisation has great
power and its members have considerable economic privileges.
This power and these privileges are justified by the alleged
necessity of defending Soviet society against the activities of
agents of hostile powers, and with any real lessening of international tension this justification would largely disappear. This
means that the many people in the Soviet secret police organisation have at least as strong a vested interest in a continuing threat
of war as armaments manufacturers in capitalist countries. Most
armament factories have some value for peace time production
but many of the special skills of a secret police agent, such as
the ability to extort confessions, would have no social value at all
in a peaceful world. And similar secret police organisations have
developed or are developing in every other country under
Communist rule.

Vested interests may be over-ruled and, in a world which is
stock-piling hydrogen bombs, action motivated by a vested
interest in war is not compatible with rational self-interest. All
the same, the failure of Communist theory to allow for the
dangers involved in the use of police state methods must count
as one serious danger for peace.

Apart from these consequences of Marx-Leninist faith for
internal developments in Communist ruled countries, orthodox

Marx-Leninist faith also has direct implications for the conduct of international relations. Even if orthodox Communists really wish to settle disputes with non-Communists by negotiation they will find it very difficult to act in a way that is likely to succeed. In so far as they think of the world as presented by the Marx-Leninist system they will continually be at cross purposes with people who judge reality by empirical standards. And the principle of democratic centralism is likely to produce rigidities in the Communist position which will make negotiation very difficult. On certain points the Communist negotiators will be tied to views or policies which cannot be modified except with great difficulty. It will be very difficult for Communist negotiators to admit the existence of alternative possibilities about the motives of other parties and to work for the clarification of these motives, adjusting their policies accordingly.

A very interesting illustration was the negotiations in China in 1946. The Communists were first rigidly conciliatory and later rigidly intransigent and in both cases the rigidity was almost certainly contrary to Communist interests. I have already argued that a major mistake in American policy was the failure to use Soviet action in Manchuria as a test of Chinese Communist good faith when it was obvious that the American policy of mediation might succeed if the Communists put loyalty to China above loyalty to Russia and was bound to fail if they did not. Communist policy in the decisive period at the beginning of 1946 can equally be criticized for failing to make a test of American and Kuomintang good faith, and on this side too there was an issue which would have made an excellent test case, namely the use of Japanese and puppet troops. A whole series of official American pronouncements had claimed that the objective of American troops in North China was to disarm and repatriate the Japanese army. In fact the Kuomintang was allowed to use Japanese troops in the civil war. As late as the end of February, 1946, the Kuomintang front within twenty or thirty miles of the main American base at Tsingtao was still largely held by Japanese troops under Japanese officers and the Japanese forces fighting for Yen Hsi-shan in Shansi were only eliminated by the Communist victory in 1949. American mediation was bound to fail unless the Americans made up their minds between the incompatible policies of settling the Chinese situation by mediation and of helping the Kuomintang to win a civil war, and the issue of Japanese troops could have been used to force a decision.

Again, both in October, 1945, and in February, 1946, Chiang Kai-shek promised to disarm and disband troops that had been in Japanese service. In fact he never did so and puppet troops played a major part in breaches of the truce agreement during 1946. It was obvious that a peaceful settlement in China was only possible if the Kuomintang leadership was prepared to repudiate those elements in the Party which had co-operated with the Japanese because they considered them a lesser enemy than the Communists. If a peaceful settlement was ever possible it would not have been endangered by insisting on Kuomintang action which was an essential part of any settlement. If a peaceful settlement was never possible the Communists stood to gain by allowing negotiations to break down over an issue on which they were clearly in the right. Suppose that negotiations had broken down in February or March, 1946, because the Kuomintang refused to disarm troops that had been in Japanese service. Given the state of American opinion at the time it would have been hard for the American government to continue support for the Kuomintang. I have discussed this question with a number of Americans who had official positions at the time and they all agreed that a Communist stand on this issue would have put the American government in a very difficult position. Several declared that it would have forced a complete reconsideration of American policy in China.

I have not been able to obtain direct evidence about the motives behind Chinese Communist policy at this period; Chou En-lai refused to answer my questions about it in 1949. On circumstantial evidence it seems most likely that the determining factor in Communist policy was the rigidity imposed by democratic centralism. In the early part of the Marshall negotiations the Party was obviously following a line of conciliation and this would fully explain the failure of the Communist negotiators to use opportunities for an experimental test of whether or not the American or Kuomintang position was such as to justify a policy of conciliation. By the late summer of 1946 the Party line had changed and the Communists again weakened their position by rigidity. There were several occasions when the Communists could have influenced both Chinese and foreign opinion simply by putting their demands in a more reasonable way without any loss of real bargaining strength, but these opportunities were never used. And instead of confining their denunciations of American policy to the points where they had a good case against the American government the Communists largely discredited their position by taking a strong stand on issues where their case was, at the least, highly controversial.

It is easy to find other instances where Communist rigidity, usually intransigent rigidity, has been a hindrance to successful negotiations. Korea provides obvious examples for the Chinese Communist Party and almost every U.N. session has provided examples for the Soviet Communist Party.

The Communist Tragedy

If this theory about Communist motivation is correct the typical Communist is a tragic rather than a villainous figure, deserving, as an individual, pity rather than hatred. Motivated by a sincere desire to serve humanity and ready to devote, or even sacrifice his life to this cause, his system of faith leads him to act in ways that are certain to inflict large scale and unnecessary suffering on the masses whom he wishes to serve. Motivated by the vision of a society in which injustice, exploitation and class distinctions will disappear, his system of faith leads him to work for the establishment of a police state in which exploitation will be more ruthless and class distinctions sharper than in most of the societies he tries to destroy because of the exploitation and class distinctions in them. Motivated by a desire for peace, his system of faith leads him to act in ways which increase the risk of war.

The usual objection to this sort of view about Communism is that no one can really believe in a system so much at variance with empirical evidence—that, whatever a Communist may say about the purity of his motives and the sincerity of his belief in orthodox Marx-Leninism, he must somehow really know that he is using his beliefs as a rationalisation for motives which he does not care to admit, such as the pursuit of power or the gratification of a grudge against society. It would not be reasonable to maintain that Marx-Leninist faith is the only source of Communist motivation. Most people act very largely from mixed motives and Communists are no exception. But this objection to a view which holds that Marx-Leninist faith is a major element in Communist motivation is an objection which will not stand critical examination.

The effectiveness of the Communist system of faith in rendering those who hold it immune from persuasion by empirical evidence has been analysed from the outside* and also described from the inside by many ex-Communists.† The results of such analysis and description provide a theory which fits the evidence about Communist behaviour much better than a view which refuses to admit the possibility of Communist sincerity.

There is a lot of empirical evidence that people can hold with sincere conviction beliefs that involve even more glaring contradictions with empirical evidence than orthodox Marx-Leninism does. By any normal scientific standards the theoretical foundations of Nazism or of Japanese militarism were ludicrous. But the evidence that has become available since the war makes it fairly certain that many Nazi leaders, though probably not Hitler himself, really believed in Nazi race theory and that many Japanese really believed in the Sun Goddess and the theories of *Kokutai no Hongi*.[13] In contrast to these systems of faith which, by empirical standards, were almost pure nonsense, parts of Marx-Leninism can be restated in the form of quite reasonable scientific hypotheses. If Marx is taken as a social scientist and not as an infallible prophet he remains a fairly important figure. A reasonable comparison would be with his contemporary, Lord Kelvin. No one would now consider Lord Kelvin's vortex theory of atomic structure, and his influential estimate of the age of the earth is now known to have been based on assumptions which were not correct. But large parts of his work have only been confirmed by further experience and remain as contributions to the scientific knowledge of today. A larger proportion of Marx's theories were wrong or based on false assumptions but important parts of his work have remained and are accepted even by people

* For instance, Professor Popper (in *The Open Society*) gives an analysis in general philosophical terms and a discussion of the more detailed process can be found in an article on *The Stability of Beliefs* by Michael Polanyi in *The British Journal for the Philosophy of Science*. November, 1952.
    The point on which I disagree with Professor Polanyi is his view that the assumptions on which science is based are arbitrary. He uses this view to explain the fact that scientists do, in practice, refuse to consider certain experimental evidence. But a more satisfactory explanation has been given by Felix Kaufmann in his *Methodenlehre der Sozialwissenschaften*. Kaufmann argued that a well established theory has a very high likelihood of being correct so that it is quite reasonable to refuse to accept experimental evidence which would overthrow a well-established theory until the correctness of this evidence and the impossibility of explaining it without abandoning the theory has been established with the same degree of certainty as the theory it would overthrow.
    † Good illustrations can be found in *The God that Failed* (Hamish Hamilton. London, 1950) or Arthur Koestler's autobiography *Arrow in the Blue* (Collins, with Hamish Hamilton. London, 1952. Chapters 28-30.)

who would not recognise their origin. And this mixture of genuine scientific theory has almost certainly been important in making Marx-Leninism more stable and more persistent than the completely irrational systems of political faith.

The ability of men to believe in theories in the face of empirical evidence is not confined to politics. One can find many examples from natural science. Aristotelianism as developed by the mediaeval scholastics was, like Marx-Leninism, a system which claimed to explain everything in the universe. And people continued to believe in theories implied by this system in the face of clear empirical evidence. For instance, it was deduced that projectiles must move in a straight line and then drop vertically to earth and this theory was accepted though anyone who threw a stone and watched its flight could see in a moment that it was false. One mediaeval writer on popular science actually maintained that it was theoretically impossible for rivers to rise during a thunderstorm and go down again afterwards.[14] Another analogy is the history of medicine. It is certain that doctors have always wanted to cure their patients, apart from a small minority of criminals and lunatics. It is equally certain that doctors have used treatments which lessened their patients' chances of recovery and have continued to do so in the face of empirical evidence that their treatment was worse than useless. Even after some unorthodox pioneers had established that wounds heal better when kept clean, doctors in Europe continued to believe that there was something wrong with a wound which did not discharge and to use treatment which ensured that all wounds became infected. Even in the nineteenth century many doctors refused to accept the evidence of Semmelweiss's work which reduced maternal mortality in hospital from over 17 per cent to under 1 per cent.

Turning to present day Western societies one can find many convinced believers in completely fantastic theories, astrology, the message of the Great Pyramid, the economic theorems of Major Douglas, and so on.*

---

* An extremely clear illustration of refusal to admit empirical evidence has been provided by the controversy in the Australian press over the proposals to allow the sale of petrol outside normal shopping hours. Writer after writer has claimed that unrestricted or extended hours would involve the owners of filling stations in heavy expenses for overtime labour or involve family businesses in intolerably long hours. These people only need to visit their national capital to see that their arguments are nonsense. The Australian Capital Territory does not restrict the hours of sale for petrol and the result

Considering all this empirical evidence about the strange theories which have been believed in the face of empirical evidence, it is quite reasonable to believe that most Communists are completely sincere about their faith in Marx-Leninist orthodoxy. This means that many of the Communist "doublethink" positions can be explained as the result of real contradictions in Communist thinking. Klaus Fuchs described his condition as one of "controlled schizophrenia" and it is easy to see how Communist thinking can become extremely complicated and confused. If Communists were simply insane they could keep an untroubled faith in the Marx-Leninist system and ignore all the aspects of empirical reality which conflicted with it. In fact, they also try to keep in touch with empirical reality and, therefore, become involved in a continuous struggle to reconcile their theoretical system of faith with their experience. The different ways in which this reconciliation can be produced can account for the considerable differences between individual Communists. Those who appear to non-Communists as fairly normal, decent, reasonable people keep in fairly close touch with empirical reality at the expense of making qualifications and interpretations to their theoretical beliefs which would really imply an abandonment of orthodox Marx-Leninism if their implications were logically and consistently thought out. Those who appear to non-Communists as fanatical doctrinaires keep close to their theoretical system of faith at the expense of refusing to admit empirical evidence or maintaining positions which are simply illogical. (I remember one argument with a doctrinaire Chinese Communist, Chou Hsiao-chou, who maintained that a proposition could be simultaneously true and false—true when asserted by a

---

is that most garages keep normal shopping hours while one stays open till midnight, and presumably find that it pays to do so. Conditions in the U.K. show the same result. Most garages and filling stations keep normal shopping hours while a few in big cities and on main trunk roads offer twenty-four hour service.

In this case the opinion which is held in the face of empirical evidence is based on almost pure prejudice. If it were explicitly formulated it would probably be based on the assumption that commercial relations are what modern theorists would call a "zero sum game", that any change which benefits the general public must inflict a corresponding loss on the other parties concerned.

The opponents of any modification of existing restrictions in New South Wales and Victoria are almost certainly fairly normal members of the Australian public. If pure prejudice can thus lead them to maintain irrational views directly contrary to empirical evidence there is nothing surprising about the greater influence of the elaborate and coherent system of Communist doctrine in leading otherwise normal people to maintain irrational views.

Marxist and false when asserted by a non-Marxist. At that time, 1943, most Chinese Communists held a fairly reasonable position and people who heard of the argument told me that Chou Hsiao-chou was a hopeless doctrinaire who needed to be told that he was talking nonsense.)

This analysis of Communist thinking could be carried a good deal further. The orthodox Communist position involves a continual struggle to reconcile contradictions and can only be maintained by a refusal to face empirical evidence or a refusal to think out logical implications. Such a strain is likely to produce psychological reactions and further details of Communist behaviour can be explained in terms of such reactions.

The interpenetration of opposites

A very similar analysis could be applied to the thinking of many extreme anti-Communists who hold views with obvious similarities to the Communist position. In many cases they start with the same basic philosophical assumptions, some form of what Professor Popper calls "essentialism", and there are often fairly close similarities in behaviour. A good illustration is the falsification of history. One can find, especially in America, falsifications of Chinese history quite as bad as anything published by the Communists and dating back to a time before the Chinese Communist Party had lowered its standards to the Soviet level.

Consider, for example, the version of Chinese history expounded by General Wedemeyer as early as October, 1946 (in a speech at a celebration of the Chinese National Day at Hotel Roosevelt, New York). He begins in the nineteenth century. "During the past hundred years within China, a similar evolution [to that of Europe] has been in progress. The Chinese empire consisted essentially of feudal dynasties, whose leaders, or warlords, paid tribute to the Emperor." In fact, feudal dynasties belong to the period before the establishment of a centralized empire in the third century B.C.; warlords belong to the period of the Republic after 1911; while paying tribute to the emperor belongs to the external relations of the empire which only recognised other countries when their representatives came as tribute bearers. Having established his complete contempt for historical accuracy by combining these incongruous elements as a picture of internal conditions in nineteenth century China,

94

General Wedemeyer continues with the more familiar myth that, "the people of China emerged triumphant in their struggle to create a unified country, dedicated to the principles of free enterprise, personal liberty and constitutional government," inspired by the "sincerity, high moral purpose and Christian humility of China's present leader, Generalissimo Chiang Kai-shek," who "followed faithfully the program envisaged by Dr. Sun Yat-sen" and who co-operated completely loyally and effectively with his allies in the war against Japan. It is true that constitutional government was the theoretical objective of the Kuomintang; by explaining away the activities of the secret police and concentrating on laws and policy statements it might even be possible to argue that Chinag Kai-shek favoured personal liberty; but neither Kuomintang practice nor Kuomintang theory could suggest a dedication to the principle of free enterprise as understood by an American audience.* Admittedly, a speech like this should not be judged by the same standards as something which claims to be serious history. But even by the standards appropriate to a speech it is pretty bad. What would people think of a Chinese official who, after holding a responsible post in America, made a speech in which he asserted that, before the Civil War, the Southern States were semi-independent kingdoms under U.S. protection ruled by European aristocrats such as Huey Long and that the United States, under Presidents Coolidge and Hoover, had dedicated itself to the principle of a planned economy? But this would be roughly equivalent to General Wedemeyer's version of Chinese history.†

* P. A. M. Linebarger describes Sun Yat-sen as an "empirical collectivist" in his economic theory and says "Sun Yat-sen's frequent expressions of sympathy with communism and socialism, and his occasional identification of the large principles of *min sheng* (people's livelihood) with them, are an indication of his desire for ultimate collectivism." (*The Political Doctrines of Sun Yat-sen*, page 153). And Linebarger is a scholar with strong pro-Kuomintang sympathies.

† Other American military politicians have revealed equally gross ignorance of China. In his speech to Congress after his dismissal General MacArthur referred to the rise of Chinese nationalism at the beginning of this century under the leadership of Chang Tso-lin (*sic*). At this time Chang Tso-lin was actually a bandit leader with Japanese connections.

Describing his meeting with Chiang Kai-shek, Admiral Leahy wrote, "Chiang Kai-shek was a slight, studious appearing man with no resemblance to the bandit he was reported to have been before the war commenced." (Admiral Leahy, *I Was There*. Gollancz, London, 1950. Page 236.)

According to correspondents in Chungking, it was only after several months in China that General Hurley realised that Chinese names put the surname first: "for months after he arrived he referred to General Chiang as Mr.

General Wedemeyer's speech is an interesting illustration not only because of its date but also because the falsification of history extends to points where the true facts are not really controversial. Since 1948 the anti-Communist falsification of recent Chinese history has become much more common and attempts are now being made to secure the general acceptance of a mythical anti-Communist Chinese history. It is also interesting to see the growth of an attitude very similar to the attitude of Communists and Fellow Travellers to the Soviet Union but orientated towards the Kuomintang and not the C.P.S.U. Just as Communist Fellow Travellers explain away all evidence of terrorism and slave labour in the Soviet Union as the fabrications of sinister capitalist agencies, so the Kuomintang Fellow Travellers explain away all evidence of Kuomintang corruption, incompetence and terrorism as fabrications by such alleged Communist agencies as the I.P.R.

It is worth examining the fallacy involved in this type of argument. The McCarran Committee Report does give evidence to show that a number of people connected with the I.P.R. had pro-Communist sympathies and, in some cases, even Communist affiliations. What it does not even try to do is to analyse how far this bias influenced the accuracy of the material published by the I.P.R.

Bias is a question of degree. It may merely influence judgment within the range within which entirely honest opinions may differ. Stronger bias may lead to the selection of unrepresentative samples or the evasion of relevant evidence. And still stronger bias may produce deliberate false statements on matters of fact. There would only be a real case against the I.P.R. if it could be shown that its bias extended to these second or third degrees. And the McCarran Report does not try to do this.

Shek." (T. H. White and A. Jacoby, *Thunder Out of China*. Gollancz, London. Page 231.)

Here again one needs to imagine similar statements about America. What would one think of responsible Chinese officials who wrote that President Roosevelt had no resemblance to the gangster he was reported to have been before his election, or who went about Washington referring to "Mr. Franklin"?

In themselves these mistakes are not important but they do reveal an ignorance of elementary general knowledge about China. There is no reason why American generals or admirals should be experts on China. But one does expect that people in responsible positions should take a little trouble to check their facts before writing books or making public speeches. It has been said "It isn't what a man doesn't know that makes him ignorant; it's what he knows that isn't so." It is alarming to think that American policy has been influenced and perhaps decided by men who reveal this kind of ignorance.

The Kuomintang Fellow Traveller position depends on an argument which, if stated explicitly, would be as follows: all statements from a biased source are untrue; statements critical of the Kuomintang and favourable to the Chinese Communists were published by sources with a pro-Communist bias; therefore, all these statements were untrue.*

It would be reasonable to say that statements from a biased source should not be accepted without confirmation. But in the case of statements alleging corruption and incompetence in the Kuomintang and much higher standards of competence and honesty among the Communists there is abundant evidence from sources with no pro-Communist bias.

Exactly similar criticisms can be made of the arguments of Communist Fellow Travellers. Many of the criticisms of Communist rule have been published by people with an anti-Communist bias, but a considerable proportion of them can be confirmed by very strong evidence, including statements in the official Communist press.

Another weakness in both Fellow Traveller positions is a belief in highly implausible theories of conspiracy. The Communist Fellow Traveller who accepts the official Soviet case against Lavrenti Beria, for example, has to believe that a man with all the power conferred by command of the Soviet secret police organisation and, presumably, with the help of Western intelligence agents, was so incompetent that his conspiracy produced no observable results and that he could be arrested without a struggle. Similarly, the Kuomintang Fellow Traveller theory that American policy in China was influenced by powerful Communist conspirators in the State Department completely fails to explain why these alleged conspirators failed to use some of the most obvious opportunities for influencing American policy in a pro-Communist, anti-Kuomintang direction. The obvious way to discredit the claims that Chiang Kai-shek was a democratic Christian leader would have been to publish the passages from Chiang's own book in which he denounces Communism

* Something very close to this position can be found in Ralph de Toledano's *Spies, Dupes, and Diplomats*. (Little, Brown. Boston, 1952.) He quotes with approval a statement by another writer that, if the Amerasia case had been pursued honestly and the pro-Communists cleared out of the Far Eastern division of the State Department, Chiang Kai-shek would have driven the Communist armies into Siberia. But though a large part of the book is devoted to supporting this thesis it gives no evidence except allegations of bias among those in control of American policy.

and Western democracy as equally unsuited to China and claims that Chinese culture will be able to absorb Christianity as it had already absorbed Buddhism and Islam. But when *China's Destiny* was published in 1943 it was treated in America as a secret document to which even congressmen were refused access, and the American public only obtained an English translation in 1946. Again, it was only after the war that any information began to appear in the American press about the large scale desertions of Kuomintang troops to the Japanese, with the approval of the Chungking authorities. An instance of the suppression of pro-Communist material was the fate of a report I wrote in 1942 which was the first account of the Communist areas by a foreign observer since 1939. This argued that co-operation with the 18th Group Army would be of considerable advantage to the Allied war effort against Japan, but it was classified as a confidential document and only became known through publication in *Amerasia* in 1944.*

It would be easy to extend the list of instances in which information which would have influenced American opinion against the Kuomintang and in favour of the Chinese Communists was suppressed by the State Department.

This indicates that the theory of State Department China policy being determined by Communist conspirators could only be true if these conspirators were so incompetent that they neglected the most obvious opportunities of furthering their aims. The evidence of infiltration for the purposes of Soviet intelligence is irrelevant on this point. It is quite probable that the Soviet authorities did not want to incur any risks to their sources of information in order to help the Chinese Communist Party. There is, in fact, a fair amount of evidence that the Soviet authorities had comparatively little interest in the Chinese Communist Party until it had become certain that it would follow orthodox Stalinism and was likely to win the civil war. General Hurley's account of his conversation with Molotov is to some extent confirmed by Marshal Tito's report of a conversation in which Stalin claimed that the Chinese Communists had been advised to dissolve their army and seek agreement with Chiang Kai-shek.[15]

* Since the *Amerasia* case is still a subject of controversy in America I might point out that *Amerasia* had quite as much right to this particular document as the U.S. Government had. The report was written for publication by a British citizen. Taking advantage of its having been entrusted to an American citizen, the American authorities appropriated it and classified it, without payment and, so far as I know, without communicating it to the British authorities.

Some of the other similarities between the doctrinaire Communists and the extreme anti-Communists are discussed in a later section. The obvious point of difference is that the extreme anti-Communists do not form a strictly disciplined organisation united by a common faith in an elaborate system of political theory. This is important in making anti-Communist extremism less dangerous than Communist extremism.

It is, of course, true that anti-Communist extremism is not confined to America but it does seem to flourish there in its most exuberant form. Senator McCarthy is a figure of world wide notoriety, Representative Keon is practically unknown outside Australia.

6

The conditions for peace

SUBJECTIVELY there are important differences between the mentality of the political gangster who wants power simply for its own sake, or to serve the interests of some special group to which he belongs, and the mentality of the political fanatic who wants power for some altruistic objective. But these subjective differences are not directly relevant to people threatened by the drive for power. Both political gangsters and political fanatics are a direct menace to peace because they present the rest of the world with no alternatives but armed resistance or submission to enslavement. And the practical results of rule by political fanatics with theoretically altruistic motives may be quite as unpleasant as those of rule by political gangsters. Many people from Europe with personal experience of both German and Russian occupation claim that Nazi occupation, with the explicit objective of exploiting so-called inferior races, was actually less unpleasant for the majority of the population than Soviet occupation, whose proclaimed objective was to liberate the masses and serve their interests. For the peasant family condemned to starvation by government requisitions of food it makes little difference whether they starve in order to build a basis of heavy industry for some hypothetical future socialist economy or to increase the private wealth of corrupt officials. And the deaths from starvation produced by the Soviet government during the First Five Year Plan were of the same order of magnitude as those produced by the Kuomintang government ten years later in the Honan and Kuangtung famines. For the man who is treated as a social outcaste through no fault of his own it makes little difference whether he suffers because one grandparent was a Jew or because one grandparent was a capitalist or landlord.

The completely doctrinaire Communist, convinced by his system of faith that he is justified in using any means to extend Communist power, presents the same sort of menace to peace as the Nazi or Japanese militarist. A great deal of the controversy on this subject is at cross purposes because people fail to dis-

100

tinguish what Communists are trying to do in terms of their system of faith on the one hand, from the probable results of their actions when judged by normal scientific standards on the other. And to make this distinction demands some analysis of just where the results of Communist power diverge from the results predicted by orthodox Marx-Leninist theory.

The Communist case

In terms of orthodox Marx-Leninist theory, the objective of Communist power is to establish regimes which will serve the interests of the masses and, in so far as people understand their own interests, Communist power will only be opposed by the former ruling classes whose elimination from power is essential for any permanent social progress. This view is not simply a rationalization to justify the power of a new Communist ruling group.

It is quite true that the vested interests of a ruling class may often be an obstacle to essential reforms and that, in many countries, these vested interests cannot be overcome without eliminating the old ruling classes from power. In so far as they stand for the carrying out of certain reforms and the elimination from power of the groups which oppose these reforms, the Communists may have genuine mass support. Orthodox Communist theory can be criticized for exaggerating the inevitability of violent revolution. If people act in terms of rational self-interest both the masses and the old ruling class can gain by compromise. The masses can gain by avoiding the losses involved in violent revolution or civil war and the old ruling class can avoid liquidation by accepting a gradual reduction of its privileges. But there is a great deal of empirical evidence that reform without revolution is only possible where there is a tradition of reasonableness and social solidarity which many countries do not possess. Many groups with anti-social vested interests have preferred to go down fighting for their privileges rather than make concessions and such an attitude makes revolution an essential condition for progress.

This means that the people who oppose Communism simply for its advocacy of violent revolution are taking up an indefensible position. In terms of some theory such as the divine right of kings it would be consistent to argue that armed revolution against an established government is always wrong. But the present governments of most Western countries owe their power to successful revolutions against legitimate authority. No Englishman who is not a Jacobite, no Frenchman who is not a monarchist and no American who does not repudiate the Declaration of Independence can be logically consistent in objecting on principle to the use of armed force to overthrow an unpopular government. And the people who claim to stand for democratic principles while they also appeal to some principle of legitimacy as the basis of opposition to a Communist led revolutionary movement become involved in hopeless contradictions and confusion.

A good illustration was American policy over Formosa. Annexe 170 of the *White Paper on China* reports President Truman saying to T. V. Soong in September, 1945, that "it should be clearly understood that military assistance furnished by the United States should not be diverted for use in fratricidal warfare or to support undemocratic administration." Annexe 169 described developments in Formosa in February and March, 1947. According to American officials, Communist influence was negligible in the rebellion which was a reaction to intolerable misgovernment and was touched off by an incident in which Kuomintang police beat to death a woman cigarette pedlar who protested against the confiscation of her money as well as her allegedly untaxed cigarettes. The Formosan leaders showed great restraint and called off the rioting after the local Kuomintang officials had agreed to make reforms and had given the most solemn and explicit promises that troops would not be brought from the mainland. These promises were immediately broken and Kuomintang troops, with American equipment, suppressed the rebellion by a reign of terror which included the typical totalitarian tactics of killing off educated natives who might be potential leaders of opposition. By every democratic principle for which the Americans claimed to stand they should have supported the Formosans. If they had done so the result would almost certainly have been the establishment of a fairly democratic regime, friendly to America, which would have had the support of democratic opinion throughout the world in resisting conquest by any totalitarian regime from the mainland. In fact, because the Kuomintang regime was a legitimate government engaged elsewhere in a struggle against Communism, the use of American aid "to support undemocratic administration" by the worst methods of totalitarianism produced nothing but private protests. American claims to stand for democracy against totalitarianism were badly discredited and Formosa has become a subject of dispute between America and her allies. (While the standards of Kuomintang administration in Formosa have greatly improved since 1947 the island is still not governed for the benefit of the Formosans. And Formosa as the seat of a rival government of China is a much greater international problem than Formosa independent or as a U.N. protectorate.)

Similar confusion and ineffectiveness arises when Communist power is opposed in terms of a theory which takes institutions of the type found in Western countries as the only criterion of democracy. I do not wish to become involved in an attempt to define the theoretical basis of democracy but I would suggest that the ordinary usage of the term would include something like the following four conditions. 1. The ordinary citizen should have security against injustice and arbitrary action by agents of the government. (Engels' definition, quoted above (page 58), of "the first condition of all freedom" could support this with the authority of one of the founders of Marxism.) 2. The public should have access to information which could enable the ordinary citizen to form his own reasoned judgment about the policies of the government. 3. The ordinary citizen should be able to influence the government to serve his interests and, if his views have majority support, to change government policy or the government itself without resort to force. 4. There should be a respect for human personality which will prevent any group of citizens being condemned to a position of permanent inferiority by social or economic distinctions. These conditions are not "all or none" qualities which are either definitely present or definitely absent in any society. They are all variables which may not reach zero even in very despotic societies and are not completely satisfied even in the most democratic.

The institutions of Western democracy—the rule of law with an independent judiciary, freedom of speech and the press, and governments chosen by elections allowing free choice between competing parties—are devices to secure these conditions for democracy, but it would be hard to prove that they are the only possible devices. There is a very strong case for maintaining that some Western democracies are the most democratic societies in the world at present, but they are obviously far from perfect democracies and it is at least theoretically possible that a society with different institutions might be equally or even more demo-

103

cratic and there is no reason to suppose that the same institutions will be equally suitable for all types of society.

In particular, there is a great deal of empirical evidence that the institutions of Western democracy do not function properly and do not lead to democratic conditions except in societies where there is some tradition of working such institutions and where the general public has a certain amount of political education. And Western political theory has very little to offer about the problem of how to promote the development of democracy in societies where these conditions are not satisfied.

There is, in fact, a great deal to be said in favour of Sun Yat-sen's theory of "political tutelage"—the theory that in some societies progress towards democracy is only possible through a period in which a more or less dictatorial government uses its power to train the people in the working of democratic institiutions. Sun Yat-sen's programme envisaged elected government starting at the *hsien* (county) level, then extending to the provinces and finally to the central government. If this programme had been carried out it would have been very like the progress through which some countries have developed from British colonies to self-governing members of the Commonwealth. Though the sample is too small to give a high degree of certainty to any generalization, the empirical evidence does suggest that progress towards democracy in societies which start with no democratic institutions and a low degree of political education has been most successful where there has been a period of political tutelage, either under a colonial power or else under some native dictatorship, as in Turkey. A realistic democratic policy for China should probably have accepted the necessity for a period of political tutelage and concentrated on the problem of how to make political tutelage work—how to ensure that the ruling group used its power for its proclaimed objective of training the people for democracy and not in order to perpetuate its own status as a privileged ruling class. In fact, the supporters of democracy in China were largely ineffective because they tended to denounce political tutelage and to press for the immediate establishment of institutions which were very unlikely to function properly under existing conditions.

(Though the Chinese Communists officially repudiated the theory of political tutelage because of its Kuomintang associations, members of the Party would admit in private conversation that Communist practice amounted to something very like political tutelage. And at one time Chinese Communist political tutelage was much more genuine than that of the Kuomintang. In some of the war-time Communist areas control of government by freely elected councils was quite effective at the village level and sometimes at the *hsien* level; and the organisation met the requirements of genuine political tutelage by making it possible for the people to extend the range of popular influence on government when they had acquired enough political experience to want to do so. The Kuomintang, under much easier circumstances and over a much longer period, did almost nothing to carry out even the first stage of Sun Yat-sen's programme by putting local government on an elective basis.)

All this means that a great deal of the normal liberal criticism of Communism is beside the point. It is quite justifiable to criticize the Communists for suppressing Western democratic institutions in a country such as Czechoslovakia which had demonstrated its capacity to make them work. But in many countries a Western type democratic constitution had been tried and had failed to work or to promote the development of democracy. In such countries the replacement of the old regime by a Communist dictatorship would not necessarily be undemocratic, provided that the dictatorship were really carrying out political tutelage which made progress towards democracy possible. The important question is whether political tutelage is developing towards democracy or degenerating towards tyranny and it is hard to draw this distinction in terms of standards which condemn all forms of political tutelage.

The real case against Communist power

The real case against Communist power turns on the truth or falsity of Communist claims. When judged by any normal standards of empirical evidence the Communists are making claims which are mainly false when they claim that orthodox Communist regimes give first priority to serving the interests of the masses, that orthodox Communist regimes are more democratic than Western democracies, and even when they claim to be exercising political tutelage which is training the masses for democracy.

Some developments under Communist regimes, such as the reduction of illiteracy, could form part of genuine political tutelage. But political tutelage would imply the gradual extension

105

of popular control over government as the people become better qualified and more interested to exercise it, and the actual trends of development under orthodox Communist regimes have been in the opposite direction. The powers of popularly elected bodies in Russia, such as Soviets and Trade Unions, were reduced after the mid-1920's. In China some Communist areas were holding elections with secret ballot and equal voting as far back as 1940, but the 1953 Election Law has abolished secret ballot and gives urban votes a weighting eight times as great as rural votes. In other countries the period of Communist power has been shorter but the general trend has always been towards the increased concentration of power in the hands of the hierarchical Communist organisation. And the existence of this trend is incompatible with claims to be exercising political tutelage.

The falsity of Communist claims to be practising democracy are even more obvious. Even from the internal evidence of official Communist publications it is clear that the ordinary citizen has very little security against arbitrary action by government officials. A good illustration is the account of the collectivization of agriculture in the *Short History of the Communist Party in the Soviet Union*. It is admitted that, in many areas, local officials tried to push through collectivization in a shorter period than that laid down by the government. It is admitted that this action was extremely unpopular and that the higher authorities had eventually to intervene to correct the situation. It can be deduced quite clearly from these admissions that the ordinary peasant had no means of resisting the orders of officials who were exceeding their legal authority or of making an effective protest against them even though he intensely disliked these illegal orders. Similar deductions can be made from many more recent reports by Communist regimes of intervention by the higher authorities to remedy the results of action by lower officials who had been behaving in ways that were both illegal and unpopular.

People under Communist control are never allowed access to information from which they could form an independent judgment about the policies of the government. For instance, expert economists making a full time study of all available published material find it very hard to deduce the sort of information about economic developments in Communist ruled countries which the governments of Western democracies make available to their citizens as a matter of course. And within

Communist ruled countries attempts to obtain such information are treated as espionage. For the ordinary citizen in a Communist ruled country it is almost impossible to obtain reliable information from which to judge the economic policy of the government except from his personal experience and immediate environment. A recent study of Soviet society concludes that Communist publicity is not only trying to persuade the masses to support the government but "it is also designed to deny to men the information and concepts which would permit them to formulate an alternative to the lines of policy they are meant to implement and support." And it is suggested that, "The system of Soviet propaganda is apparently designed, in part, simply to exhaust the intellectual and political energies of men"[1] in order to prevent the rise of any opposition to the regime. The accounts of life in China with interminable meetings and discussion groups which appear, to the non-Communist, carefully to avoid the discussion of most really interesting or important questions seem to show the same pattern.

Admittedly, orthodox Communist regimes claim to base their power on popular support but they also show very clearly by their practical policies that they are not prepared to allow this claim to be subject to any experimental test. In spite of their propaganda system orthodox Communist regimes are never willing to allow any developments which might make it possible for the people to express their preferences for policies or methods of government other than those of the Communists. The whole Communist attitude on such questions is yet another example of "doublethink." On the one hand it is claimed that the workers have a class status which gives them a unique power of correct political judgment. On the other hand, the arguments used to justify Communist publicity or the Communist refusal to allow free elections imply that the majority of the actual workers in Communist ruled countries cannot be trusted with the information necessary to form a judgment and would use a free election to vote for parties which, according to orthodox Communist theory, wish to enslave and exploit them and not for the party which, according to orthodox Communist theory, wishes to liberate them and serve their interests. In terms of any empirical standards this attitude is quite incompatible with any claim to stand for democracy. It can be explained either as a rationalization to justify the indefinite pursuit of power by the Communist Party or else as one result of the inevitable conflict between empirical reality and a system of Marx-Leninist faith which implies that the Party is infallible.

Any fairly efficient totalitarian regime can obtain popular support of a kind. When the government has a complete monopoly of publicity which works to present the regime and its policies in a favourable light and to suppress all information and ideas which would allow the people to formulate an alternative to them, and when an elaborate security organisation works to destroy any nuclei of potential organised opposition, then a majority of the population can normally be induced to support the government so long as it does not make living conditions intolerable. And to run an efficient totalitarian regime requires genuine devoted support from a small minority, perhaps 10 per cent, of the population. The real question is whether the support obtained by orthodox Communist regimes is different from the support obtained by right-wing totalitarian regimes such as those of Hitler in Germany or Peron in Argentina. Judging from circumstantial evidence, which is the only evidence available, it would seem that the difference is very small. There is strong evidence that some orthodox Communist regimes have started with widespread and genuine popular support but, in every case up to now, there has been a more or less rapid degeneration of the Communist Party into a dominant minority only able to maintain its power by totalitarian methods.

It is very unlikely that any existing orthodox Communist regime, with the possible exception of the Chinese, would be able to survive in an environment where the masses were able to form and support organisations offering an alternative to Communist power. And there is strong evidence that orthodox Communist regimes have been unable to prevent the existence of bitter opposition from a considerable proportion of the population under their control. In parts of the Soviet Union the German armies were first welcomed as liberators and not only the Reichswehr leaders but also the less doctrinaire Nazi officials considered that it would have been possible to obtain large scale support from the Russian people against the Russian government. In fact the experiment was never tried because of Hitler and Himmler's insistence on their doctrinaire racial theories which demanded that all Slavs should be treated as human animals to whom tolerable living conditions could not be offered. However, it is unlikely that Germans in responsible positions would have taken the considerable risks of pressing for policies contrary to the wishes of the top Nazi leadership unless they had very good reasons to believe that policies designed to win the support of the Russian people would have had an extremely high chance of succeeding. Even as it was, the record of such organisations as the Vlasov Army shows that many Soviet citizens considered the Germans to be a lesser evil than the Soviet government. And, in the post-war period, the Soviet government showed itself very afraid of allowing contacts which would have enabled considerable numbers of Soviet citizens to make an empirical comparison between conditions in the Soviet Union and those in non-Communist societies.

Again, between 1945 and 1950, about a quarter of the entire population of North Korea ran away to the admittedly bad conditions of South Korea. And, if a quarter of the population disliked the regime so much that they were ready to abandon their possessions and take the risks of flight in order to live under a corrupt and oppressive but non-Communist regime, it is fairly certain that a much higher proportion of the population of North Korea would have expressed their dislike of Communist rule if they had been able to do so at less risk and expense.

Yet again, the revolts of June, 1953, in East Germany and Czechoslovakia showed that the Communists had failed to keep the support even of the industrial working class to whose interests they were in theory specially devoted.

These are only a few samples of the sort of evidence which can be very simply explained by the hypothesis that orthodox Communist regimes have not been able to base their power on the support of the masses, as they should be according to Marx-Leninist theory. In contrast, the attempts to defend the official Communist position do not meet the requirements of a satisfactory scientific hypothesis. They have either to deny the authenticity of reports which, by ordinary standards, would appear to be quite reliable or else to explain the facts by all sorts of unsatisfactory and implausible hypotheses. For instance, the official Communist explanation of the East German revolt of June, 1953 as the work of Western agents would not be a satisfactory explanation even if the leadership of such agents could be established, which it has not been. Under a regime with an elaborate security service, agents from outside could not produce such a widespread movement of revolt unless they had been able to obtain large scale and spontaneous support from the masses for any move against Communist rule.

This failure of orthodox Communist regimes to retain popular support is largely the result of their failure to serve the interests of the masses. In part this failure has been the result of doctrinaire policies. For instance, most orthodox Communist regimes have pushed the collectivization of agriculture without regard for the conditions under which collectivization could lead to higher productivity. And every Communist regime has planned economic policy in terms of a very low rate of discount of the future* for which it could almost certainly not obtain popular support. An obvious slogan for a popular opposition movement in any country under orthodox Communist rule would be "Plan for the living and not the unborn"; that is, increase the relative priority of such production as housing and consumer goods which

* Many economic decisions involve a choice between the present and the future, or between the near and the remote future. The decision must depend on the relative valuation of present and future. Most people value the present more highly than the future and this relative preference can be expressed as a "rate of discount of the future." For example, if someone is indifferent between £100 now and £110 in a year's time his rate of discount of the future is 10 per cent. and the ordinary theory of compound interest can extend this to cover more complicated cases.

Under conditions near full employment any investment project involves a diversion of present national income in order to increase national income in the future. For example, the Snowy Mountains scheme in Australia involves large expenditure which will not yield any return until the power stations and irrigation projects come into operation, while the same expenditure differently used, might do much to overcome present housing shortages. On any rational economic plan the rate of discount of the future will determine how far it is worth while making such present sacrifices to secure future benefits.

Mr. Maurice Dobb, defending the Communist position, argued that "since planning attempts to take a long view and has small reason to discount the future, there is little to qualify the priority that is assigned to the task of equipping future decades with productive instruments more richly than the present is equipped." (*Soviet Economic Development since 1917*. Routledge London, 1948. Page 28.) This low rate of discount of the future explains the Communist policies, slightly modified in 1953, which have compelled the citizens of Communist ruled states to accept low standards of living in the present in order to build up productivity for the future. Mr. Dobb's apparent suggestion that planned economy should have a zero rate of discount of the future would logically imply an economy with the slogan "Jam tomorrow but never jam today" because the number of possible investment projects which would increase productivity in the indefinite future is indefinitely great.

The idea of rate of discount of the future can be extended outside economics. Many political decisions involve a similar choice between present and future, between taking risks now and facing probably greater risks in the future, between present gains and possibly greater future losses. The concept is less definite because the things involved are even less measurable than economic quantities. All the same, to talk of a high or a low rate of discount of the future is a convenient way of describing different attitudes towards political or even personal decisions.

benefit the present generation as compared with heavy industry and long term projects which can only raise the standard of living in the more or less remote future.

Besides this, the actual policies of orthodox Communist regimes give the present day interests of the masses a lower priority than the maintenance of Communist power. The study of Soviet society quoted above summarises the position as follows—"The citizens of the Soviet Empire, including its European satellites, are regarded as units to be molded if possible, but certainly to be controlled, so as to contribute to goals determined independently of their inclinations. The system is designed to operate indefinitely in the face of the wishes of its citizens while doing what it can to identify the wishes of its citizens with the goals of the regime . . . What is distinctive about the Soviet regime is the extreme priority it accords to the pursuit of the goal of its own power, as opposed to a national program reflecting the aspirations of its citizens. In particular, the regime is marked by an almost total lack of inhibition in the means it is prepared to use to effect this priority."[2] Given the assumptions of orthodox Marx-Leninist faith this priority is quite logical. In the long term interests of the masses it is of supreme importance that power should remain in the hands of the Party which represents their class interests, whatever sacrifices this may involve of their short term interests.

This case against Communist power is often spoilt by exaggeration. It is quite possible that the interests of the masses may be better served by a second priority under Communist rule than by an equally low priority under some equally undemocratic non-Communist regime. A single closely organised group with a monopoly of power, even if it is primarily concerned with its own power, will be forced to accept responsibility for the condition of the masses and will have an interest in maintaining conditions good enough to enable the masses to work with efficiency and to prevent discontent with its rule from rising to a dangerous level. The changes in policy in 1953 in the Soviet Union and the European satellites can be interpreted as the results of a realisation that discontent with Communist rule might rise to a dangerous level if more attention were not given to the immediate interests of the masses. These restraints on the exploitation of the masses may not operate in an undemocratic non-Communist regime and a society in which several different groups are all trying to exploit the masses is much more likely to push exploitation to a point where efficiency declines seriously and discontent becomes so strong as to threaten the regime.

In many countries Communist rule has made some real reform which benefit the masses not only when judged in terms of Marx-Leninist theory but also when judged by empirical standards If the only alternative to orthodox Communist rule were a return to something like the old regime it is quite possible that the people might prefer the Communists. But there is no reason to suppose that these are the only possible alternatives. A move towards greater democracy which gave the people more power to force the government to consider their interests would be preferable to either. This is one of the many points on which orthodox Communists and extreme anti-Communists join forces in trying to confuse the issue. Both try to present the situation as if the only alternative to orthodox Communist rule were to return to something like the pre-Communist regime or as if socialism necessarily implied something like orthodox Communist rule.

Though the case against Communist power is often spoilt by exaggeration, it remains a strong one even when these exaggerations have been discounted. And there is nothing inexplicable about the failure of orthodox Communist regimes to retain mass support or to govern in the interests of the masses. To anyone who does not think in terms of orthodox Marx-Leninist faith the degeneration of Communist rule into that of a dominant minority primarily concerned with its own power and governing by terrorism and deception is a natural and inherently probable result of certain aspects of orthodox Communism—the refusal to admit the possibility that a Communist Party may be corrupted by power, the failure to realise the dangers inherent in the use of police state methods, the rigidities imposed by democratic centralism, the tendency to believe in Party infallibility, and so on.

The threat to peace

All this means that there is an irreconcilable conflict between doctrinaire orthodox Communists and the rest of the world Subjectively, the Communists may be trying to extend their power from entirely altruistic motives and may sincerely believe that they are justified in using any methods to overcome opposition which can only spring from the vested interests of ruling classes trying to preserve their power to enslave and exploit the masses

To anyone who judges Communism by empirical standards the extension of orthodox Communist power is a threat to the interests of the masses just as much as to those of the ruling classes. In societies where pre-Communist administration has been exceptionally oppressive the masses may benefit from Communist power in the short run. In the long run the only people who stand to gain by it are those who manage to obtain a position in the new Communist ruling group, and even they will only gain if they rate the enjoyment of power fairly high as compared with security. Judging from the frequent purges which have marked the history of every Communist Party except the Chinese, most Communist leaders would greatly increase their expectation of life if they could exchange their present positions for one similar to that of political leaders in democratic societies.

It is this practical empirical objection to Communist power which Communists seem to find extremely hard to understand. An analogy might help to make it clear. Imagine a doctor whose medical theories lead him both to refuse to accept the empirical evidence behind the work of Pasteur and Lister and also to advocate surgical treatment for almost every case. Such a man might be entirely sincere in wishing to help his fellow men and he might even quite often be correct in diagnosing that an operation was essential. But anyone with an elementary knowledge of modern medicine would be acting quite rationally in going to almost any lengths to avoid his treatment. By empirical standards it is practically certain that his operations would be followed by infection with a very high mortality rate. Only people whose condition without operation was hopeless and who could not obtain treatment from anyone else would be justified in accepting his services. To make the analogy complete it would also be necessary to suppose that this doctor did everything possible to discourage the practice of rivals with more empirical theories of medicine and that, while his motives in forcing his services on people were largely altruistic, he also made a very good income from his practice. Similarly, the Communist treatment of social ills would be rejected by anyone who has studied the actual results of Communist rule in Eastern Europe, even by someone belonging to the class to whose interests the Communists profess to be specially devoted. The only case in which rational judgment would lead to the acceptance of the leadership of an orthodox Communist Party is where the existing social situation is intolerable and where there is no prospect of essential reforms being made except by the Communists.

This medical analogy is not entirely imaginary. An Austrian doctor who worked in China has published a horrifying description of the results of Communist dogmatism in medical work. While his experiences are probably not typical I would be inclined to accept his account as authentic because, even during the war, I heard some very critical accounts of medical work in this particular area.[3]

The impression one gets both from Communist statements and from the accounts of people who have visited China recently is that the Chinese Communists find it almost impossible to understand that anyone can sincerely doubt their good faith in wanting peace. But if they want to get peace it is essential that they should understand that many people believe that it is almost impossible for any Communist to behave in a way that can lead to peace. Many non-Communists would be inclined to question the value of this whole discussion of Communist motivation. They might quote the saying of Hume: "Nothing is more requisite for a true philosopher than to restrain the intemperate desire of searching into causes; and, having established any doctrine upon a sufficient number of experiments, rest contented with that, when he sees a further examination would lead him into obscure and uncertain speculations. In that case his inquiry would be much better employed in examining the effects rather than the causes of his principle."[4] Having established by strong empirical evidence that Communists try to extend their power by every possible means and that this drive for power endangers world peace, we would be much better employed in considering the best methods of countering this Communist threat than in obscure and uncertain speculations about the motives behind Communist behaviour.

This sort of view is very widely held, not only by anti-Communist extremists but also by serious scholars. As an illustration, consider the following passage from a book sponsored by the Russian Research Centre at Harvard. "Communism in action is today a very intricate religion of power . . . Collectivization, political terror, industrial planning, and mass education and indoctrination are not separate items of a political program, either as relics of earlier idealism or as results of today's corruption, but they all fit together into the composite picture of the Communist understanding of political power . . . It follows, therefore, that Communism as a social and economic reform movement has become an illusion. It has no social or economic postulates save as they are considered the means of achieving and perpetuating political power."[5]

If this view of Communism is correct it implies that peaceful co-existence is impossible. If any powerful organisation is determined to use every possible means to extend its power the best that can be hoped for is an armed truce. If the rest of the world is sufficiently well armed and sufficiently determined, the drive for power may be restrained by the realisation that it can only be pursued at the cost of a war which will probably end in defeat and complete loss of power. In so far as the Communists are committed to unqualified support for the extension of the power of the C.P.S.U. or of orthodox Communism in general they present a threat to the peace of the world similar to that presented by Nazism and Japanese militarism in the recent past, or Assyrian militarism and Mongol imperialism in the remote past.

However, it is possible to criticize this view of Communism, though not in terms which orthodox Communists would accept. For both Nazism and Japanese militarism the extension of power was an explicit objective justified by concepts such as historic destiny or divine mission which are outside the range within which beliefs can be either confirmed or refuted by rational argument or empirical evidence. And the basic philosophy of both Nazism and Japanese militarism was irrationalist. The arguments about the economic unification of Europe or the Greater East Asia Co-prosperity Sphere were little more than propaganda devices whose truth or falsity was not essential to the system. If people simply say "We belong to a group which has a right to rule the world" it is not possible to prove by rational argument that they are mistaken; it is only possible to defeat by force any attempts to assert this claim. On the other hand, Communism does not make the pursuit of power an explicit final objective. If people say "We believe that our organisation has a right to rule the world because this would produce 'the maximum good for the greatest number'" it is at least theoretically possible that they could be induced to modify their claim by a demonstration that this basis was false. And, on a common sense view, the question of whether or not certain policies are

115

likely to produce "the maximum good for the greatest number" is a question to which rational argument and empirical evidence can be applied.

In practice, faith in orthodox Communism depends on "doublethink" positions, which means that any statement about the ultimate objective of Communism can only be based on an estimate of how Communists would act if they ceased to use "doublethink". No orthodox Communist would admit that there could be a conflict between extending the power of the Communist Party and serving the interests of the masses, and would use "doublethink" and other forms of irrationalism to maintain this position. But, if he were to admit that the two objectives might be incompatible, which would he choose? Until this estimate has been made it is not possible to say whether orthodox Communists are acting rationally but in bad faith or in good faith but irrationally. Such an estimate of what answer Communists would give to a question which they actually refuse to consider cannot be based on anything more than indirect evidence and it is very likely that the answer would not be the same for all Communists. Some Communist ruling groups have acquired a very strong vested interest in the continuance and extension of Communist power and, in the Soviet Union, this has lasted long enough to allow the development of a social tradition. If the leaders of the C.P.S.U. could be subjected to some form of compulsory psycho-analysis it is quite likely that many of them would admit that power was their ultimate objective and the service of the interests of the masses only a rationalization. But some scholars such as Isaac Deutscher with considerable inside knowledge of Soviet Communism seem to doubt whether such an answer would be unanimous even for this sample. There is a great deal of empirical evidence that many Communists are more altruistic and less cynical than the present Soviet ruling group and it is quite possible that a majority of Communists would, if they were forced to choose, put the interests of the masses before the extension of Communist power.

In terms of this analysis the possibility that Communists might act in a way which would allow "peaceful co-existence" as opposed to an armed truce depends on two unknowns. Firstly, the relative influence within the Communist organisation of those whose ultimate objective is to serve the interests of the masses as compared with those whose ultimate objective is simply power.

Secondly, how far it is possible for those Communists who wish to serve the interests of the masses to modify their orthodox Marx-Leninist faith enough to allow them to work for their objective with functional rationality.

Both doctrinaire Communists and extreme anti-Communists tend to assume that Marx-Leninism is a coherent system which must be either totally accepted or totally rejected by some act of faith. Both tend to accept the irrationalist philosophy according to which beliefs are never influenced by rational judgment and consequently deny the possibility that a Communist may make progressive modifications in his beliefs in order to bring them into closer accordance with logic and empirical evidence. The most doctrinaire Communists admit that some people of non-proletarian origin may repudiate their class status and accept Communism and some of the most extreme anti-Communists are former members of the Communist Party, but such cases are thought of as exceptions which only prove the general rule that beliefs produced by class status or Communist indoctrination are unchangeable.

As against this I would maintain that most people have a real though limited power of rational judgment and that the standards of rational judgment are objective. While beliefs may be greatly or even mainly influenced by such factors as class status, indoctrination, cultural tradition or the way in which people were treated when they were babies, they are also influenced by a tendency to accept beliefs which meet the requirements of a satisfactory scientific theory—which are logically consistent, which explain and co-ordinate empirical evidence and which lead to predictions confirmed by empirical evidence. At the one extreme a system of beliefs entirely determined by rational judgment is a theoretical ideal case never realised in practice. And indeed the use of rational judgment depends on assumptions about the nature of the world which cannot be proved by reason. At the other extreme, a system of beliefs entirely uninfluenced by rational judgment is a sign of insanity.

If the world is such that rational judgment can be applied to it, the influence of rational judgment will be increased in the long run by the greater effectiveness of systems which encourage it as compared with systems which discourage it. Here again parts of George Orwell's *Nineteen Eighty-four* can be paraphrased as a perfectly serious discussion when he argues that the completely

117

totalitarian state can maintain a system of faith almost entirely divorced from empirical reality only when competition has disappeared.

A Communist whose ultimate objective is power will maintain the irrationalities and "doublethink" positions in his system even when he does not really believe in them. So long as he retains the ability to recognise them when their practical consequences would be inconvenient, they can serve as functionally rational parts of a policy to extend Communist power. On the other hand, a Communist whose ultimate objective is to serve the masses can only maintain his faith in orthodox Marx-Leninism by a continual struggle to evade or explain away empirical evidence and to avoid thinking out implications which would make "doublethink" positions untenable.

It is not reasonable to expect that Communists should show a degree of rationality far above the average and suddenly abandon a system of beliefs to which they have a strong emotional attachment. Indeed, a considerable proportion of the sudden conversions from Communism cannot be explained as the result of rational judgment because many ex-Communists only change their Communist faith for some system of beliefs equally in conflict with logic and empirical evidence. On the other hand, it is reasonable to expect that many Communists may retain enough power of rational judgment to make them desirous of modifying their system of beliefs and that, especially with encouragement, this modification might eventually go far enough to make them no longer a danger to peace. If one looks at the history of natural science one finds that explicit modification in basic beliefs is often the last stage of a process of development. For a long time people may continue to express new knowledge in terms of an old theory with which it is really incompatible and the same is likely to be true of political beliefs. The obvious first stage for any Communist who starts to think is something like Titoism, and there was a time lag of about two years between the Yugoslav Communist Party taking the decisive first step of breaking with the Cominform and the modification of officially accepted orthodox theory to bring it into line with the empirical evidence about the Soviet Union.

In the case of the Chinese Communist Party there is a great deal of evidence indicating that devotion to the service of the masses remains very powerful as an ultimate objective. Many reports by non-Communist observers agree in describing an atmosphere of devotion and enthusiasm among members of the Communist organisation. A good recent example is Basil Davidson's *Daybreak in China*.[6] There is no reason to suppose that his account of the mental state of supporters of the Chinese government is wrong although he seems to be completely uninterested in the question of whether many of the enthusiastic beliefs which so much impressed him have any rational basis and he does not make the obvious comparison with the early years of the Soviet Union when many observers reported a similar enthusiasm.

The Chinese Communist Party is also exceptional among Communist parties in the extent to which its history has shown instances of rational judgment. Mao Tse-tung's first important work *A Report on an Investigation of the Peasant Movement in Hunan* was a criticism of accepted Communist orthodoxy in terms of rational judgment. On the basis of the empirical evidence obtained through his study of the peasant movement he criticized the orthodox view that the peasantry could not become an independent revolutionary force. Until Mao Tse-tung's views had proved their obvious success in practice they were considered heretical and, at one time, Maoism was denounced as a heresy in *International Press Correspondence*. And although the element of rational judgment was never completely dominant over orthodox Marx-Leninist dogmatism it was sufficiently prominent in the Chinese Communist party at one period to make the behaviour of the Chinese Communists noticeably different from that of other Communists. This was not only my personal impression comparing the Chinese Communists with Communists I had known in England. It was also the impression of foreign journalists and members of the U.S. Army Observers Section at Yenan who were able to compare the Chinese Communist Party with the Communist Party of the Soviet Union. And, while General Hurley is not a reliable witness, his account of Molotov's views about the Chinese Communists suggests that the Soviet leaders may possibly also have recognised the difference.[7]

The theoretical position of the Chinese Communist Party about rational judgment was always inconsistent. There are considerable parts of the "Cheng Feng" movement which seem to be arguments in favour of the use of rational judgment but they were never taken entirely seriously even by Mao Tse-tung himself. A good illustration is the lecture given in 1941, *The Reconstruction of Our Studies*. The main theme of the lecture is a plea for an objective scientific spirit in study which would

119

seem to be quite incompatible with doctrinaire Marx-Leninism.
But at the very end of the lecture Mao Tse-tung suddenly refers
to the official *Short History of the Communist Party of the
Soviet Union* as ". . . the highest synthesis and summary of the
world Communist movement in the last hundred years, a model
for the union of theory and practice; in the whole world this is
still the one perfect model."[8] According to everything he had
said previously he should have cited it as the perfect model of
what to avoid, the deliberate distortion and falsification of the
facts to fit them into a preconceived theory. And the attitude
of many people in the Party to the whole "Cheng Feng" movement was a good illustration of the self-perpetuating forces in
a system of dogma. The warnings against taking Marx-Leninist
writings as a system of sacred dogma were often taken simply
as additional bits of sacred dogma. An amusing story on this
was told me by a friend in the New China News Agency. A
phrase in one of Mao Tse-tung's lectures, "to gain favour by
rousing the mob", became garbled in transmission to South East
Shansi and was received there as, "to gain a jewel from the fog".
(Chinese characters are transmitted as four-figure groups so that
a mistake in transmission produces a different word and not just
a wrong spelling. In this case three characters out of four
were changed.) Although one main theme of the lecture was a
warning against uncritical reverence for Communist writings,
the editors of the local paper did not say to themselves, "This
really doesn't make sense." With uncritical reverence for the
supposed words of Mao Tse-tung they wrote an editorial
expounding the deep inner meaning of gaining a jewel from the
fog.

The element of rational judgment in Chinese Communist
thinking has certainly greatly decreased since 1946 but it is still
true that the modifications in the orthodox Marx-Leninist position
which would make the Chinese Communist Party capable of
acting with functional rationality for peace are implied by sayings
of Mao Tse-tung which still remain in the recent editions of his
writings. For instance, suppose the Chinese Communists were
to take seriously the slogan, "If you have done no investigating,
you have no right to speak."[9] This would imply a complete
revolution in their conduct of foreign affairs. Instead of reproducing without question the accounts of the non-Communist
world given by Soviet propaganda or local Communist leaders
and refusing opportunities for contacts or discussion with

informed non-Communist opinion, they would take every opportunity for making the widest possible contacts and joining in the
widest possible discussion in order to find things out for
themselves.

Even more revolutionary would be the results of taking
seriously Mao Tse-tung's slogan, "Seek the truth by referring to
fact."[10] Such an attitude in any study of the European situation would certainly lead to the acceptance of something like
the Titoist analysis of the Soviet Union as an imperialist power.
In the study of America it would lead to a complete redrawing
of the line between friends and enemies of China and between
people working for and against peace. In Far Eastern affairs
it would lead to a repudiation of previous Chinese policies on
such issues as the Korean war, voluntary repatriation and so on.
And in internal Chinese affairs it would almost certainly lead to
radical revisions of policy.

In *Coalition Government* Mao Tse-tung said, ". . . we Chinese
Communists, who take the most vital interests of the broadest
masses of the Chinese people as their starting point, believe that
their cause is entirely one of justice, feel no regret in sacrificing
everything we have and are ready to give up even our lives for
the sake of their cause. Can there then be any thought, viewpoint, opinion, or method of work which is erroneous and does
not correspond to the necessity of the people which are too dear
to us to give up?"[11] If this were applied to faith in orthodox
Marx-Leninism it would certainly lead the Chinese Communists
to modify their beliefs sufficiently to enable them to act with
functional rationality to serve the Chinese people. And this
would certainly include acting in a way which would make
possible peaceful co-existence and the settling of disputes by
negotiation rather than war.

As against the view that it is inherently impossible for Communists to behave in a way which would lead to peace I would
maintain that, at least for the Chinese Communist Party, the
necessary modifications of orthodox Marx-Leninism were difficult
but not impossible.

7

Some confusing theories

BEFORE discussing the kind of policies most likely to promote peace it may be worth while criticising two theories which are widely believed and which cause a great deal of confusion and which, I believe, have a common origin.

The Marxian theory of war

This whole discussion of the conditions for peace, in terms which imply that the major obstacles to peaceful co-existence come from the Communist side, will appear strange to many people. Marxist theory explains war in terms of economic conflicts, especially the struggle for raw materials and markets between acquisitive capitalist societies, and maintains that such conflicts will disappear under Communism.[*] To people who accept this view it seems obvious that the main danger of war must come from capitalist countries. And some form of this theory is very widely accepted even by many non-Communists. For example, most of Sapper's "Bulldog Drummond" novels are violently anti-Communist but the plot of *Bulldog Drummond at Bay* (published in 1935) depends on a crude version of this Marxian theory—unscrupulous capitalists plotting to start a war to serve their economic interests. However, there are at least two strong arguments against this popular Marxian view.

Firstly, there is no real reason to suppose that economic conflicts tending to produce war would disappear with the abolition of capitalism, though they might take different forms. To put the case at its lowest, it is not theoretically impossible that one

---

[*] A very clear summary of this view was given by Bukharin in 1936. "What creates wars is the competition of monopoly capitalisms for raw materials and markets. Capitalist society is made up of selfish and competing national units and therefore is by definition a world at war. Communist society will be made up of unselfish and harmonious units and therefore will be by definition a world at peace. Just as capitalism cannot live without war, so war cannot live with Communism." (Quoted in *Tito and Goliath*. By H. F. Armstrong. Victor Gollancz, London, 1951. Page 9.) Very similar views can be found in the section on pacifism in the third edition of the Soviet *Small Philosophical Dictionary* published in 1952.

socialist state could use its superior power to divert to its own use some of the national product of another state. The Soviet government has admittedly diverted some of the national product of Eastern Germany to the Soviet Union in order to obtain reparations. And, though Communists deny it, there is extremely strong evidence that the economic relations between the Soviet Union and other Communist ruled states involve similar exploitation without the justification of reparations. The Yugoslav leaders have published fairly detailed accounts of the type of exploitation which the Soviet Union tried to impose in the period between 1945 and 1948. This included such devices as trading agreements which allowed the Soviet Union to exchange commodities at rates more favourable than those prevailing on world markets, and joint companies in which the Soviet share of the capital was over valued and the native share under valued and which claimed special monopoly rights and extraterritorial privileges. For countries still under Communist rule the evidence is less detailed but it is still fairly clear that similar arrangements lead to a considerable degree of exploitation for the benefit of the Soviet Union. (When, for example, the Soviet Union bought Bulgarian tobacco at a price fixed by a trade agreement and sold it to other countries at a higher price there was clearly a diversion of income from Bulgaria to the Soviet Union. And there is some evidence of similar exploitation of China.)

Thus the exploitation of one country by another is still possible even when both are under Communist rule. So even in a world where capitalism had been entirely replaced by Communist rule wars could still be caused by the use of military force to impose or to resist this type of exploitation.[*]

Similarly, vested interests favouring at least the threat of war can be found in Communist ruled as well as in capitalist countries. There is a lot of evidence, such as the often cited fall in stock exchange values with the Korean truce, to show that some interests in capitalist countries gain by the continuing risk of a major war. It is also possible to make a fairly strong case for holding that the maintenance of full employment without large scale armament expenditure might present some capitalist economies with fairly difficult problems of adjustment. But the

---

[*] It is possible to preserve a definition of socialism as incompatible with exploitation by saying that the Soviet Union and other countries under orthodox Communist rule are not examples of socialism but of "state capitalism." But this is simply a matter of terminology, which does not affect the facts of the situation.

123

Communist arguments that capitalism could not adjust to a peaceful world depend on the assumption that such problems are not difficult but insoluble. And this would only be true under governments committed to strict pre-Keynesian capitalist orthodoxy. On the other hand, the transition to a state of peaceful co-existence would present Communist ruled countries with problems that might be quite as difficult to solve. It has already been argued that some groups in Communist ruled countries, such as the very powerful secret police organisations, have a very direct vested interest in the continuance of a threat of war. And the ability of an orthodox Communist regime to survive without the threat of war has yet to be demonstrated. In the past some capitalist societies have functioned fairly effectively for considerable periods during which the war or preparations for war had very little influence on the economic or social system, while the Soviet government, throughout its history, has used the danger of a capitalist military attack as the justification for a great deal of its economic and social policy. As in the case of capitalist countries there is no reason to suppose that the adjustment to a peaceful world would be impossible for a Communist ruled country, but there are good reasons for supposing that it might prove very difficult.

All this means that the economic forces tending to produce war may take different forms with different social systems. But they have certainly not disappeared in Communist ruled countries and only a detailed factual analysis could show whether they are greater or less than in capitalist countries. Many of the Communist arguments on this point are obviously fallacious. For example, it is often argued that large projects of national reconstruction are clear proof of the peaceful intentions of Communist governments; and precisely the same argument was frequently used before 1939 to prove the peaceful intentions of the Nazi government. One cannot at present definitely disprove the Communist claim that Communist rule will eventually produce a new pattern of human behaviour in which men will no longer strive for economic advantage at the expense of other people. One can only say that the existing evidence does not seem to support such a theory.

Secondly, there is a very important difference between a theory which maintains that economic conflicts have been an important and sometimes a dominant influence in causing wars and a theory which maintains that war can be explained entirely in terms of economic conflicts. The former view can be supported by a great deal of evidence, the Communist belief in the latter view is a good example of what I called pre-Newtonian thinking —the inability to think in terms of functions of more than one variable.

In the nineteenth century a theory which explained war in terms of capitalist interests seemed fairly satisfactory. In many cases capitalist interests could make obvious gains through war without incurring any great risks of direct suffering as the result of war. Fighting was usually left to the lower classes officered by professional soldiers while ruling class life at home continued comparatively undisturbed. And there is a great deal of evidence that many people have few scruples about promoting their economic interests by methods which involve suffering for other people. But even in the nineteenth century the Marxian theory of the origins of war was not always satisfactory. To take an extreme case, the war of 1865 to 1870, in which Paraguay fought Uruguay, Brazil and Argentina, can be explained very simply by the megalomania of a dictator in a country whose history had made the population exceptionally submissive to authority. It is extremely unlikely that any economic interests in Paraguay gained from a war which reduced the population by no less than five-sixths.

The war of 1914-18 showed that a major war was likely to leave even the victor powers worse off than before and would involve heavy casualties among the ruling classes as well as among the masses. Capitalist interests might still gain from small scale local wars, but the possibility of economic gain from a major war was doubtful and only a few people are prepared to pursue even less doubtful economic interests to a point which involves an appreciable risk of death or disablement for themselves or their families. At present, when every major centre is within reach of atomic bombs, it is extremely unlikely that rational considerations of self interest, however unscrupulous, would lead anyone deliberately to start a war.

Thus, while economic conflicts may provide motives for war, the increasingly high costs and dangers of modern war for everyone concerned provide even stronger motives for settling such conflicts by compromise rather than by fighting. It follows that a necessary condition for a major war is that, at least in one country, power should be in the hands of people who do not act in terms of rational economic self interest. A major war will only be started by leaders who are so irresponsible or deluded that they are unable to envisage the most probable consequences of their actions, not only for their country but also for themselves; or else by leaders so devoted to some non-economic objective that they are prepared to pursue it even though this involves a high probability of ruin and destruction. (For instance, the main lines of Hitler's policy can be explained by devotion to his slogan "World Power or Ruin." They are hard to explain as directed to the economic interests of Germany or even of the German ruling group.) An exceptional case is when people are ready to fight because they feel that their present situation is intolerable and are therefore ready to accept a high probability of death in trying to change it. But these cases are likely to produce revolutions or civil wars rather than international wars.

All this means that the Marxian analysis of war is unsatisfactory as a guide to action for peace in the modern world. It fails to explain why capitalist interests, which are normally ready to compromise when the costs of unrestricted competition become too high, should sometimes indulge in this most ruinous form of competition. In the modern world, economic rivalry does not provide a sufficient condition for war and, in the case of some wars, may not even be an important factor. And it is almost certainly wrong in its assumption that economic conflict could be reduced to zero through the replacement of capitalism by Communist rule.

It is also possible to suggest an explanation of why so many people believe in the theory even though it is unsatisfactory. It is extremely unpleasant to face a danger one does not understand and to feel that action must be taken to meet this danger without knowing what action to take. The Marxian analysis offers a simple explanation of the danger of war which fits some of the evidence and which indicates a very simple course of action to meet it, namely to take sides with the forces of socialism working for peace against the capitalist interests working for war. The same reasons explain the attractive power of the extreme anti-Communists who offer an equally simple course of action to meet the danger of war, namely to join the crusade against the Communist conspiracy for world power.

Power politics theory

The other type of theory about the origins of war which is very widely held is what might be called the power-politics theory. This assumes that it is natural and inevitable for every nation or group to act in pursuit of its interests, that these interests are normally in conflict and that wars occur when these conflicts cannot be resolved by compromise. On this theory the way to prevent war is to work out compromises which correspond to the balance of power. Because of the high cost of war, there will normally be a range within which a compromise will leave both parties better off than if they had fought. The fact that wars occur even though both parties would have gained by a compromise is explained by the refusal of some people to accept the real nature of the international system. The danger of war is ascribed to the "utopians" who insist on operating in terms of principles instead of in terms of interests and thereby reduce the range of possible compromise so much that it cannot be kept in adjustment with the balance of power.

The clearest statement of this theory I have come across was in E. H. Carr's *Twenty Years Crisis*.[1] It is not often stated so explicitly because non-Communists are much less inclined than Communists to formulate their theoretical position, but it does seem to form the operational theory of a great many people concerned with international politics and can be found as an implicit assumption behind a great many statements by statesmen of Western countries. It is, however, quite as unsatisfactory as the Marxian analysis.

The possibility of peaceful adjustment to a changing balance of power depends entirely on people in responsible positions pursuing the interests they represent with functional rationality. If one party to a dispute makes a completely unreasonable estimate of its relative strength there will be no agreement as to what the balance of power really is and peaceful compromise will become impossible. (An obvious instance of this was the belief of the Kuomintang leaders in 1946 that they could win a complete victory in a civil war within a matter of months.) Peaceful compromise is also impossible when one party has unlimited objectives. (The Nazi slogan "World Power or Ruin" ruled out any possibility of peaceful settlement and Chamberlain's policy can be explained as a blind adherence to power-politics theory in face of the evidence that Hitler's behaviour simply did not fit the pattern of normal power-politics bargaining.*)

At the present time the arguments that peace can be preserved through the North Atlantic Treaty Organisation, the European Defence Community or similar arrangements in other parts of the world depend entirely on the assumption that Communist leadership will act rationally in terms of power-politics and become willing to accept a peaceful compromise when their chances of winning a war become small. This is a doubtful assumption. If the Communist leaders really believe their own propaganda they might even be inclined to provoke a war before the completion of what they believe to be preparations for an attack on them, especially if they believe that the Western powers would be weakened by widespread strikes and sabotage. These measures would also fail to prevent war if Communist leadership is motivated by a determination to extend Communist power at whatever cost. This means that, while such defence preparations can be defended as insurance against losing a probable war, it is only on certain assumptions that they could, by themselves, prevent a war.

There are other equally serious objections to power-politics theory. It is possible to have a situation in which everyone is sufficiently rational to realise that they would gain by compromise

---

* E. H. Carr's account of the Munich Agreement (*op. cit.*, pp. 282-3) is a good example of the completely unrealistic position of people who prided themselves on being hard headed and realistic. He argues that "The negotiations which led up to the Munich Agreement of 29 September, 1938, were the nearest approach in recent years to the settlement of a major international issue by a procedure of peaceful change. . . . The change in itself was one which corresponded both to a change in the European equilibrium and to accepted canons of international morality." Hitler's attitude was "psychologically understandable as a product of the methods employed by the Allies at Versailles," and the failure of Munich to "inaugurate a happier period of international relations in which peaceful change by negotiations would become an effective factor" is ascribed to the violent attacks on the Agreement "by a section of British opinion" which produced recriminations from the German side.

Even in September, 1939 (the date of the preface), this argument was unrealistic and the evidence which has become available since the war shows that it was based on a complete misunderstanding of Nazi motivation. This evidence shows that the only policy which might have averted war would have been one based on the very policies which Carr condemns as likely to produce war. A firm stand in the summer of 1938 might have led to Hitler's overthrow by the German army; and the army leaders were men who would have been prepared to bargain in the way required by power-politics theory.

rather than war but in which compromise is almost impossible because no one will trust anyone else to observe an agreement.*

An essential condition for the working of a system in which sovereign states settle their disputes by compromise rather than war is the existence of a convention that agreements will be observed. For the system as a whole such a convention is very valuable; it enables everyone to serve their interests more effectively. But any individual member of the system can advance its interests at the expense of other members by operating rather below the accepted standards of honesty and finding excuses to repudiate any obligation it considers inexpedient. It follows that a pure power politics system is almost certain to end in war through a progressive decline in the standard of respect for agreements. Hobbes drew the logical conclusion that the only stable equilibrium in a pure power politics system would be one in which all power had become concentrated in the hands of a single member.

A system in which respect for agreements has disappeared is a very unpleasant one for everyone in it. There can be no guarantees that the strong will not use their power to exterminate or enslave the weak and no one can afford to make any concessions involving loss of power because this would start a process which would put them at the mercy of their opponents. No one may want a war and everyone may realise that a compromise would be to their advantage but people may still feel that war offers at least a small chance of survival under tolerable conditions, while anyone who makes concessions to secure a compromise is certain to end before a firing squad or in a forced labour camp. The people of the Baltic states might be better off now if they had fought Russia in 1940.

* This point was clearly stated three hundred years ago by Hobbes. "If a Covenant be made, wherein neither of the parties performe presently, but trust one another; in the condition of meer Nature, (which is a condition of Warre of every man against every man,) upon any reasonable suspition, it is Voyd: But if there be a common Power set over them both, with right and force sufficient to compell performance; it is not Voyd. For he that performeth first, has no assurance the other will performe after; because the bonds of words are too weak to bridle men's ambition, avarice, anger, and other Passions, without the feare of some coercive Power, which in the condition of meer Nature, where all men are equall, and judges of the justnesse of their own fears, cannot possibly be supposed. And therefore he which performeth first, does but betray himselfe to his enemy; contrary to the Right (he can never abandon) of defending his life and means of living." (*Leviathan*. By Thomas Hobbes. Andrew Crooke. London, 1651. Page 68.)

There are examples of systems which have got into this sort of state. Under the late Roman Republic it became the accepted thing for the party in power to kill off all its more prominent opponents and the series of civil wars ended in a way which fitted Hobbes' theory—the concentration of power in the hands of Augustus and his successors. And parts of the modern world have reached nearly the same situation. Such an unpleasant condition in which peaceful change has become impossible is the natural result of everyone acting in terms of power politics and accepting either the right-wing or left-wing versions of totalitarian philosophy which revive the old claim of the Greek sophists that "Justice is that which serves the interests of the stronger." (Thrasymachus in Plato's *Republic*.)

Peace dependent on a balance of power can also break down through a progressive armaments race. It is an axiom of power-politics theory that all countries act to further their national interests and any country can further its interests by increasing its bargaining power through stronger armaments— by negotiating from a position of strength, to use the modern term. This may be done with the sincere hope that these armaments will never be used, that their existence will be enough to secure a satisfactory compromise. But here again there is a situation in which the general interest is in conflict with all particular interests. All countries would gain by keeping armaments at a low level; but any particular country can gain by increasing its armaments. So long as all countries act in terms of power politics it is very unlikely that any agreement or limitation of armaments can be reached; even in the much calmer period of the 1920's most disarmament conferences failed. And a balance of power dependent on steadily increasing armaments all round is very unlikely to be stable. In theory there might even be a point at which the expected costs of a war would be less than the present value of indefinitely continued peace-time armament costs, and long before this point was reached it is likely that international tension would so increase that any irresponsible subordinate on either side could precipitate a war.

The people who believe in power politics theory and believe that peace can be maintained by the balance of power very seldom face these problems. In consequence the policies they advocate are often likely to postpone the outbreak of war but seldom offer any prospect of preventing a gradual drift toward war.

Pre-Freudian psychology

If one argues with people who hold either the Marxian or the power politics theories about the origins of war one often finds that the real basis of their beliefs is a theory about psychology—that all human action or at least all economic and political action, can be explained in terms of the pursuit of interest.

The idea of basing a science of human behaviour on the principle that people always act so as to further the interests of themselves, or their group, is one which has attracted a whole series of philosophers from the Greek sophists up to Machiavelli, Hobbes and Marx. And the theory is attractive because in many instances it is able to explain and predict human behaviour. Some of the Marxian analysis explaining historical developments in terms of the conflict of class interests has become generally accepted even by non-Marxist scholars. But all sorts of difficulties arise when the hypothesis, that human behaviour can often be explained and predicted in terms of the pursuit of interest, is generalised into the theory that all human action is determined by the pursuit of interest.

In many cases it is not clear what peoples' interest really is, and the theory can only deal with such cases by sacrificing precision or sacrificing accuracy. By defining interest sufficiently widely the theory can always be made to fit the evidence, but the wider the definition of interest the less precise is the action implied by its pursuit. In the extreme case where interest is defined as that towards which human action is directed the theory becomes formally true by definition but ceases to have any verifiable implications. By giving a narrow definition of interest the theory can be made precise. But it will then often be false that human action is directed to interest, so defined. The people who try to make the theory precise usually define interest simply in terms of gains in power or material wealth. But there is a great deal of evidence that the pursuit of interest defined in this way has very unpleasant long term results. Which means that only people with a very high rate of discount of the future will be behaving rationally if they act as the theory demands.

Again, even when there is no disagreement about what people's interests are it is often not clear what course of action would be most likely to promote these interests. In such cases the theory cannot determine which possible course of action people will take, and it is noticeable that people who believe in the theory are very reluctant to accept this implication. A great deal of Communist argument, for example, depends on the assumption that all disagreements must be disagreements about objectives. Communists always maintain that those who disagree with them do so because they do not share the Communist objective of promoting the interests of the masses. They will seldom, if ever, admit that people might share the Communist objective and yet disagree with Communist policy because they consider it unlikely to promote the interests of the masses.

An even more serious objection to the theory is that it cannot explain why people should make mistakes. In a great many cases people act in ways which obviously do not promote their interests (unless interest is defined so widely as to include results contrary to any normal meaning of the word). Often there is an obvious common sense explanation of such actions in terms of some form of irrationality, such as prejudice or wishful thinking. But the consistent believer in the theory that all action is determined by the pursuit of interest will argue that, despite all appearances to the contrary, such action must really have been determined by the pursuit of interest.

An important result of this view is a belief in elaborate theories of conspiracy. The process of deduction could be summarized as follows: all men act so as to further the interests of the group which they represent; some actions by group A have in fact furthered the interests of a rival group B; therefore, the people in group A who are responsible for such actions must really be representatives of group B.

These points can be illustrated from the recent history of China. On any long or even medium term definition of interest it was obviously in the interests of the Kuomintang leaders to make the reforms which were essential for their survival. As far back as the beginning of 1941 a very well informed American supporter of the Kuomintang had written ". . . the base of Communism has been widespread peasant revolt. If the conditions of peasant revolt are eliminated, Communism will not be much more of a threat to China than it is to the advanced countries of Europe." But even when it had become obvious to any reasonable person that the alternative to making reforms was defeat by the Communists the essential reforms were not made.*

* On the necessity for reforms, see the Wedemeyer Mission of 1947 (U.S. White Paper Annexes 133 to 135) and William C. Bullitt's article in Life of 13 October, 1947.

The Marxist explanation in terms of class interest is not satisfactory. The ruling group in the Kuomintang acted to secure short term advantages in power or wealth by methods which involved a very high probability of complete loss of power, wealth and even life within a few years. There is no reason to suppose that the Kuomintang leaders decided in the mid-1940's that they were not interested in what would happen in five or ten years time. But except in terms of such a decision their behaviour cannot be explained in terms of action designed to promote their interests.

The refusal of many American and British writers to accept the evidence that Kuomintang defeat was mainly caused by Kuomintang mistakes and their preference for explaining it in terms of Communist influence on American policy is a good illustration of how far the "conspiracy" theory can influence even reputable scholars. (An example chosen at random is an article by George Catlin in the *New Leader* of 2 November, 1953.)

It would be easy to give other instances to show that the theory which explains all human action in terms of the pursuit of interest is not really satisfactory and can only be made to fit the evidence by similar highly implausible assumptions.

It is likely that the reasons for a belief in such theories could be traced back one stage further and related to a philosophical belief that the world is such that it can be completely explained in terms of simple general principles which are already known. But it is not necessary to make this analysis. The view of human motivation which forms the basis of the Marxian and the power politics theories of the origins of war is not only unsatisfactory when judged by its implications in the field of political behaviour but is also in conflict with most of the developments in psychology for the past fifty years or so. Whatever the value of Freud's particular theories, the developments started by Freud have produced a mass of empirical evidence to show that human motivation is far too complicated to be explained in terms of some crude simple principle such as the pursuit of interest.

In the future psychological theory may develop to the point where it becomes capable of explaining political behaviour in terms of some unified general theory. But if one is concerned with the immediate practical problem of analysing the causes of war and suggesting appropriate policies it is essential to realise that a general system capable of giving a satisfactory theory of political behaviour does not yet exist. It is only possible to operate with a number of partial hypotheses each of which can co-ordinate and explain some of the evidence and make prediction possible in certain cases. The view of behaviour being influenced by the pursuit of interest is valid as such a partial hypothesis provided it is recognised that this influence is modified and sometimes completely over-ruled by other influences.

The discussion of Communist motivation in previous chapters suggests two other partial hypotheses; that the attempt to realise the vision of some ideal future society may provide a very powerful motivation for political action, and that people tend to act in terms of the world as it should be according to their theories even when these theories are in conflict with the empirical evidence. And these hypotheses can explain non-Communist as well as Communist behaviour.

To return to the illustration already used, these hypotheses can explain a good deal of the evidence about Kuomintang behaviour which cannot be explained by the Marxian class interest analysis. There is a lot of evidence to show that Chiang Kai-shek and his closest associates were deeply influenced by a belief in Confucianism. Many of Chiang Kai-shek's speeches and writings, apart from those intended specially for the foreign public, show a strong emotional attachment to the traditional Chinese society and devotion to an ideal which would combine most of the values of Confucianism with nationalism and the use of Western technology to make China into a great power. The ideal on which he seemed to base his behaviour, analogous to the Super-ego of individual psychology, was probably modelled on the greater Chinese emperors who had restored order, driven out barbarian invaders and made possible a new flowering of Chinese culture. And this vision of China's destiny was shared by many of his closest associates. Ch'en Li-fu, for example, was avowedly a neo-Confucian.

Even more directly than a faith in Marx-Leninism these beliefs were incompatible with functionally rational behaviour. Aspects of the Confucian tradition were incompatible with the effective use of modern technology necessary to make China into a great power in the modern world and a political party whose leaders had a strong emotional attachment to the traditional social structure was seriously handicapped in competition with a rival which had no inhibitions about using Western techniques of political organisation and administration.* And the Kuomintang

* For a discussion of these points and of the totalitarian elements in the

was further weakened by a lack of unity about basic objectives. What the believers in Confucianism wanted was a system which would be honest and efficient but also paternalistic and authoritarian, democratic only in the sense that it was the duty of the rulers to serve the people. But a high proportion of the men who were capable of providing honest and efficient administration did not share this belief in Confucianism and wanted some system much closer to Western democracy. As a result, Chiang Kai-shek continually faced a choice between supporting men who could provide honest and competent administration but who did not share his social ideals and supporting men who might be dishonest and incompetent but shared his ideals or were personally loyal to him. Again and again honest and competent men would be appointed to official positions but they never received effective support when they came into conflict with others who were dishonest or incompetent but personally loyal to Chiang Kai-shek. When forced to choose, Chiang Kai-shek would always subordinate other considerations to his Confucian ideals.*

The result of this situation was to produce an atmosphere of frustration in the Kuomintang system. Functionally rational behaviour to ensure Kuomintang survival would have implied a change in the basic beliefs of the dominant group in the Kuomintang leadership; but the dominant group in the Kuomintang leadership was devoted to its basic beliefs, and there was no way in which an alternative leadership could replace it, except perhaps through American assistance which was never given. In the final stages this frustration was recognised by many Americans,[3] but by then it was too late to do anything.

There is abundant empirical evidence that frustration produces irrational behaviour, not only in human beings but even in animals. As the situation became more critical and the frustration more marked it was natural for the Kuomintang leadership to become increasingly unwilling to face unpleasant realities. And when there seemed to be no practical possibility of making the changes necessary for long term survival it was natural for people in the Kuomintang organisation to concentrate increasingly on short term personal advantages.

traditional Chinese system see the author's Morrison Oration for 1953. (Australian National University. 1954.)

* This hypothesis about Chiang Kai-shek's motivation was formed on the basis of indirect evidence but it was accepted as probably true by Dr. J. Leighton Stuart who had had close personal contacts with him for a considerable period.

This hypothesis does not claim to give a complete explanation of Kuomintang behaviour but it does co-ordinate a great deal of the evidence which other theories fail to explain. It can also explain the improvements in Formosa since 1949. Benevolent despotism which is an unworkable system in a country of over 450,000,000 inhabitants is far more satisfactory in a community of some 8,000,000.

8

A programme for peace

WHILE the Communist-inspired peace campaign has defects which make it, on balance, an influence increasing rather than lessening the risk of war, it is based on a sound general assumption. It assumes that the vast majority of people in all countries do not want war and that, if this public opinion could be effectively mobilized, it could exert a decisive influence. In the past it was possible for a government to get into a war with little regard for public opinion which was willing to leave the conduct of foreign affairs in the hands of those who claimed to be experts. The situation in the modern world was summed up by the French historian Marc Bloch: "The masses no longer obey. They *follow*, either because they have been hypnotized or because they *know*."[1] Even governments which show a complete contempt for the opinions or wishes of the masses still take a great deal of trouble over propaganda to win support for their policies and would be seriously embarrassed if this proved impossible.

It is very unlikely that the majority of the population in any country would support a war, if they were able to form their own judgment. The only exception would be the case in which people had reason to fear that the alternative to war was enslavement or extermination, which was true for the last war against Germany and Japan and might be true for a future war against the Communist powers. This implies that a government whose policies are influenced by an informed public opinion is extremely unlikely to start a war.

Again, while the Communist inspired peace campaign is largely wrong in its selection of the people it denounces as warmongers, it is true that a campaign for peace cannot be based on the objective of obtaining universal agreement. It must involve opposition to certain groups and certain interests. There are people who are so deluded or irresponsible that they would be quite likely to start a war without intending to do so; and people so fanatical that they would pursue their objectives even by methods which involve a high risk of war. And there is abundant empirical evidence that such people can gain control of governments and use their power not only to start a war but also, by deception and propaganda, to build up a considerable measure of popular support for their policies. It follows that a campaign for peace must involve the destruction of the power of such people and, when they are in control of a government, it must include measures to undermine the power of such a government.

A distinction which is important in such a campaign against the influences making for war is that between irrational behaviour and fanatical behaviour. People are acting irrationally when it can be predicted, from the knowledge available to them, that their actions are not those most likely to produce the results they intend. For example, the policies of the British government towards the Axis powers in the 1930's were almost certainly irrational. It is clear that no British government of the period wanted a war. It is also clear that their refusal to face the evidence about the intentions of the Axis powers led them to follow policies which were very unlikely to prevent a war, policies which, in so far as they had any theoretical basis, seemed to depend on unquestioning acceptance of the assumptions of power politics theory. The policies of the Comintern were even more irrational in considering the Social Democrats to be worse enemies than the Nazis in the early 1930's, and in urging local Communist Parties to oppose the war effort against Germany between 1939 and 1941. Whatever the views of the Comintern about the prevention of war, it is certain that it did not wish to put Germany under a militaristic government whose basic objectives included the conquest of *"Lebensraum"* at the expense of the U.S.S.R. and, later, that it did not wish to ensure the defeat of the U.S.S.R. by Nazi Germany, which would have been almost inevitable if the British workers had followed the British Communist Party. To give a later example, it is certain that the American government did not intend to assist the Chinese Communists in rousing anti-American feeling in China and that the Soviet government did not intend to induce the American public to accept the costs of a major rearmament programme. But these have been the results of American and Soviet policies, results which were correctly predicted at the time. The list of instances could be extended almost indefinitely.

On the other hand it is possible for people to act with a considerable degree of rationality for objectives which must almost inevitably lead to war. This was to a large extent true of Hitler up to 1941. Consider the verdict of one historian.

"His ultimate purpose was indeed clear to those who did not willingly deceive themselves: he aimed at the destruction of European civilization by a barbarian empire in Central Europe—the terrible hegemony of a new, more permanent Genghis Khan: 'a new Dark Age,' as Mr. Churchill called it, 'made more sinister, and perhaps more protracted, by the lights of a perverted science.' But when we have admitted the bestiality of his ambition, we must admit that he set himself to realise it with political genius . . . His purpose was clear, his policy consistent, his methods various, adaptable, and effective."[2] And here again it would be easy to give many other instances of people who have had some ultimate objective of conquering large parts of the world or who have been determined to secure the spread of some religion or social system by every means including war.

Irrational behaviour is a fairly definite concept and the greater the degree of irrationality the more clearly can it be demonstrated in terms of normal scientific standards. At some much deeper level it may be true that fanatical behaviour is also irrational but it is not possible to demonstrate in terms of scientific standards that people are mistaken in having a determination to conquer the world or in giving the objective of spreading some system of faith a priority over every other consideration. What can be demonstrated is only that action determined by such objectives is certain to produce war.

The two types of behaviour are not mutually exclusive. People are often both fanatical and irrational. But, in so far as they are distinct, the appropriate action of a peace campaign towards each is very different. In so far as people are endangering peace simply by irrational behaviour they will change their behaviour if they can be brought to understand its probable results, though the process of persuasion may be very difficult. Irrational behaviour may come from deep seated causes and have a strong emotional basis and persuasion may be a problem in psychiatry rather than a problem of diplomacy or rational argument. All the same, persuasion is theoretically possible. On the other hand it is doubtful whether fanatical behaviour can be modified. The genuine fanatic will pursue his objectives even if he clearly realises that an almost certain result of his policies will be a general war, indeed he may even consider war desirable.

Any peace campaign which is to be effective must make this distinction between potential allies and irreconcilable enemies.

People who endanger peace simply by irrational behaviour are potential allies because they want peace but only fail to realise how to obtain it. People who endanger peace by fanatical behaviour are irreconcilable enemies; if they do not want war they want things which can only be obtained through war. An important corollary of this is that an effective strategy for peace must be prepared to take into account the divisions within states and within governments. The extreme conventional diplomatic attitude which is reluctant to recognise divisions within a government or between a government and the people it claims to represent is incompatible with an effective peace campaign.

In some cases it may be necessary to recognise that the prevention of war is almost impossible. If the government of some country is under the control of a fanatical group committed to objectives which cannot be realised without war, and if this group cannot be removed from power except by war, then, in the long run, war is inevitable. A balance of power may postpone the war if these fanatics are sufficiently rational to avoid provoking a war which they are likely to lose. But peace dependent on a balance of power is unlikely to be stable and there cannot be any lessening of international tension so long as the drive for objectives involving war remains. The case in which it is completely impossible to prevent a war may be uncommon because the power of genuine fanatics usually depends on an irrational following, who would not support the fanatical policies if they realised their implications. When this is so there is a theoretical possibility of destroying the power of the fanatics without war though the chances may be very small.

These points can be very clearly illustrated from the history of the 1930's. The evidence that has become available since 1945 shows fairly clearly that war was inevitable so long as the men who determined German and Japanese policy remained in power. A better balance of power might have postponed a war but no long term peaceful agreement was possible with either the Nazi leaders or the Japanese militarists. On the other hand, if the leaders of the democratic powers had realised this, as they could have done even from the evidence available before the war, then there might have been a small possibility of avoiding the war. There were divisions in Germany between the Nazis and the army leaders and in Japan between the militarists and the emperor and politicians. If it had been made quite clear that any attempt by the Nazis or Japanese militarists to realise their ambitions would be met by effective armed resistance and if it had also been made clear that non-fanatical ruling groups in Germany or Japan could obtain satisfaction for reasonable national interests through peaceful negotiation, then it is possible that the German and Japanese governments might have been changed without war. It cannot be proved that a rational strategy for peace would have prevented war but it would have substituted the possibility of peace for the certainty of war.

Going further back, the period also illustrates the importance of economic factors as an indirect cause of war. The rise to power of both the Nazis and the Japanese militarists was greatly assisted by the Great Depression. In Germany a whole series of election results showed that the support for extremist parties rose whenever the economic situation seemed hopeless. The sense of frustration produced by the crisis made people behave irrationally and become ready to accept Nazi leadership. Similarly, in Japan the crisis had an important effect in discrediting the more liberal political leaders and in enabling the extremists to obtain support. The economic factors did not directly cause war but they did produce a situation in which power could be captured by groups whose objectives involved war. (Even here an explanation in terms of one variable is incomplete. The economic crisis largely explains the rise of the Nazis to be the largest party in the Reichstag, but support for the Nazis was actually declining when Hitler obtained his appointment as Reichskanzler through intrigues in the circles round President Hindenburg.)

A non-Communist peace campaign

It would in theory be possible for an effective peace campaign to be conducted by either Communists or non-Communists but, under present conditions, the situation is not symmetrical. A Communist peace campaign conducted with functional rationality would be almost certain to succeed. While the opportunities for Communist publicity in the major non-Communist countries are restricted they are still considerable. There is a considerable body of comparatively well-informed opinion among people who are not afraid of using their own judgment and if a Communist peace campaign were trying to put over a case which appeared convincing to reasonable people and which was defensible under criticism it is fairly certain that it could gain powerful and rapidly growing support. In most important non-Communist countries governments are comparatively sensitive to public opinion and pressure from public opinion in favour of policies that were clearly and demonstrably likely to produce peace could almost certainly overcome the influence of those who persisted in irrational behaviour and of the small minority of fanatics. However, the discussion which follows on the conditions for an effective peace campaign will show that it is extremely unlikely that such a campaign could be conducted by orthodox Communists who would have to make important changes in their basic beliefs.

A peace campaign from the non-Communist side faces much greater difficulties, but the chances of its being carried out are much greater. And this case is, therefore, discussed.

It is first necessary to face the real difficulties. If serious students of Communism are right when they maintain that "Communism in action is today a very intricate religion of power" and that "What is distinctive about the Soviet regime is the extreme priority it accords to the pursuit of the goal of its own power . . . In particular, the regime is marked by an almost total lack of inhibition in the means it is prepared to use to effect this priority." (See above, pp. 111 and 114), then the present leaders of world Communism must be treated as irreconcilable enemies of peace. The possible subjective altruism of their motives does not alter the fact that an unqualified drive for power by people controlling strong military force is certain to produce a war. (The adjective "unqualified" is important. The hypothetical case of a Communist Party which tried to extend and maintain its power, in so far as this could be done by winning and retaining popular support, would not be a threat to peace.)

The only hopeful feature of the situation is the possibility that a high proportion of Communists are more irrational than fanatical—that for possibly a majority of Communists the drive for power is not an ultimate objective but the result of irrational behaviour produced by a faith in Marx-Leninism. This means that the chances of preventing war can only be estimated when it has been discovered how far Communist behaviour is the result of irrationality and how far the result of devotion to power as an ultimate objective. It also means that the only possibility of obtaining peaceful co-existence and the settlement of disputes by negotiation rather than war is to induce those Communists for whom power is not an ultimate objective to modify their system of beliefs enough to enable them to co-operate for peace with functional rationality.

What is needed might be described as psychological warfare, provided it is clearly realized that psychological warfare aimed at inducing people to use rational judgment not only has very different objectives from totalitarian psychological warfare but also needs to use very different methods. All forms of totalitarian psychological warfare have the aim of inducing people to hold beliefs which would not stand up to critical rational examination. In other words, their aim is to prevent people from thinking. As against this the basic objective of psychological warfare for peace should be to encourage critical rational thinking. One of its slogans should be: "Any Communist who starts to think is a possible ally." Any Communist who gives peace or the interests of the masses a higher priority than the extension of Communist power as an end in itself, and who starts to use rational judgment, is bound to find that his system of Marx-Leninist faith is inconsistent and has implications incompatible with empirical evidence. He is bound to find that he can only work for peace or the interests of the masses by modifying his system of faith and this must lead him to oppose both those Communists who give the highest priority to Communist power and also those who are acting irrationally against peace because they refuse to modify their system of faith.

Totalitarian psychological warfare must involve some inconsistencies or conflicts with empirical evidence because it is trying to secure acceptance of views which would not stand critical examination. And Hitler's theory about the advantages of the big lie indicates that it does not even need to keep its inconsistencies to the unavoidable minimum. So long as they are not too glaring, inconsistencies can help in promoting the atmosphere of general confusion and frustration which is favourable to the uncritical acceptance of beliefs. The case is completely different for psychological warfare aimed at extending the influence of rational judgment. In so far as it is successful in encouraging people to think it will make them aware of all inconsistencies. Someone who starts to use critical judgment will not only see the weak points in the orthodox Communist position but also those in non-Communist positions. And this means that it is impossible to make an effective attack on Communist threats to peace without being equally ready to expose and attack non-Communist threats to peace. Attacks confined to the weak points of the Communist position, combined with a refusal to attack the weak points in non-Communist positions, are unlikely to be convincing. Even if they were convincing they would only produce people who were completely sceptical about the good faith of all parties, whereas what is needed is people who are ready to co-operate for peace.

An important corollary of this is that the publicity for an effective peace campaign cannot be conducted by people who think in terms of commercial advertising. A great deal of commercial advertising, like totalitarian psychological warfare, has the aim of inducing people to hold opinions which would not stand critical investigation and is very seldom willing to admit the defects in the product or cause which it supports.

An essential condition for psychological warfare aimed at winning support from an informed and critical public opinion is to avoid becoming involved in the defence of indefensible positions. This has very direct relevance to the case against orthodox Communism quite apart from the issue of peace. It has already been argued that the real case against orthodox Communism is that its claim to serve the interests of the masses is simply false, that the interest of the masses is in fact given a lower priority than the power of the Communist Party. But there are people who oppose orthodox Communism, not because its claim to serve the masses is false, but because they believe this claim to be true, or because at some particular period or in some particular field it is actually supporting mass interests against some non-Communist vested interest. A good deal of anti-Communism fits the Marxian theory as defending the interests of a ruling class against the masses. Any alliance between these two forms of anti-Communism cannot be more than an opportunist tactical move. It is not possible to combine effective opposition to Communism, on the ground that ruling Communist Parties are dominant minorities exploiting the masses and maintaining their power by terrorism and deception, with support for non-Communist dominant minorities doing much the same.

It is not possible to predict the chances of success for a non-Communist peace campaign. The evidence about the relative power of fanaticism and irrationality in the Communist threat to peace is not at all satisfactory. (An important task for a peace

144

campaign would be to obtain more experimental evidence on this point.) It is also not certain how far it would prove possible to induce those Communists who give a higher priority to peace than to Communist power to modify their beliefs enough to enable them to act rationally in terms of this priority. (Here again experimental work is badly needed.)

However, the case for trying a peace campaign is still strong even if its chances of success are small. Even a thousand to one chance of peace would be preferable to the certainty of war, and the chances are almost certainly better than this. Also, a properly conducted peace campaign would serve a useful purpose even if it failed in its main objective. Even if it failed to change the Communist policies likely to cause war it might at least weaken support for them. More important, it would provide a great deal of evidence about Communist motivation. If it is true that peace is impossible because Communist policy is unshakably controlled by people who give the expansion of Communist power a higher priority than peace, then the sooner and more clearly this can be demonstrated the better. A very important cause of disunity and indecision in the non-Communist section of the world is uncertainty about Communist intentions. Many people who believe that Communist intentions are incompatible with any real peaceful settlement argue quite logically from these beliefs to deduce appropriate policies. (Mr. W. C. Wentworth's pamphlet *Time and the Bomb* is a good example.) And these people are often strongly critical of any peace movements on grounds which have been discussed above (page 67). But the obvious obstacle to the adoption of the policies which they advocate is that public opinion is not prepared to accept the premises about Communist policy from which they argue, because the evidence for them is not really conclusive. If such people were acting rationally they should support a peace campaign, which might prove them to be wrong, but which, if they were right, could win them general support by providing almost conclusive evidence that their views about Communist motivation were correct.

There is, of course, a certain range within which policies aimed at modifying Communist behaviour would conflict with policies designed to restrain the drive for power from unmodified Communist behaviour. Some people, for example, argue that Soviet behaviour has been determined by a fear of attack from the West and could be modified by the abandonment of Western military preparations. But an attempt to modify Soviet behaviour in this way would leave Western Europe defenceless against Soviet pressure if Soviet behaviour did not change. In this particular case the weight of evidence is strongly against expecting the policy to succeed. The period of war-time co-operation between 1941 and 1945 showed that the maximum goodwill and concilia-tion from the Western powers failed to remove a solid core of hostility, suspicion and aggressiveness in the attitude of the Soviet authorities. In other cases, however, there might be a real problem in deciding whether the probability of some policy succeeding was high enough to justify the risks involved if it were to fail. But this is only true within a certain range and there is a much wider field in which the policies implied by a peace campaign would not conflict with policies designed to resist an unalterable Communist drive for power.

The obvious weak points of orthodox Communism are its "doublethink" positions and these are closely related to the threat to peace from orthodox Communism. A peace campaign should attack these "doublethink" positions for two reasons. Firstly, so long as Communists continue to indulge in "doublethink" there is no possibility of reaching a peaceful agreement with them. An agreement is valueless if it does not rule out actions incompatible with its terms. And it is doubtful whether it is even possible to make a contract in the ordinary sense of the term with some-one who can hold two contradictory beliefs simultaneously. Unless it is possible to make an agreement with Communists which has a fairly definite and unambiguous meaning and unless there is some reason to suppose that, after making an agreement Communists will not act in ways which are incompatible with it no settlement by peaceful agreement is possible. And at present Communist "doublethink" positions greatly restrict the range within which agreements are possible. Secondly, an attack on "doublethink" positions is one obvious way of finding out which Communists really want peace and which Communists give peace a lower priority than the expansion of Communist power. So long as Communists are able to maintain "doublethink" positions they can refuse to admit that these objectives are incompatible. Attacking "doublethink" positions is, therefore one way of inducing them to make the choice between these two incompatible objectives. It may not always be successful when one "doublethink" position becomes indefensible Com-munists may simply retreat to a more complicated evasive position. But such a retreat will involve a loss of effectiveness. The point of "doublethink" is "to deny the existence of objective reality and all the while to take account of the reality one denies" and a retreat from the more obvious "doublethink" positions can only be into a world of fantasy still further removed from objective reality. And this will make it harder to act effectively in the real world.

"Doublethink" positions are fairly easy to maintain in an environment where they are not challenged. If no one asks awkward questions it is fairly easy to secure acceptance for views which involve internal contradictions or conflicts with empirical evidence. (And the accounts of discussions in present day China indicate that awkward questions are very seldom asked.) It would be much harder to secure acceptance for an irrational case if its exponents had to face questions from people who would draw implications and point out the resulting contradictions or press for explanation of claims which conflict with empirical evidence.

When one is dealing with people who have strong emotional attachments to some system of faith it is not enough simply to point out inconsistencies and leave it at that, because most people have a strong tendency to forget or explain away inconsistencies or mistakes with unpleasant emotional associations. Someone once told me that he had found the only effective way of arguing with his Communist friends was to make them bet on their predictions. Merely to point out the inconsistencies in successive Communist pronouncements was not effective because they could usually wriggle out of the difficulty by arguing that the original prediction had been qualified or was capable of different interpretations. (And it is noticeable that a high proportion of published Communist statements are characterized by vagueness or ambiguity.) But when Communists had been driven to make predictions sufficiently definite to form the subject of a bet, and when a series of such bets had almost all been lost, the result was that they became considerably less confident about their Marx-Leninist faith.

This particular technique could not be used in international affairs. But it would be possible to do far more than is now being done to use opportunities of repeatedly and emphatically calling attention to the contradictions in the Communist position. In very many cases comparatively slight modifications in policy, or even in the wording of statements, would make the contradictions between Communist claims and logic or empirical evidence very much harder to explain away. If non-Communist leaders thought a little about how their actions or statements would appear to people who were trying to fit their experience into a picture of the world as it should be according to Marx-Leninist theory, they could make the task of people trying to retain their orthodox Marx-Leninist faith very much more difficult. As a single illustration, consider the case when the Soviet Union offered a non-aggression pact to Norway as an alternative to Norwegian entry into the N.A.T.O. The most effective reply to this offer would have been to ask the Soviet government to explain how the proposed non-aggression pact would differ from the non-aggression pacts between the Soviet Union and Finland or the Baltic States which had not prevented the total or partial annexation of these countries by the Soviet Union. A rejection expressed in this way would have been far harder for Soviet propaganda to misrepresent and explain away. And it would be easy to give many similar instances.

One essential condition for an effective appeal to those Communist supporters who still retain some powers of rational judgment is the avoidance of inaccuracy and exaggeration. Only a small part of the evidence on which any political judgment is based can be obtained from direct experience. To a very large extent everyone has to rely on indirect reports and make estimates about how far different sources of information can be trusted. The obvious tests which can be applied to any source of information are firstly, its internal consistency, and secondly, the accuracy of the sample of its statements which can be checked by direct evidence. A source which contradicts itself is obviously not reliable and if some source makes false reports in the field within which it can be checked by more direct evidence it is reasonable to suppose that it is equally inaccurate in the wider field within which it cannot be checked.

Any intelligent Communist is almost certain to realise that official Communist sources of information are not objectively accurate. It is likely that he will find frequent reports whose falsity he can check from his direct observations and, if he has a reasonably good memory, he will know of many cases of inconsistency. However, this will not shake his faith in orthodox Communism if he believes other sources to be equally inaccurate. He will merely accept the more sophisticated Marx-Leninist theory according to which objectivity is a meaningless concept and all sources of information merely make statements which are expedient for the interests which they represent. If the standard of objective accuracy offers no grounds for preferring one source of information to another, a Communist can feel justified in preferring those sources which, according to his theories, represent the "interests of the masses" or "the inevitable course of history." This is the kind of argument one actually hears from more intelligent Communists.

What would be incompatible with orthodox Communism would be a demonstration that non-Communist sources of information can be distinguished from Communist sources by a superiority in objective accuracy. For some non-Communist sources this can be done provided it is made clear that accuracy is a "more or less" quality which cannot be described in terms of the "all or none" logic which Communists are inclined to use; and provided it is admitted that non-Communist sources show a wide range of variation in accuracy. For example, a comparison between the *Jen Min Jih Pao* and the *New York Times* would show that the reader of the latter is vastly better informed on world affairs than the reader of the former, even though the *New York Times* is certainly biased and not always accurate. To give an instance where the facts are not a matter of interpretation, the reader of the *New York Times* will be given the complete texts of most important international statements, both Communist and non-Communist, while the reader of the *Jen Min Jih Pao* will seldom learn of non-Communist statements except through Communist comments on them. On the other hand, a comparison between the *Jen Min Jih Pao* and *Time* would provide an instance which fits Marx-Leninist theory by showing that different types of political bias can be accompanied by similar standards of accuracy. And it would be possible to give instances of non-Communist sources whose standards of accuracy were even lower than those of most Communist sources.

It is possible to make a convincing case for the claim that the ordinary citizen in the British Commonwealth or in America who is interested in world affairs can, by taking a little trouble, obtain far more complete and accurate information than is available to the citizens of any Communist ruled country. But this case would be completely discredited by an attempt to defend all non-Communist sources of information. (At the conference on Freedom of Information in 1948, the representatives of the Western powers were seriously handicapped in stating an

149

effective case against the Communist representatives by their reluctance to admit that some of the Western press was even worse than the Communist press.)

For psychological warfare against the aspects of Communism which threaten peace, anti-Communist publicity with low standards of accuracy is a serious hindrance. Like Communist publicity, it may be quite effective in rousing the enthusiasm of the converted; but its effect on others is usually to strengthen rather than weaken any attachment to Communism. People who find that a considerable proportion of the accusations made against Communism are demonstrably untrue are inclined to believe that all accusations against Communism are untrue and the more exaggerated type of anti-Communist propaganda is used with considerable effect by Communist publicity in just this way.

This can be very clearly illustrated in the case of China. The anti-Communist propaganda put out by Kuomintang and right-wing American sources has contained a high proportion of statements that were demonstrably false. An amusing example of obvious absurdity was one Kuomintang publication which gave a list of Kuomintang officers allegedly killed by the Communists between 1938 and 1943. According to two items on this list, Sun Chung-wen, commander of the "Min Tuan" in Yenshan hsien, Hopei, was atrociously murdered by the Hsing Jen-fu unit of the 18th Group Army both in November, 1938, and on 12th January, 1940. [3] Lin Yu-t'ang's The Vigil of a Nation[4] contained many statements almost as absurd. For example, General Lu Cheng-ts'ao is removed from his command in Central Hopei and sent to Yenan "to receive training" in March, 1939, but reappears in the narrative six pages later leading his troops against the Kuomintang general Chang Yin-wu in June, 1939. (It would have been just possible to get to Yenan and back in the time, but only just.) The statement in the Bolton Report that the Chinese Communists "slackened their efforts against Japan" between September, 1939, and June, 1941, could be refuted from the record of press conferences in Chungking at which National Government spokesmen reported the results of the Communist "Hundred Regiment Campaign" in 1940, and the Report discusses Communist land policy in terms which show complete ignorance of the great modification of this policy in the period between 1937 and 1946.[5] In a recent book, a foreign missionary claims to have "lived among the Reds" from 1937 to

1943, when he was interned by the Japanese, but does not mention that his mission station came under Japanese occupation in 1939 and shows surprising ignorance on such elementary points as the name of the Communist region in which he was living.[6] It would be easy to extend the list of instances to show that, at least for the period from 1937 to 1946, a very high proportion of those who attacked the Communists showed themselves to be unreliable sources of information by making statements which they must have known to be false or whose truth or falsehood they had not troubled to investigate.

An effective criticism of Chinese Communism during this period would have admitted its real successes and concentrated on its real weaknesses—its uncritical following of the Soviet line on world affairs, its reluctance to generalize from the success of its actual policies to an open repudiation of its extremism before 1937 and of the undemocratic elements in orthodox Communist theory, and the occasional cases where it could be demonstrated that Communist action was incompatible with Communist claims. Actual anti-Communist publicity had an important influence in discrediting any real case against Communism. Any supporter of the Chinese Communist Party in 1945 or 1946 would know from fairly direct evidence that a high proportion of the accusations against the Chinese Communist Party were false or at least wildly exaggerated. From the evidence available to him he had no reason to believe similar accusations against the Communist Party of the Soviet Union even though a much higher proportion of these accusations were, in fact, true. To quote my own personal reactions, I was sceptical about the reports of widespread atrocities during the extremist land policy of 1947 until I had been able to confirm them by fairly direct evidence because I had read so many reports of Communist atrocities which I knew from my own experience to be false. (For example, between 1941 and 1944 I met a number of the people whom Lin Yu-t'ang alleges were liquidated by the Communists in 1939.) The readiness of educated Chinese opinion to accept Communist rule in 1949 was greatly strengthened by the obvious contrast between direct observations of the Communists and the descriptions of the Communists given by Kuomintang and American propaganda. Even now, the real evidence of a decline in Chinese Communist standards is hard to disentangle from the falsity and exaggerations of anti-Communist propaganda.

151

All this has very definite implications for a peace campaign. Anti-Communist propaganda containing falsehoods and exaggerations may produce its intended results among people who are already inclined to be anti-Communist, but among people who are inclined to be pro-Communist it will weaken the influence of rational arguments against Communism and tend to strengthen any faith in orthodox Marx-Leninism. The objective of a peace campaign should be to induce supporters of Communism to modify those parts of their beliefs which lead them to support policies incompatible with peace. The realization of this objective will be hindered by extreme anti-Communist propaganda just as much as by Communist propaganda trying to maintain a faith in orthodox Communism. Even if it is believed that the major threat to peace comes from Communism it will still be necessary to make clear that the extreme anti-Communists are not allies but enemies—that, whatever their intentions, the actual result of their actions is to strengthen the influence of orthodox Marx-Leninist Communist leadership.

An uncompromising attack on policies and objectives incompatible with peace is only one side of a peace campaign. The other side must be a demonstration of readiness to co-operate with anyone who both wants peace and is prepared to do what is needed to promote it without regard to disagreements not directly relevant to peace. This again is incompatible with the extreme anti-Communist position. A peace campaign will be anti-Communist in so far as Communists refuse to modify those parts of their beliefs which lead them to work against peace. It will be quite ready to co-operate with Communists who have made the necessary modifications in their beliefs and policies and it might even be pro-Communist if Communists working for peace came into conflict with non-Communists working against it.

Many of the extreme anti-Communists think in terms of the same basic assumptions as Stalin did, a classifying logic dealing with "true" definitions. Because they make these assumptions they refuse to admit the possibility of any important modification of Communism, so long as it can be correctly defined as Communism. They would, therefore, denounce this kind of discriminating policy as appeasement and some discussion of this highly controversial term is necessary to deal with this point.

What is appeasement?

Taking Mr. Chamberlain as the classic type of appeaser, the characteristic of his policy was to make real concessions in return for promises which were very unlikely to be kept. Some of his concessions were not unreasonable in themselves, others involved a real betrayal of principles, but in every case the evidence available at the time indicated that it was very unlikely that Hitler or Mussolini would keep their side of the agreement.

An analogy for the appeaser would be a man who proposed a non-aggression pact between human beings and tigers, from which both parties could really benefit in a tiger infested country, and refused to admit that tigers could not be induced to keep an agreement.

On the other hand, it is not appeasement to make concessions which do not involve a betrayal of principle in return for promises which are likely to be kept. While Chamberlain made war inevitable by appeasing Hitler, Poincaré played a large part in bringing Hitler to power by refusing concessions to German governments which were likely to keep agreements and which did prefer international co-operation to war.*

It is also not appeasement to decide a case on its merits. It is reasonable to argue that people should not be allowed to enjoy advantages from principles whose obligations they refuse to accept. But the view which denies that any case can be settled on its merits and claims that "justice is that which serves the interest of the stronger" is a view which implies the inevitability of war. Some official Soviet writings explicitly state this sort of view. For example "In our epoch, in which all roads lead to Communism, all those who declare themselves for the Soviet Union are historically correct. All those who declare themselves against the Soviet Union are historically incorrect. They are attempting to arrest the wheels of history."[7] And it has already been argued that this sort of Communist claim rules out any

* cf. Stresemann, in April, 1929, a few months before his death: "If you had given me one concession, I could have carried my people. I could still do it today. But you have given nothing, and the trifling concessions you have made have always come too late. . . . Sir Austen (Chamberlain) is a gentleman; I know he means well. But for the last ten years Europe has been suffering from gentlemen who mean well . . . nothing remains now except brute force. The future is in the hands of the new generation. And the youth of Germany, which we might have won for peace and for the new Europe, we both have lost. That is my tragedy and your crime." R. H. Bruce Lockhart, *Retreat from Glory*. Putnam, London, 1934. Pages 361-3.)

possibility of peaceful settlement except through other people submitting to the Communists. But the same sort of claim is just as incompatible with peace when it comes from the non-Communist side. If, in some dispute, the Communists have a good case in terms of standards which both sides accept, then it is not appeasement to decide the dispute in favour of the Communists. More generally, an essential condition for the peaceful settlement of disputes is objectivity, the application of the same standards to both sides.

In terms of this discussion of appeasement, Western policy towards the Soviet Union during what might be called the Yalta period was a border line case. In the light of the evidence now available there is a strong case for holding that the Western powers made concessions which were not justified. But a great deal of this evidence did not exist at the time. The question is whether the evidence available in 1944 should have led Roosevelt to realise that the Soviet leaders were among the exceptional 10 per cent in his principle that "If you treat people right they will treat you right 90 per cent of the time."[8] The case for believing in 1944 that a conciliatory policy towards the Soviet Union would evoke good faith from the Soviet leaders was certainly much stronger than the case for believing before the war that it was possible to evoke good faith from the Nazi leaders. A real defect in Western policy was that the public was not kept informed. Conciliation towards Stalin could have been defended as a calculated risk, worth taking in spite of some indications of Soviet bad faith. If this had been made clear it would have given the Soviet leaders a clear warning that Western conciliation would change to hostility if Soviet policy were not modified and, with an informed public opinion, Western policy could have been changed much more rapidly.

At the present time one of the hardest problems for a peace campaign would be to decide what could be taken as evidence of a real modification in the Communist position making possible co-operation for peace. To give a complete answer would need a lot of investigation but it is possible to suggest the sort of tests which might be applied. One obvious test would be the standard the Communists themselves use, namely attitude to the Soviet Union. No one who defends the methods by which Soviet power has been expanded and maintained since 1938 can be expected to co-operate with practical good faith for peace because the continuance of such methods is bound to lead to war

154

The obvious question to ask the Chinese Communists is "How do you expect anyone to believe your denunciations of imperialism so long as you give unqualified praise and support to Soviet imperialism?" For the Soviet government a possible test would be readiness to abandon collaboration with the Nazis and to purge the Soviet organisation in Germany of those responsible for such collaboration. Also, because Communists attach such great importance to ideology, Communist statements might have considerable value as evidence. If Communists were willing to accept general formulae about the conditions for peaceful co-operation which implied a clear and unambiguous repudiation of those parts of orthodox Communist theory leading to claims of infallibility and justifying the unqualified Communist drive for power, it would be evidence of a real change in the Communist position. International discussions on such philosophical disputes would be highly unconventional. But there is good reason to suppose that these philosophical questions are at least as directly relevant for peace as many of the topics which are discussed at international conferences at present.

A peace campaign which did not insist on satisfactory evidence of the essential modifications in the orthodox Communist position would be guilty of appeasement. On the other hand, it would have to be made clear that, in so far as Communists proved themselves willing to accept common standards necessary for the peaceful settlement of disputes, they would gain the benefits as well as assume the obligations implied by such standards. In particular it would have to be made clear that Communists could obtain security by showing themselves ready to co-operate for peace. Preparations for defence are largely indistinguishable from preparations for aggression, and if non-Communist defence preparations were continued against Communist countries which had given clear evidence of their desire for peace the Communists would have a real justification for feeling insecure. It would, for example, need to be made clear that the Soviet government could obtain satisfaction for its demand for the abandonment of American bases capable of attacking the Soviet Union, by giving clear evidence that these bases would not be needed for defence against Soviet aggression.

The problem of communication

One common objection to suggestions for this sort of non-Communist peace campaign is that it could not make contact with the people it is designed to influence. In Communist ruled countries all means of publicity are controlled by the Communist Party and seem to be firmly in the hands of people committed to strict Communist orthodoxy and all forms of contact with the non-Communist world not approved by the Communist leadership are fairly effectively restricted. Many people would agree that most of the population under Communist rule would be ready to co-operate for peace, and even that this might be true for considerable sections of many Communist Parties, but argue that nothing can be done under such circumstances.

It is true that the restrictions on contacts between populations under Communist rule and the outside world are a serious obstacle to an effective non-Communist peace campaign, but the people who take this as a reason for not even trying a peace campaign are almost certainly too pessimistic. Psychological warfare aimed at encouraging people to think for themselves has certain inherent advantages over totalitarian psychological warfare and should be able to compete with very much smaller opportunities for contact. The views for which it should be trying to secure acceptance are those which people would reach for themselves if they once start to use rational judgment, which means that they will be self propagating if once they can be introduced. If some source of information can once establish its reputation for accuracy, people in a totalitarian country will often go to considerable risk and trouble in order to keep in contact with it, because they know that the official sources of information available to them cannot be trusted. On the other hand, because the objective of totalitarian propaganda is to secure acceptance for views which will not stand critical examination, it has to rely on continual repetition and is only really effective with a complete monopoly of publicity.

Also some points in the orthodox Communist position are very vulnerable to attack. It has already been argued that the points in the orthodox Communist position which endanger peace are related to the belief in the infallibility of the Communist Party. And a claim of infallibility is difficult to sustain, even though orthodox Communists make it implicitly rather than explicitly. While orthodox Marx-Leninism contains defence mechanisms

156

against attack by rational argument it would probably prove much more vulnerable to ridicule. Most Communists are notably lacking in a sense of humour about anything concerned with their faith. To find their views meeting with disagreement or even hatred is something for which they are fully prepared; to find that their beliefs have implications which expose them to public ridicule would be much more damaging to their faith. And this weapon of ridicule has so far been little used.

To put it another way, the system of beliefs built up by totalitarian propaganda and indoctrination may be very impressive but it is often to some extent unstable. If people once start to ask certain questions or to face certain empirical evidence then the whole system of beliefs may collapse. In exceptional cases the asking of one question may produce the collapse of a system of faith. I remember, for example, a story my brother told of his experiences interrogating prisoners of war. One German N.C.O. was a fanatical Nazi and began by giving all the regular answers of Nazi propaganda, including the claim that British soldiers were cowardly because they never tried anything like the Russian "human wave" tactics. He was asked, "Have you ever thought about the relative populations of England and Russia? How could the British ever win a war if they threw away lives like that?" His reaction was to burst into tears. And having once started to think and having realised that at least one claim of Nazi propaganda would not stand examination his whole attitude changed. In most cases the stability of a system of irrational beliefs produced by indoctrination is higher than this and for some individuals it may be very great, especially if the system of beliefs has defence mechanisms against attack by rational argument. But without a lot of experimental work it would not be possible to say how stable the average result of Communist indoctrination is. There is a certain amount of evidence to indicate that in many cases degree of stability may be fairly low.

Communist governments go to a lot of trouble to isolate the populations under their control from the outside world. For example, there is the very high expenditure on the jamming of broadcasts, even those from short wave stations which could only be received by a minute fraction of the population. More important, even Communist Party members in fairly responsible positions, such as diplomatic staffs and members of international organisations, are discouraged from having contacts with non-Communists. By comparison the pre-war German and Japanese governments were much less afraid of their systems of indoctrination being destroyed by outside contacts. If such Communist policies have a rational basis, which is of course uncertain, it would indicate that the stability of Stalinist indoctrination may often be quite small even for Communist Party members. Again, there is the evidence of the prisoners of war in Korea. The Chinese armies certainly took a lot of trouble to indoctrinate their men, but this indoctrination proved unstable for about 70 per cent of Chinese prisoners. By contrast, the beliefs of men in the U.N. forces proved much more stable. After active Communist efforts at indoctrination only 3 per cent of prisoners refused repatriation. Of course the prisoners were not a fully representative sample and circumstances were exceptional. Even so the case provides some evidence of a low stability of Communist beliefs for a fairly high proportion of those subject to Communist indoctrination.

If the stability of Communist beliefs in Communist countries is low, then an effective use of even the present limited possibilities of exerting influence from outside might have considerable results. Which means that, while the chances of success for a non-Communist peace campaign may be small they are not negligible.

The arguments against trying a peace campaign because its chances of success may be small often depend on the assumption that a strategy is not worth trying unless it can be predicted with reasonable assurance that it will, by itself, lead to complete success. But to judge strategies by such a standard is quite unreasonable. The right test of a correct strategy is whether or not it is likely to produce a more favourable situation, whatever the response of the other side. To give an analogy, it is only in the simplified final stages of a game of chess that it is possible to say that some strategy will certainly produce checkmate in a given number of moves. In the early stages of the game good strategies can seldom produce a certain checkmate but they can produce situations in which checkmate can only be avoided by responses which increase the chances of checkmate in the future. Similarly one cannot predict the Communist response to a peace campaign. The most desirable result would be the modification of those elements in Communism which threaten peace. But the Communist leadership might react by restricting still further the contacts through which a peace campaign could reach the population under Communist rule and using their monopoly of publicity to secure acceptance for a view of the non-Communist world still further removed from reality. Though this response would prevent the peace campaign from exerting an immediate influence on Communist policy, it would only do so by making the system of Communist indoctrination still more unstable and by reducing the ability of Communist publicity to influence opinion outside Communist control.

These points were very clearly illustrated by the controversy in Australia over participation in the Peking Peace Conference in 1952. Most of the people who opposed Australian participation did so on the grounds that it was unlikely that the Conference had been called in good faith (as opposed to using "peace" for Stalinist propaganda), and unlikely that any Australian delegation could modify Chinese policy towards peace, even over the points which were preventing a truce in Korea.

One obvious argument against this view was that even a small chance of influencing Chinese policy towards peace was worth taking. An equally important argument was that a representative and well informed Australian delegation could have accomplished a great deal even if the Conference was not called in good faith. If the organisers of the Conference were firmly committed to orthodox Marx-Leninism and interested, not in peace, but only in using talk of peace to weaken opposition to the expansion of Communist power, then one competent and well informed non-Communist delegation would have presented them with a serious dilemma. If the delegation had been allowed to function the result would have been public criticism in China of the aspects of orthodox Communism incompatible with peace, a challenge to Communist "doublethink" positions, an exposure of imperialist Soviet policies and so on. The publicity would only have reached small numbers directly but, for the past thirty years or more, the intelligentsia of Peking have exerted an influence on Chinese politics out of all proportion to their numbers. And in the uniformity of a totalitarian state any demonstration of dissent stands out in a way which people living in the variegated political atmosphere of a democracy find hard to imagine. In Western countries a Communist demonstration with placards denouncing the local government and America causes little comment. An Australian delegation with sufficient courage to go to the conference hall in Peking with a placard saying "Chinese people struggle for peace! Refuse to serve as cannon fodder for Soviet imperialism!" would have created a sensation which would have been reported by word of mouth over large parts of China. Even less courageous action in the form of frank speeches in the conference hall would have been the sort of challenge to orthodox Communism indoctrination which Communist governments take great trouble to prevent. On the other hand, if the delegation had not been allowed to function the result would have been to discredit the propaganda value of the Conference and of the Communist inspired peace movement in general in countries outside Communist control. If a representative Australian delegation had been refused entrance to China or if, having reached Peking, they had not been allowed to speak to most of the items on the agenda, this would have provided conclusive evidence for the Australian public that the Conference had not been called in good faith, that its sponsors did not wish to discuss peace but only to use peace as a device for Communist propaganda.

In fact, the Communists were able to win an almost complete victory in psychological warfare. The Australian government was manoeuvred into using the totalitarian device of refusing passports to its citizens and acting in a way which Communist propaganda could plausibly represent as a warmongering capitalist government refusing to allow even the discussion of peace. Because there were no well-informed non-Communist delegates, the Conference was able to allow great freedom of speech without this producing any criticism of the indefensible points in the orthodox Communist position. The result was that the reports of those Australians who were able to attend strengthened rather than discredited the Communist inspired peace movement, and, because the relevant questions were never discussed, the Conference did nothing to promote peace.

A reasonable argument against Australian participation was that Australia, like most Western countries, does not possess the organisation necessary for effective psychological warfare. It would have been difficult to ensure that an Australian delegation did not grossly over-represent the minority of Communists and Fellow Travellers and there was no organisation to produce a well-informed delegation by providing adequate briefing. If participation had been opposed on this reasonable ground it would have shown that Australia, like most Western countries, was making a serious mistake in devoting large resources to preparations for resisting Communist aggression by actual warfare while grudging a minute fraction of this effort to psychological warfare which might undermine the basis of Communist aggression. In fact, because participation was opposed on fallacious grounds, the Communist victory did not even provide a lesson for the future.*

* The arguments against participation used by the Parliamentary Foreign Affairs Committee depended on demonstrably false statements of fact. It was claimed that "neither the Australian Government nor any Australian organisation *can* send any delegation to Peking" because "the choosing of the individuals who would make up this limited delegation is in the hands of the Preparatory Committee now sitting in Peking. (See Annexure C.) In short, the Communists can decide the make-up of any delegation leaving Australia, and consequently Australia can send no delegation, and certainly not the 'impartial, strong and well-informed' delegation which is usually suggested." In fact, the document reproduced in Annexure C. only shows that the Preparatory Committee had power to allot a quota of delegates to each country and says nothing about the procedure by which this quota should be chosen. The actual choice of delegates in Australia was conducted in a way which could have been influenced by any group prepared to take a little trouble.

It was then argued that even an "impartial, strong and well-informed" delegation could do nothing to expose Communist bad faith at the Conference because "with the agenda decided in advance, with an assured majority to prevent it being changed and to control debate, no question could be discussed unless the Communists so desired. And there would be nothing to 'expose', because the result would be achieved by ostensibly normal Parliamentary procedure." In fact, the agenda, also reproduced in Annexure C., shows that on almost every item a competent non-Communist delegation could have criticised indefensible aspects of the Communist position in strictly relevant speeches. (*First Report from the Joint Committee on Foreign Affairs relating to the Peking Peace Conference.* Canberra. 1952.)

The arguments against participation used by some leaders of the Australian Labour Party were equally fallacious. It was alleged that an Australian delegation might enable the Chinese Communists to obtain information of military value which would be harmful to the Australian troops fighting in Korea. But normal postal communication existed between Australia and China through which the Chinese Communists could obtain information from contacts in the Australian Communist Party and the withdrawal of Australian passports did not prevent the Conference being attended by Australian delegates who had U.K. passports. In these circumstances an attempt to restrict the flow of information by withdrawing Australian passports from some delegates was like carefully closing a gate between two paddocks while large sections of the boundary between them remain unfenced.

If the Australian authorities had been able to secure a unanimous refusal to participate in the Conference because its good faith was doubtful, this would have been an effective gesture. But such a response could only be obtained in a totalitarian society. By making half-hearted use of totalitarian methods the Australian authorities actually only got the worst of both worlds.

9

Actual Western policies

ACTUAL Western policies have been very far removed from the strategy implied by this sort of peace campaign. This can be illustrated by a discussion of policies in China where Western policy, and especially American policy, failed on both sides of a peace campaign. The Communists were never seriously challenged on the indefensible points in their position and were never clearly given the opportunity of obtaining peaceful co-operation by demonstrating their willingness to behave in a way which would make peaceful co-operation possible.

American policy

I have already mentioned the failure to challenge the Communists over the issue of Soviet behaviour in Manchuria and, in this particular case, the failure is hard to explain in terms of purely Chinese factors. A possible explanation is that, at the beginning of 1946, U.S. policy was still influenced by a tendency to appease the Soviet Union. On every issue, however, the failure of American policy to challenge the indefensible points in the Chinese Communist position can be explained by the fact that any such challenge would also have involved a challenge to the Kuomintang, which America was determined to support. Both the main parties in China claimed to be in favour of democracy and civil liberties, and the Communists could well have been challenged over their reluctance to repudiate those parts of Marx-Leninist theory incompatible with such claims or over some aspects of their actual practice. But on almost every issue the Kuomintang record was worse than the Communist. American policy could only have made an effective challenge to the Communists if it had been willing to admit that the Kuomintang was largely a totalitarian party, maintaining its power by secret police terrorism,* and that Chiang Kai-shek's belief in Confucianism

---

* Cf. General Wedemeyer's statement "Secret police operate widely, very much as they do in Russia and as they did in Germany." (*U.S. White Paper*, page 762). So long as the American government refused to face the

162

was quite as incompatible with democracy and the interests of the Chinese people as Mao Tse-tung's belief in Stalinism.

While American policy failed to challenge the weak points of the Communist position it failed even more completely to provide the Chinese Communists with any evidence for believing that they could obtain the opportunity to work peacefully by rational methods for the service of the Chinese people if they gave up those parts of orthodox Marx-Leninism incompatible with a peaceful settlement in China or, later, incompatible with world peace.

Even during the war, many American actions seemed to show that the Chinese Communists would be faced with American hostility regardless of their behaviour. There were many points at which co-operation would have been of obvious advantage for the common war effort against Japan but the Americans were not prepared to consider such co-operation on its merits and in several cases showed definite bad faith. Several schemes were suggested by the U.S. Army Observers Section at Yenan through which the Communists were induced to divert a considerable amount of man power and scarce resources into some project only to find that the Americans refused to carry out their share of the scheme. I can illustrate this from a project with which I was personally concerned. As soon as the Americans reached Yenan in July, 1944, they were interested in obtaining a lot of information from the front-line areas. Much of this, such as weather reports, was information which 18th Group Army headquarters had no interest in collecting for its own use and a scheme was worked out for a network of radio stations over North and Central China feeding information to American Intelligence. The Americans repeatedly promised that stations working mainly for them would be supplied with suitable American equipment but asked the 18th Group Army to send the information through it own communications network until this could be arranged. The result was that an appreciable part of the very scarce radio equipment of the Communist forces was tied up in sending information for the Americans, while the promised suitable equipment never materialized. In the spring of 1945 several plane loads of equipment were at last delivered

---

contradiction between such admissions and its claims to be supporting democracy it could not challenge the Communists over their claims. (In this case General Wedemeyer's statements have some value as evidence because he was assisted by expert advisers.)

to Yenan but the sets were of a type which the Americans had been clearly told was quite unsuitable for the front-line areas.*

Under another scheme the Communists were induced to build a number of airstrips which then remained unused except, in a few cases, to save rescued American airmen the trouble of walking back to Yenan. And while the Kuomintang government was paid for airfield construction, often at prices grossly inflated by the artificial exchange rate, the Communists were not paid.

Of course, this policy represented the attitude of only a certain section of the American organisation. Meanness is a very untypical American failing. The U.S. Army Air Force made considerable deliveries of medical supplies to show their gratitude for the rescue of American airmen and there were many Americans who would have liked to join in genuine co-operation against the Japanese. Unfortunately the dominant group in the American Army command at Chungking seemed determined to give support for the Kuomintang a higher priority than the war effort against Japan.†

* In the areas east of the Yellow River the staff of a radio station had often to move carrying their equipment, sometimes on night marches in mountain country. The American sets weighed 230 lb., of which 140 lb. was a converter to get power from a truck battery, though it was known that none of the front line areas had any trucks. Even when this was discarded the main unit still weighed 50 lb., and had too small a frequency range to give reliable communication from the more distant areas. A much smaller delivery of hand generators and components from which suitable sets could have been made would have been satisfactory.

† This was not true of General Stilwell but, judging from his published diaries, General Stilwell had a very limited appreciation of the complexities of the situation. For example, although his diaries are violently abusive against Chiang Kai-shek and the Kuomintang army leadership he says nothing about the large scale desertions of Kuomintang troops to the Japanese, though these were often very prominently reported in the Japanese controlled press, and the American Air Force, at least, knew that the Kuomintang command maintained relationships with these generals in Japanese service. (The American Air Force asked for a map showing areas where it would be safe for American airmen to make forced landings. The Kuomintang command produced a map which showed all Communist areas as "enemy territory" and showed as safe only some areas held by Japanese puppet troops. In reply to protests General Ho Ying-ch'in said that these puppet units had comparatively few Japanese attached to them and he had sufficient authority with them to secure the return of American airmen.) If General Stilwell had known of this evidence of Kuomintang-Japanese collaboration it seems very unlikely that he would not have commented on it in his diaries. (The Stilwell Papers. Edited by Theodore H. White. William Sloan, New York, 1948.)

I can give an instance of American simple-mindedness during the Stilwell period from my own personal experience. I wished to get in touch with British or American Intelligence and when Mr. G. M. Hall of the National City Bank escaped from Peking and passed through Shansi-Chahar-Hopei I gave him plans for a code and radio schedule to make contact with the

The Communist reaction to such American behaviour was irrational. They were never willing to make a frank statement of their grievances, which could have won them support from those Americans who did not approve of subordinating the war effort against Japan to considerations of Chinese politics. For example, in the case just described they could very well have said "If the repeatedly promised suitable equipment is not delivered we will be compelled to consider how far our limited communications network can continue to carry its present load of American traffic." Instead of this they simply became sulky and obstructive. Meteorological reports were handed over a day late, the small amount of apparatus supplied unofficially by the Americans at Yenan was not properly used, and so on. These tactics not only failed to influence American policy but also alienated those Americans who were in favour of honest co-operation. This was an example of action which was irrational in the real world but would be rational in the world of Communist theory and similar action does explain Communist behaviour over more important issues at a later period.

An even worse instance of American bad faith was provided by General Hurley in November, 1944. Proposals for a Kuomintang-Communist agreement, including several points suggested by General Hurley, were signed on 10 November, 1944. According to both Chinese and American eyewitnesses, General Hurley signed the proposals saying that, though he could not commit his government, he was signing to show that he pledged his full personal support for the proposals. Within a few weeks he had repudiated this pledge.* General Hurley may have been wrong in pledging his support for these proposals but, having done so, his only honourable course would have been to admit

---

British or American authorities in Chungking. It proved impossible to establish the connection, though tests with the 18th Group Army station in Chungking showed that there were no technical difficulties. When the U.S. Army Observers Section reached Yenan more than a year later I was told that the American authorities had entrusted the contact to a station with operators provided by General Tai Li's organisation, the very organisation that was responsible for maintaining the blockade of the Communist areas.

* It is an interesting example of the cowardice of the State Department against its critics that the U.S. *White Paper* says that General Hurley only signed "as a witness" (page 74). General Hurley's attacks on the State Department for being too favourable to the Communists would have been effectively discredited by revealing that, at one time, General Hurley had pledged his support for a Kuomintang-Communist settlement on terms which his own suggestions had made slightly more favourable to the Communists than the original Communist demands.

that he had pledged his support for proposals which his government would not support. As it was, the Communists were given good reason to believe that the pledged word of an American ambassador was worthless when it was a matter of keeping faith with Communists.

Instances accumulated in the post-war period to show that the American authorities were not prepared to apply ordinary standards of objectivity or observance of pledges where Communists were concerned. For example, the American government replied to charges that it was intervening in the Chinese civil war by claiming that American troops were sent to North China to secure the full surrender of Japanese forces. But, through the fiction that American troops were only assisting the Kuomintang, Japanese forces were not disarmed so long as the Kuomintang wished to use them in the civil war. According to an informant who served in U.S. Headquarters at Peking, the Japanese command in North China offered to deliver all Japanese troops at the ports to await evacuation if only the Americans would persuade the Kuomintang to allow them to withdraw. And the Americans would not do this. As a result, Japanese forces remained active for months even near the main American bases and, in Shansi, the final surrender of Japanese forces was only secured by the Communist capture of T'aiyuan in 1949. (In this case published American reports confirm that the Japanese command asked the Americans to be allowed to withdraw.)[1]

The handling of U.N.R.R.A. provided a still more striking example of refusal to apply objective standards. U.N.R.R.A. claimed to be operating on the principle of relief without political discrimination, but the Communist areas, with about half the population eligible for relief, obtained less than 3 per cent. of U.N.R.R.A. supplies. And the Communists claim that the damage, caused when the Yellow River diversion project was perverted to cause deliberate flooding of large areas under Communist control, was far greater than the total value of U.N.R.R.A. supplies to the Communist areas.[2]

In these circumstances the Chinese Communist leaders showed considerable courage, for which they have seldom been given credit, in accepting General Marshall's mediation in an attempt to avoid civil war. American writers now argue that the Marshall mission was bound to fail because the Communists were determined to seize power.[3] These arguments depend on an over-simplified view of Communist motivation. It is probable that Communist motives were always mixed but there are many points in Communist behaviour, at least up to May, 1946, which are very hard to explain except on the hypothesis that they really hoped for a peaceful settlement to avoid the civil war and were prepared to make considerable concessions to get it. But, whatever the merits of these arguments, the Marshall mission was also bound to fail because the Communists were never given any reason to believe that they could obtain security except through victory in a civil war. The agreements reached through General Marshall's mediation could only have been effective if American policy had been objective and had made it clear that either party breaking the agreements would meet with American opposition. But the Communists were never given reason to believe that, even if they showed complete good faith in carrying out the agreements, the Americans would support them against the Kuomintang if the Kuomintang broke the agreements. Later developments showed that even the 1946 constitution gave no security to opposition groups without a private army to protect them. General Marshall himself said in his final report that "The reactionaries in the Government have evidently counted on substantial American support regardless of their actions."[4] But this was a natural deduction from American behaviour.

All this is directly relevant to the much discussed question of possible Titoism in China. Marshal Tito was actually appointed by the Comintern to bring the Yugoslav Communist Party into line with strict Stalinist orthodoxy, while Mao Tse-tung rose to leadership of the Chinese Communist Party in competition with rivals preferred by the Comintern. But Tito had the war-time experience of co-operation in good faith from the Western democracies. When Churchill said that his primary objective was to defeat the Nazis he was prepared to make this the criterion of co-operation. It is very likely that Tito's decision to break with the Soviet Union was influenced by his experience showing that the Western powers would co-operate in so far as this was of mutual advantage without making political conditions. He had reasons for believing that the alternative to subservience to Russia was not the complete abandonment of Communism. For China, even such a strong anti-Communist as Freda Utley considered that the Chinese Communists may have wanted to break with the Soviet Union in 1946.[5] But Mao

Tse-tung had been given no reason to suppose that he could obtain any alternative to reliance on the Soviet Union except through the complete abandonment of Communism.

According to Brigadier Evans Carlson, President Roosevelt suggested to him that he should return to China and try to win over the Communists from a pro-Soviet to a pro-American alignment, a suggestion which he refused. (Statement made to the author in 1946.) The contrast between the hostility towards the Chinese Communists of actual American policy between 1944 and 1946, and the extremely conciliatory attitude towards the Soviet Union, is hard to explain definitely. American policy can only be explained as the resultant of several rival pressure groups and the Kuomintang may have been more effective in exerting pressure than anti-Communist forces in Europe. Also, in so far as there was Communist influence within the American government, it may have been pro-Soviet rather than pro-Communist and inclined to follow the Moscow line in underestimating the Chinese Communists. But these are only speculative suggestions.

American policy in 1949 did seem to be moving towards a more reasonable position which would have enabled the Chinese Communists to obtain satisfaction for reasonable Chinese interests, in so far as they abandoned the elements in Communism incompatible with peaceful international co-operation. But the Korean war reversed this trend. The policy of declaring that under no circumstances whatever will the Peking government be allowed to obtain the U.N. seat obviously offers the Chinese government no inducement whatever to modify its doctrinaire Communist position in favour of a policy of trying to obtain reasonable Chinese objectives by behaving more reasonably.

It should be made clear that this criticism of American policy could not consistently be made by anyone who believes in orthodox Communism or some other form of totalitarian philosophy. Someone who denounces objectivity cannot honestly complain of the lack of objectivity in American policy. In terms of the standards implied by Göring's claim that "Right is that which serves the German people" (as interpreted by the Nazi Party), or the similar claims that "Right is that which serves the workers" (as interpreted by the Communist Party), there was nothing wrong with American policy except that it did not succeed, as it might have done if it had been considerably more dishonest and unscrupulous. The real case against American policy in China is that it was never based on the principles for which the American government claimed to stand. Instead of using the real strong points of the democratic position it tried to influence a struggle between two totalitarian parties by half hearted and amateurish use of totalitarian methods, thereby both failing to attain its objective and also discrediting the case for democracy against totalitarianism. If the American government had followed the advice of its expert China Service officers instead of dismissing them for alleged disloyalty it might have produced a Titoist China. Even if it had still failed to prevent the victory of a doctrinaire Stalinist Communist Party it would still have been very much more difficult for the doctrinaire Stalinists to win support from the Chinese people.

American policy in China is also an illustration of the inadequacy of the orthodox Marxist explanation in terms of class interest. Not only has American policy completely failed to serve American capitalist interests but this failure could be, and was, correctly predicted before the event. If American policy had been anything like as cunning and unscrupulous as Communist propaganda claims, it would have acted to remove the Kuomintang leadership centred round Chiang Kai-shek, both because this leadership was clearly incapable of preventing a Communist victory and also because its policies would not have been very favourable to American capitalism even if it had won the civil war. The economic policies envisaged in *China's Destiny* or *Chinese Economic Theory* were not likely to promote the interests of the Chinese people but they were also unlikely to favour foreign capitalism. And American business interests in China, who found their operations hampered by the Kuomintang, were actually strongly critical of American policy. As in most cases, it is not possible to give an adequate explanation of policy in terms of any one single influence and it is possible to select evidence to support the Marxian theory. But, while capitalist interests may have influenced American policy, it is doubtful whether they were as important as influences not dependent on economic interests. The completeness of the American failure in China is hard to explain without allowing for the influence of the Kuomintang Fellow Travellers. Alfred Kohlberg's motives can be explained in terms of economic self interest but the "China Lobby" could not have obtained anything like its actual influence without the services of men like Congressman Walter Judd, who seems to have acted in the service of a foreign political party from motives quite as altruistic as those of Communist Fellow Travellers. The assistance of such sincere fanatics was essential for channelling the traditional sentimental American feeling for China built up by missionary activities into support for a particular group in Chinese politics.

British policy

The British authorities started in 1945 with the disadvantage of almost complete ignorance about the Communist areas. Sir Archibald Clark-Kerr had been interested in getting information from as wide a range of sources as possible, even though this rather shocked his more conventionally minded subordinates, but the situation changed under his successor. In November, 1945, what struck me about the British Embassy at Chungking was that most people not only knew nothing about the Communist areas but also made it clear that they did not wish to know anything except what the National Government or the American authorities wanted them to know, which was very little. (By contrast the Australians and Canadians had much smaller facilities for getting information but were interested to get what they could.) The Americans were glad to receive reports from British Intelligence, which was good in South China, but they deliberately excluded the British from all the information coming from the U.S.A.O.S. at Yenan.* When General Hurley gave orders that no British representative was to visit Yenan Sir Horace Seymour did not challenge the right of an American ambassador to issue orders to British officers but accepted the situation without protest.

The resulting degree of ignorance can be illustrated from General Carton de Wiart's autobiography. General Carton de Wiart was the Prime Minister's special representative at Chungking and, presumably, received all information available to the

---

* I can illustrate this from my personal experience. I wrote a letter to the head of British Intelligence at Chungking saying that, in case he was not getting all the information he wanted through the Americans, I had arranged with General Yeh Chien-ying for copies of all the material given to the Americans to be made available to British Intelligence. Colonel Barrett of the U.S.A.O.S. promised to take this to Chungking for me and when I got no reply I assumed that this meant that my help was not required. On reaching Chungking, I found that my letter had been suppressed by the American authorities there and that no information from Yenan had been passed on to British Intelligence.

British Embassy. But he discussed the Chinese Communist problem in terms which assume that the Communist areas were the same in 1945 as they had been in 1937.*

This ignorance gradually diminished after 1945 but British policy completely failed to use its opportunities. Britain had little military or economic power in China, but could have exerted a great influence on Chinese opinion by taking a stand for principles which would have been supported by the vast majority of the British people. British policy was not hampered by powerful pressure groups at home devoted to some particular Chinese party and could have publicly expressed disapproval of secret police terrorism practised by either left-wing or right-wing governments. Such a position would have had a strong appeal for very large sections of Chinese opinion and publicly expressed disapproval for known Kuomintang terrorism would have made people ready to believe British reports of Communist terrorism. It would also have been a direct challenge to the orthodox Communist theory which claims that no government really disapproves of terrorism but only denounces its use by the other side as a propaganda device. British officials claim that disapproval of Kuomintang terrorism was expressed in private protests to the National Government. But when it is known that unheeded private protests will not be followed by publicity or some other sanction they are very unlikely to produce any effect. From the evidence available to the Chinese public it appeared that the British government was ready to express its public disapproval of secret police activities and elections with no opposition candidates in Europe, where the Communists were responsible, while similar behaviour by a right-wing government

---

* Adrian Carton de Wiart, *Happy Odyssey*. (Jonathan Cape, London, 1950.) Pages 268-271. He says, ". . . the organisation of the Communists was good, but their forces were concentrated into a specific area which made matters easier for them. The Central Government suffered from the drawbacks of geography . . . with a transport problem which was insoluble." In fact, the Communist forces were scattered all over North and Central China and their base areas were separated and cut up by strips of Japanese held territory along railways and motor roads, often heavily fortified, and transport was mainly by pack animals or porters. The Kuomintang areas, though larger, were continuous until the latter part of 1944 and had a network of motor roads, some navigable rivers and sections of railway.

Later he argues that Chiang Kai-shek could have crushed the Communists in June, 1945, if he had continued his attacks. In fact, several of the largest Communist bases could not have been reached by Kuomintang troops unless they had obtained permission from the Japanese command to operate across Japanese held territory.

171

in China produced no protests. That is, the British government appeared to be acting in exactly the way that Communist theory predicted that a capitalist government would act.

The British government showed similar cowardice over U.N.R.R.A. Individual British employees of U.N.R.R.A. did a great deal to raise British prestige in China by establishing a reputation for fairness and honesty, but their efforts to combat some of the worst scandals in U.N.R.R.A. administration received no official British support.

Up to 1948 the Communists appeared to welcome foreign contacts and there were a number of precedents for securing at least unofficial British representation with a *de facto* government that controlled a considerable part of some country. And such British representatives might have exerted considerable influence. The possibility of directly influencing Communist policy was not negligible. The Chinese Communist leadership was very badly informed on world affairs. It obtained its information mainly from the monitoring of news services but could only evaluate this information in the light of Communist theory with very little background knowledge. Few of the Communist leaders had had any direct contacts with Western societies except as students in the early 1920's. In these circumstances, British representatives able to win the respect of the Communist leadership and able to provide more complete and accurate information might have had considerable influence. Apart from this such British representatives could have made a direct challenge to some of the indefensible points in the Communist position. The Communists claimed to be in favour of freedom of the press and this claim could have been tested by putting out strictly factual publicity about Soviet actions in Eastern Europe, from which anyone in North China would have drawn the obvious analogies between Soviet and Japanese behaviour. If the accuracy of such reports had been challenged the Communists could have been invited to send an investigating commission to visit Germany under British auspices where they could have been presented with witnesses giving first hand accounts of widespread looting and rape by the Soviet forces and could have been challenged to ask the Soviet authorities to allow them to investigate the concentration camps in the Soviet Zone. Either of the possible Communist responses to this strategy would have been favourable. If such publicity had been allowed it would have made it much harder for the doctrinaire Stalinists in the Chinese Communist Party to secure acceptance of their extreme pro-Soviet line. If it had not been tolerated it would have demonstrated that the Communist claims to stand for freedom were false and the public outside the Communist areas would have been given evidence that Communist practice in this field was as undemocratic as that of the Kuomintang.

In fact, British policy between 1945 and 1949 seems to have concentrated on finding excuses for doing nothing. Even attacks by the Kuomintang air force on British ships carrying U.N.R.R.A. supplies failed to produce any active protest. The British authorities seem to have accepted the crude power-politics view—that it was futile to stand for any principles and that alliance with America implied uncritical acceptance of any American policy in a country which had been recognised as an American sphere of influence.

From 1949 on British policy has come much nearer to satisfying the requirement of showing that a readiness by the Chinese Communists for peaceful co-operation would be reciprocated from the British side. There has still been a good deal that could be criticized. It is possible that if the British authorities had acted sooner or if they had acted with more courage and more tact, they might have changed the course of events. But when all criticisms have been made, the record of British policy since 1949 as offering the possibilities of peaceful co-operation remains far superior to the record of the Peking government. The Chinese criticisms of lack of active support for Chinese claims in the U.N. are cancelled out by criticisms from the opposite point of view. For example "Already in 1950 the British canvassing for votes in the U.N. to bring about the seating of China had produced considerable tension between London and Washington . . ."[6] The weakest point in British policy was the failure to restrain General MacArthur. Even before the fiasco of the advance to the Manchurian border, about which the British authorities had the gravest misgivings, there was a very strong case on the simple issue of military discipline. The British government could well have said that British troops could not continue to serve under a commander who was showing himself to be disloyal and insubordinate. The American government could have been warned that if General MacArthur was not brought under effective discipline the British commanders in Korea would be told not to accept any orders with political implications from him until they had made certain that such orders came within his terms of reference as commander of the U.N. forces.

(Going further back, both Britain and Australia were very cowardly in resisting the indefensible aspects of General MacArthur's record in Japan, such as the prevention of criticism by expelling foreign correspondents and the molestation of British citizens by American military police. It could have been argued that, as Supreme Commander Allied Powers, General MacArthur was bound by the terms of the inter-allied occupation directive and that action to restrain freedom of the press and information was *ultra vires*. This sort of argument would have been a strong one for American opinion and if General MacArthur had refused to accept it the expelled correspondents could have returned with diplomatic status and diplomatic facilities for transmitting their messages. A more unscrupulous policy might have brought a few competent detectives to Japan and reinforced British influence by the threat of public exposure for the very shady transactions in which, according to general rumour, many of General MacArthur's close associates were involved.)

On the other hand, British policy has still failed to make use of the opportunities for challenging the indefensible points in the Communist position, even though these opportunities have been limited. So far as I know, the British government has never made a public statement of the case against the Chinese arguments for refusing diplomatic relations. There has certainly been no active publicity to show the British public and such sections of the Chinese public as can be reached that the arguments used by the Chinese government to justify its policy are completely unreasonable. The British authorities have tended to consider Chinese behaviour as evidence that the Chinese government does not really want any improvement in Sino-British relations and have simply accepted this situation.

Such a publicity campaign would almost certainly have been attacked by such bodies as the Britain-China Friendship Association with the argument that public criticism of the Chinese government was incompatible with trying to improve Sino-British relations. This raises an important question of principle. This whole discussion of conditions for an effective peace campaign has implied that demonstrations of desire for peaceful co-operation and attacks on the indefensible points in the position of the other party are not incompatible but complementary. If certain policies or certain beliefs are really incompatible with peaceful co-operation then they must be moved before peaceful co-operation becomes possible. And obstacles can seldom be removed by pretending that they do not exist. To put it another way, there is a great deal to be said for letting sleeping dogs lie, when they are not in the way. But a sleeping dog in a position where it is certain to be trodden on has to be removed and attempts to ignore its existence are likely to have unpleasant consequences. For instance, a great deal of confusion and bad feeling could have been avoided if the Western leaders in 1944 had tried to insist on operational definitions of such concepts as "free elections" instead of accepting agreements that only concealed fundamental disputes by using terms which had completely different meanings for Communists and non-Communists.

Of course it is important to make correct judgments of relevance and irrelevance. If everything is considered relevant to every question then co-operation is only possible between people who are in complete agreement. And the Communist tendency to think of everything in terms of a single, rigid, all-embracing system does make it difficult for them to co-operate with non-Communists. A more scientific outlook would admit that, in some sense, everything in the world may be inter-related but would also recognise that it is nearly always justified to neglect the more remote inter-relations and that most problems can be considered in terms of a limited number of relevant variables. This means that co-operation in a particular field only demands a limited range of agreement. To estimate this range for any particular field of co-operation will involve a great deal of skill and judgment. Looking back, one can say that Chamberlain was certainly wrong in considering that the philosophy of the Nazi leaders was irrelevant to the problem of reaching a peaceful settlement in Europe. And the more simple minded people who hope for peaceful co-operation with unmodified Stalinism are probably making a similar mistake. On the other hand, many American writers at present almost certainly go too far in the other direction when they argue that any form of belief in Communism is incompatible with peaceful co-operation.

In this case the refusal of the Chinese government to establish diplomatic relations has very direct relevance to possible peaceful co-operation. And there is reason to believe that a strong public attack on the indefensible Chinese arguments would increase the chances of an improvement in Sino-British relations. The possibility of any improvement depends on there being people in the Chinese government who want better relations— better relations, that is, with actual British governments and not with some hypothetical future British government which has been forced by the "British people" into accepting the Communist line. There are reasons for supposing that such people exist, and I will assume for the sake of the argument that they do exist. It must be very difficult for them to exert any influence against their more doctrinaire and intransigent colleagues in favour of a policy which could be represented as making concessions to an imperialist capitalist government. Suppose, however, that the British government were effectively to publicize the unreasonableness of the Chinese position. Any Chinese leaders in favour of peaceful co-operation would then be able to point out to their doctrinaire colleagues that Chinese intransigence was making the Chinese government an object of ridicule, and that a change of policy was not just making concessions to a capitalist government but was essential to preserve Chinese prestige.

Another obvious anomaly is that British information services are completely prohibited in China while the New China News Agency operates in British territory. The British authorities have been quite rightly unwilling to prohibit the operation of the New China News Agency, which would simply be retaliating against totalitarianism by using totalitarian methods. And this is a form of competition in which a government hampered by some scruples about honesty and justice is almost certain to get beaten by a purely totalitarian organisation. On the other hand it would be possible to make very effective retaliation without sacrificing democratic principles. The New China News Agency, and papers under Chinese Communist control, could be allowed to continue but could be compelled to print with every item criticizing the British government or its allies a statement saying, "We must remind our readers that this item can be published owing to the real freedom of the press which exists under British rule and that no similar item could be published in China or other countries under Communist rule." And it could be made clear that the regulation would at once be removed when the Chinese government showed that the required statement was no longer true by allowing British information services to operate in China.

Another point in the Chinese position which needs to be challenged is the claim, which is frequently made by Chinese publicity, that any conciliatory British behaviour is not evidence of British goodwill but only evidence of British fear of Chinese strength. An obvious opportunity to do this was provided by the question of visas. Even official applications for replacements for British diplomatic or consular staff in China have often been delayed for months by the Chinese government while the British authorities have often been requested to grant Chinese official visas at very short notice. It would be possible to demonstrate that British reasonableness was not the result of fear by including in the application form for official Chinese visas an item "Reasons for requesting treatment more favourable than that granted by the Chinese government to similar British applications." It could be made clear that applicants who gave a satisfactory answer on this point would get a visa in a reasonable time by British standards while an applicant who refused to give a satisfactory answer would be treated with strict reciprocity. This again would strengthen any reasonable people in the Chinese government against their intransigent colleagues. In fact, when the British authorities did restrict visas for Hong-kong it was handled in a way which inflicted considerable hardship on Chinese students in England who wished to return home and almost no hardship on the Communist officials against whose bad treatment of British citizens it would have been reasonable to retaliate.

The Korean war provided a number of other cases in which far more could have been done to challenge the indefensible points in the Chinese position if the British authorities had been ready to act with more imagination and initiative.

These are only a few examples of the sort of action which would be implied by a discriminating strategy. On the one hand such a strategy would expose the indefensible points in the Communist position and would refuse to allow indications of goodwill or adherence to democratic procedures to be mis-represented by Communist publicity as signs of weakness. On the other hand it would demonstrate its readiness to respond to any genuine Communist desire for peaceful co-operation. In effect such a strategy would say to the Chinese government, and such sections of the Chinese public as could be reached "We would prefer peaceful co-operation; we would prefer to settle any disputes by the civilized procedure of frank discussions between representatives of our countries and objective investigation of disputed matters of fact. On the other hand, if you insist on conducting diplomacy by public press statements and if you insist on misrepresenting any signs of conciliation as evidence of weakness we will be compelled to take account of your preference for conducting international relations according to these conventions. We will make clear to the public that your statements are unreasonable and will show that we refuse to be intimidated by threats of hostility."

Admittedly the direct effects of such a strategy would be limited. But the people who argue that limited gains are not worth making nearly always neglect the possibility of feed back effects. A shift between a situation in which the democratic powers are always on the defensive and a situation in which the intransigent elements in the Chinese Communist Party would be on the defensive might have very large cumulative effects, unless the present dominance of the intransigent elements in Chinese Communism has a very high stability which is not certain.

It is possible to give small scale instances from recent Chinese history of the effectiveness of imaginative retaliation and of a firm stand on principles. In the period from 1937 to 1940 French real power in the Far East was far smaller than American and smaller even than British but the French were usually able to protect their interests in China more effectively against Japanese encroachment. America and Britain nearly always reacted by making formal diplomatic protests which were nearly always ineffective, partly because they were backed by no sanction except an ultimate threat of war which the Japanese army had little reason to believe would be used and partly because the Japanese Foreign Office was almost completely unable to control the Japanese army. Such ineffective protests merely made the Japanese civil authorities still further lose face as against the military and encouraged the military extremists to believe that they could act against American and British interests with impunity. On the other hand the Japanese knew that interference with French interests would probably produce rapid retaliation which they could only avoid if they were prepared to use the threat of war against France. For example, after some Japanese provocation at Shanghai a Japanese military convoy had the humiliating experience of waiting for the greater part of a day on the Shanghai Bund because of alleged irregularities in its permit to pass through the French Concession and it became known that interference with French shipping in Japanese occupied ports usually produced delays for Japanese shipping in French ports. With the complete disproportion between Japanese and French power in the Far East this strategy could only produce limited results and resistance to Japan became impossible after the French surrender in Europe. However, an equally imaginative strategy by America might have produced decisive results. Even before the event it was clear that a military challenge to America would involve very serious risks of a total Japanese defeat and America was in a very strong position to use economic sanctions without any serious risk of war. For example, the Japanese government could have been told that failure to give public and exemplary punishment to officers or officials interfering with American interests in China would be followed by the collection of exemplary damages by levies on Japanese trade with America. James Forrestal argued later that World War II might have been prevented if America had been ready to fight over the *Panay* incident.[7] But it might not even have been necessary to fight if American policy had used every opportunity to humiliate and discredit the Japanese military extremists.

On a much smaller scale Dr. Leighton Stuart's defence of Yenching University against Japanese pressure was a masterpiece of strategy. He had no real power behind him except that, up to December, 1941, the Japanese were reluctant to offend American opinion. On the other hand the Japanese had strong reasons for refusing to tolerate Yenching. The continuance of effective academic freedom in a university which refused any acknowledgment of the authority of the Japanese sponsored local government was a standing challenge and threat to the Japanese system of propaganda and indoctrination in the occupied areas of North China; and the Japanese rightly suspected that Yenching was a centre of underground anti-Japanese activities, though they were never able to prove it. Dr. Stuart was successful because, on the one hand he stood absolutely firm on any point of principle and made it clear that the Japanese could not obtain any concessions except by forcibly closing the university; on the other hand he was careful to avoid any unreasonable challenge to the Japanese. For example, great care was taken to show that students sponsored by the Japanese army were rejected because, in the entrance examination, the best Japanese candidate did worse than many rejected Chinese applicants. (As the examination required both Chinese and English it was impossible for the Japanese military to find candidates who could qualify in it.) Again, with an international faculty, there was no reasonable case for refusing a Japanese professor, but attempts by the military to introduce an agent on the faculty were frustrated by the appointment of a distinguished Japanese scholar who refused to act as a spy. (Professor Torii showed such courage in assisting his Chinese colleagues after 7 December, 1941, that he was invited to resume his post when the university re-opened after the Japanese surrender.)

These are only small scale instances but they indicate that imaginative retaliation and policies based on careful discrimination can be more effective than conventional diplomacy and policies based on the allegedly realistic power-politics view which does not admit the distinction between reasonable and unreasonable positions and cannot, therefore, be conciliatory to the one and hostile to the other.

Again, one cannot predict the results of this sort of strategy towards the present Chinese government. But it could be made much harder for the Chinese Communist Party to avoid the dilemma of either having to behave more reasonably or else face the cumulative discrediting of its claims to want peaceful co-existence, not only among the foreign public but also among the overseas Chinese to whose opinions it attaches considerable importance.

Western policy in Europe

A proper discussion of Western policy in Europe would need a book to itself but it is possible to give several examples to show that it has had similar defects, in particular a failure to challenge the indefensible points in the Communist position. (I discuss this in terms of a sample taken largely from Germany simply because this is a field in which I have been interested.)

One important issue was Communist-Nazi collaboration. In the post-war period there were many instances of Germans with bad S.S. or Gestapo records being dismissed from positions in the British Zone and immediately being given more responsible positions in the Soviet Zone. The allegedly complete de-Nazification in the Soviet Zone has been simply a matter of definition—someone ready to work for the Russians cannot be a Nazi. One Communist leader in the American Zone actually complained to one of my colleagues at Harvard that the Americans were very unreasonable in refusing to allow that a Nazi who was willing to join the Communist Party had thereby proved his complete repentance and political reliability and should not be penalized by de-Nazification procedures.

Large scale and carefully accurate publicity on this post-war Communist-Nazi collaboration could have exerted an important influence on public opinion, especially in countries which had suffered from German occupation. Czechoslovak opinion was very much influenced by memories of the Munich Agreement and by Communist publicity alleging that the Western powers were still inclined to tolerate the Nazis and that only the Soviet Union was resolutely opposed to a revival of German militarism. A clear demonstration that, in fact, the Soviet organisation in Germany was the most deeply involved in continued relations with the Nazis could have considerably reduced pro-Communist feeling in Czechoslovakia and might even have prevented the Communist seizure of power.

In fact, for several years it was official British policy that these cases of Soviet-Nazi collaboration should be given no publicity, though this did not prevent the British from being attacked by Communist publicity for alleged failure in de-Nazification. No doubt effective Western publicity would have provoked more violent counter-charges from the Communist side but, on balance, the Western powers could almost certainly have got the better of the exchange. They would have had to admit that their record was not spotless but a high proportion of the Soviet charges could have been exposed as demonstrably false. (At one British-Soviet meeting the Soviet representatives were challenged to substantiate their charges and produced a list of Nazis allegedly holding positions in the British Zone. The British were able to show that many of the names were fictitious and that nearly all the rest had actually been dismissed by British de-Nazification tribunals. The Russians were not able to disprove a corresponding British list of Nazis in the Soviet Zone.)

Western publicity has been equally defective over the issue of German rearmament. On 23 May, 1950, the Western powers sent notes to the Soviet government complaining that an armed force was being established in the Soviet Zone of Germany

181

organised on military lines and equipped with tanks and artillery. Other reports claimed that its officers included many men who had been Reichswehr commanders under the Nazis. In so far as Communist publicity has not been able to evade this issue it has taken the quite indefensible line that an army does not count as long as it is not called an army but only claims to be "Commando units" (*Bereitschaften*) of a security police organisation. (This might be taken as an instance of the Communist tendency to attach a magical importance to words, see page 83.) The Soviet position has been equally indefensible over the rearmament of the states which were Nazi satellites and are now Soviet satellites whose armies had been increased by 1952 to roughly four times the limits imposed by the peace treaties. On these points the Western powers have been inclined to let the matter drop after registering an initial protest.

There has been very active Communist publicity denouncing the Western powers for proposed rearmament of Western Germany in violation of previous inter-allied agreements. The obvious answer to this has been that such agreements had already been broken by the actual rearmament of East Germany and the satellite states. If one reads Western statements carefully one can find this point made. But during the Berlin Conference in February, 1954, it was surprising to find how many quite well informed people did not see the obvious trick in Mr. Molotov's proposals for withdrawal of all foreign armies from Germany—that it would leave the Communists in control of a force with military training and equipped with tanks and artillery which could only be opposed by a smaller force of West German security police with little equipment beyond pistols and rifles.

A still more curious failure to challenge indefensible Soviet positions has been the willingness of the Western powers to accept the excuse from Soviet representatives that kidnappings and other illegal activities were committed by "forces not under our control." There is little doubt that this excuse was actually true. At many inter-allied meetings in Germany the reputable regular officers of the Soviet army have obviously been ashamed of their inability to control the actions of men who were nominally their subordinates but had positions in the Soviet secret police organisation. But this is no reason why the Western powers should have tolerated the situation. The Soviet authorities could have been notified that failure to restrain their secret police organisation and further use of this excuse would be followed by full publicity that the official representatives of the Soviet government had to admit that they were unable to control the Soviet secret police organisation. Even at the Berlin Conference Mr. Molotov could have been challenged on this point. He could have been asked what security the Western powers could have for the observance of any agreement on Germany by a government which had openly admitted its inability to control its own organisation in Germany.

It should be stressed that a challenge to the Soviet position on these points would not have been incompatible with attempts to secure a real lessening of international tension. If the Soviet government is really not willing or able to ensure that agreements into which it enters will be observed by the Soviet secret police organisation then there are many fields in which the Soviet government is incapable of making agreements with any practical value. And, since it is probable that the Soviet secret police organisation represents a strong vested interest in favour of continued international tension, evidence that the Soviet government is willing and able to control it is extremely important. Similarly, collaboration with the Nazis is a good instance of the complete lack of scruple in the policies which the Soviet government is prepared to use to maintain its power. Willingness to make a clear repudiation of this policy would be a good test of Soviet good faith in wanting better international relations. Again, at the Berlin Conference Mr. Molotov could have been challenged by an offer to abandon proposed West German rearmament provided that the Soviet Union disbanded the actual East German army and the excess over treaty limits in the armies of Rumania, Bulgaria and Hungary and accepted some system of control to ensure that the new agreements were observed as the old ones had not been. If this offer had been accepted it would have provided a reasonable alternative to West German rearmament. If, as is more probable, it had been rejected, it would have demonstrated that the Soviet government had no objections to rearmament in violation of treaty obligations but only to non-Communist rearmament; a demonstration which would have had important effects on public opinion especially in France.

Of course the Soviet authorities would denounce this type of strategy and try to maintain that any challenge to the Soviet Union was evidence that the Western powers did not really want peaceful co-operation. (At the time of the Paris Conference in 1948 a representative of the Soviet Embassy in London told a British M.P. that an article in the *Daily Herald* criticising conditions in the Soviet Zone of Germany was evidence that the British government did not want the Conference to succeed.) But the use of this sort of argument is evidence of a Soviet position quite incompatible with peaceful co-operation. The Soviet view implied by such arguments is that international problems should be settled by power politics bargaining with complete disregard for both public opinion and the merits of the case in any dispute. This Soviet attitude showed very clearly at Yalta. For example "When Bohlen observed that the U.S. delegation at Yalta had to keep in mind the concern of the American people that the rights of the smaller nations should be protected, Vyshinsky replied, 'The American people should learn to obey their rulers.' "[8] Even if the Soviet leaders sincerely believe that the conduct of international affairs on such principles is likely to produce peace, their belief is almost certainly mistaken. It is more likely that they realise it would give a great advantage to an unscrupulous totalitarian government as against governments inhibited by some regard for honesty and justice and by some influence from an informed public opinion.

The weakness of the Western powers has been that they have not always been ready to make a stand for their own principles and have sometimes been ready to accept totalitarian views. Churchill's agreement in 1944 to divide the Balkans into spheres of influence on a percentage basis was an example of the crudest kind of power-politics bargaining and successive British governments have been influenced by totalitarian arguments that suppression of criticism should form part of a policy to improve international relations. This applies to pre-war attempts to restrain criticism of the Nazi government just as much as to post-war attempts to restrain criticism of the Soviet government.

The real case against such totalitarian arguments is that the best guarantee of peace is an informed public opinion. And the weakness of the Communist demands for the prohibition of "warmongering" is that they make no distinction between true and false criticism. There is certainly a great deal of publicity, both Communist and non-Communist, which simply makes assertions calculated to produce hostile feelings without regard for whether they are true or false, and the suppression of this type of publicity would improve international relations. But when criticism is accurate what is necessary to improve international relations is not suppression of the criticism but remedies for the defects which are criticized. The history of the 1930's and of the Yalta period provides very clear evidence of the futility of trying to base international co-operation on restriction of justifiable criticism.

Resolutions calling for action in all countries to prohibit propaganda for war and international hatred have formed a regular part of Communist publicity. They have appeared at most meetings of the World Council of Peace and at the Peking Peace Conference. The record of the Communist controlled press in trying to rouse international hatred makes it very doubtful whether these resolutions have been made in good faith, but they have been quite effective publicity because they have never been challenged by any better suggestions. At the 1948 Conference on Freedom of Information the Western representatives quite rightly denounced the information services of Communist ruled countries but were rather disingenuous in defending the system in their own. They would have been in a much stronger position if they had admitted that the standards of some publicity in Western countries were quite as low as those of Communist publicity; and if they had recognised that the rousing of international hatred through false statements was a danger to peace in all countries. The French proposal that a government should be able to obtain publicity for official denials of statements to which it objected was not satisfactory because it took no account of the vital distinction between true and false criticism.

An imaginative non-Communist strategy would meet the Communist resolutions with proposals for an international agreement which would provide sanctions against the publication of untrue statements calculated to cause international hatred, with an operational definition of "untrue". The general requirements of such a scheme would be to put in some category of libel the making of purely malicious statements to rouse international ill-feeling when there was no basis of evidence for supposing them to be true; and to allow a government to obtain retraction of false criticisms provided that it were prepared to allow the facilities for investigation necessary to establish whether the criticisms were true or false. Such a scheme would involve many problems such as, how to define standards of proof or disproof, how to meet the costs of investigation, how to ensure that a government does not get the benefits of the agreement while refusing to accept its obligations, and so on. It would certainly require unconventional features, such as the right to send investigating commissions into a country to check the claims made by its government, and it might only be workable with an international tribunal. All the same these problems would be worth facing. If some such scheme were accepted it would make a real contribution to world peace. It is more likely that the Communists would reject it because any effective restriction of propaganda for international hatred would affect Communist publicity considerably more than non-Communist publicity. In this case it would provide a clear exposure of the bad faith in Communist claims to oppose "warmongering".

Disarmament is another issue which provides a good example of the lack of imagination in Western strategy. The Soviet government had repeatedly claimed that it is in favour of disarmament and had repeatedly put forward its proposal for a one-third reduction in existing armaments. The trick in this proposal has been that it would perpetuate the greater relative strength which the Soviet government obtained in the immediate post-war years when it made comparatively limited reductions in its armed forces at a time when the Western powers were reducing theirs to a small fraction of their war-time strength. If one reads Western statements carefully one can find passages which point this out but it has never been effectively publicized. The result has been that the Soviet government has been able to win a certain amount of support from general public opinion by appearing to take a strong stand in favour of general disarmament while actually advocating a policy designed to secure continued Soviet military superiority. The obvious challenge to the Soviet proposals would be a proposal for a much larger proportionate reduction, not on present strength, but on full mobilization strength in 1945, so as not to benefit powers which did not reduce their forces to peace-time strength after the defeat of Germany and Japan. Such a proposal would expose the bad faith of the Soviet position in a very clear and simple way which it would be difficult for Communist publicity to misrepresent. And some definite basis like full war-time strength would be more likely to lead to a reasonable disarmament plan which would not benefit any particular power.

The issue of U.N. powers over colonies and trust territories provides another case in which non-Communist powers have allowed themselves to be manoeuvred into a false position through lack of courage and imagination. The administering powers have believed with some reason that many of the governments which have supported demands for increased U.N. powers of inspection and investigation have been motivated by a desire to make trouble rather than by any concern for the peoples of colonial territories. They have, therefore, always tried to restrict the powers of the U.N. as far as possible because of their fear that these powers will be misused. But this is not really a defensible position. If the U.N. is ever to become an organisation capable of preserving world peace its powers will need to be extended and not restricted. And as a general principle it is highly desirable that the U.N. should have the power to investigate the situation in non-self-governing territories and to prevent the exploitation of subject peoples whenever it occurs. The real defect of the present situation is that the powers of the U.N. are restricted to areas in certain purely formal categories. Non-self-governing territories which are nominally independent or which are nominally parts of another state are exempt from all U.N. jurisdiction. The situation would be very different if proposals were made to give the U.N. effective powers of inspection in all non-self-governing territories, which would include the power to make investigations to find out what territories were, in fact, non-self-governing. Such proposals would almost certainly call the bluff of those governments which have so far been most active in pressing for increased U.N. powers of inspection. If U.N. investigating teams were likely to inspect Mongolia, the non-Russian republics of the Soviet Union, the East European satellite states or the native Indian areas of South America it is fairly certain that most of the governments which have so far been pressing for increased U.N. powers would at once reverse their attitude and reveal themselves strongly opposed to any investigation whatever of their administration in what are, in fact, their colonial territories.

It would be easy to continue with instances showing the same general pattern. On most international issues a careful examination of the Communist position will usually show that important points in it are indefensible and imply a lack of objectivity or a subordination of peace to Communist power which must make any peaceful agreement very difficult. But the Communists will also be found taking a great deal of trouble to make their case as plausible as possible and to present it in a way designed to influence public opinion. The non-Communist position will seldom be entirely defensible but the modifications in it required to make peaceful agreement possible will usually be less vital than those required in the Communist position. On the other hand, non-Communist governments will usually be found on the defensive in publicity and reluctant to present their case in a way designed to appeal to public opinion. In particular, they usually seem to be afraid of making any imaginative proposals which could form the basis for genuine peaceful co-operation and which would imply the abandonment of the indefensible points in the Communist position but which would also imply the abandonment of the lesser indefensible points in the non-Communist position.

And this non-Communist lack of imagination and initiative extends far outside the field of regular diplomatic negotiations. To give a comparatively trivial illustration, why should the Australian Communist Party be allowed a virtual monopoly of propaganda by wall slogans? At the level of simplification required by wall slogans the democratic case could be accurately stated by a very simple slogan of four symbols and one word: "(hammer and sickle) = (swastika) = war." (In more detailed language: "The similarities between different forms of totalitarianism are more important than the differences; and totalitarianism in any form is the greatest threat to peace.") To put this simple slogan on the walls of Melbourne and Sydney now carrying only Communist slogans would be much more effective anti-Communism than most of the present activities of the extreme anti-Communists in Australia.

Of course, this whole discussion of non-Communist strategy is speculative. The general strategy suggested for a non-Communist peace campaign is based on a number of hypotheses for each of which there is a fair amount of evidence but by no means conclusive evidence. The strategy has been described largely in terms of particular illustrations because description in general theoretical terms would have been much more difficult and very much harder for any reader to follow; but every particular illustration involves further uncertainty because the analysis is based on limited knowledge about the facts of each particular case and might require revision in the light of more complete evidence.

What can be said with a fair amount of assurance is that

there is a very strong case for some new strategy. The strategy of conciliation towards the Soviet government which was followed between 1941 and 1945 was fairly clearly a failure. The Western strategy of more recent years may have halted the expansion of Communist power in Europe but offers little hope of producing anything better than a balance of power situation which may postpone war but is very unlikely to prevent it. A public opinion survey in America indicated that 53 per cent believed that a major war was almost certain within the next twenty-five to thirty years, and this is not really a tolerable situation.[9]

At present the Communist leaders claim to be working for peace and persuade many people to believe them; they may even believe it themselves. They also refuse to face the incompatibility between working for peace and working for the extension of Communist power. So long as this situation continues there is little hope of any genuine peaceful co-existence. The kind of non-Communist strategy which has been suggested, with careful discrimination and emphasis on effective publicity, would be at least one way of trying to alter this situation. It could make it harder for the Communist leadership to maintain "doublethink" positions, and put pressure on them to choose between readiness to accept genuine peaceful agreements or the progressive discrediting of Communist influence in non-Communist countries and the growing instability of beliefs even in Communist ruled countries. Any groups within Communism in favour of genuine peaceful co-existence would then have a much better chance of exerting influence than they do now. And even if such a non-Communist strategy failed to produce the necessary changes in Communist policy it would still yield a great deal of experimental evidence which would make the future planning of strategy much easier than it is now.

This sort of strategy is also one which would have some chance of being adopted. The survey of American opinion referred to above showed that 59 per cent were in favour of doing everything possible to reach peaceful agreement while keeping up armed strength, which indicates that support could be obtained for a policy which offered the possibility of peaceful co-operation while clearly avoiding anything that might reasonably be called appeasement. As against this the minority in favour of pure conciliation was even smaller than the minority in favour of a preventive war, 4 per cent against 6 per cent. And in other

Western countries the potential support for this type of strategy would probably be even greater.

Other types of new non-Communist strategy might be possible and these suggestions will have served a useful purpose if they do no more than stimulate the discussion of such possibilities.

10

The Communist peace campaign

THE same general principles could be applied to a Communist peace campaign if allowance is made for the very different structure of non-Communist societies. The threat to peace from non-Communist societies does not come from a single highly developed system of political faith leading to fanatical or irrational behaviour. There are certainly some dangerous fanatics but their beliefs, which are seldom as systematic as those of the Communists, vary over a considerable range. And these fanatics do not have the same power as their opposite numbers in the Communist system. It would be quite reasonable to argue that, if Senator McCarthy had the same power as Liu Shao-ch'i or Molotov, America would be a greater danger to peace than the Communist powers. But in fact he clearly has not. And irrational behaviour which endangers peace in non-Communist countries usually takes the form of irresponsibility. The nearest equivalent to Marx-Leninism as a threat to peace is the "essentialist" theory of Communism. Just as orthodox Communists believe that it is theoretically impossible for a capitalist society to co-operate in good faith for peace so many people, especially in America, believe that peaceful co-operation is inherently impossible for any Communist system. In both cases these views imply that it is never worth while making the slightest sacrifice of power positions to make peaceful agreement possible if the other side really wanted it; or even to make proposals for peaceful agreement except as propaganda, because it is theoretically impossible for the other side really to want peace. But even here the situation is not symmetrical. The non-Communist theory, at least in its more reputable forms, is an empirical generalization from Communist statements and Communist behaviour, and could be modified by fresh evidence which was incompatible with it. Beliefs forming part of the general system of orthodox Communist theory are not easily modified by empirical evidence.

The test of good faith which a Communist peace movement should reasonably demand from non-Communists is not so much the abandonment of certain beliefs as evidence of readiness to oppose and ability to control the fanatical or irresponsible minorities in non-Communist countries. For example, the experience of the Chinese Communists would give them fairly reasonable grounds for demanding evidence that an American government was willing and able to maintain its announced policies against fanatical or irresponsible pressure groups, and willing and able to enforce discipline on fanatical or irresponsible generals. And, while the American government may be especially weak in resisting pressure from dangerous but vocal minorities, other non-Communist governments have shown similar weakness.

The Communist inspired peace movement claims to seek the co-operation of all who desire peace whatever their political views and to discriminate between the "warmongers" and the peace loving groups in all countries. If these claims were true the movement would be highly desirable. The case against it is that these claims are quite incompatible with its actual record. The Communist inspired peace movement cannot make a convincing attack on any threats to peace because it is completely unwilling to attack Communist threats to peace or even to admit that they exist. Though Communists may sincerely believe that no threats to peace exist on the Communist side this should not prevent them from giving some reasoned arguments for this belief, which would involve giving some satisfactory alternative explanation for the evidence which leads people to believe that important aspects of Communist policy do threaten peace. But this is what the Communist inspired peace movement is never prepared to do. The argument that Communist ruled states are inherently incapable of aggression is only cogent for people who are already convinced believers in orthodox Marx-Leninism, but this is the only serious argument the Communist inspired peace campaign ever uses. The evasion and question-begging on which it mainly depends to answer any criticism of Communist policies inevitably create a presumption that it could not refute such criticisms by any rational arguments.

A study of the Communist inspired peace movement will reveal many instances of evasiveness or distortion of the facts which can easily be explained by the hypothesis that peace is given a lower priority than support for world Communism. It was possible to make an experimental test of this in connection with the world wide Peace Petition of 1950. The British Peace

Committee circularized branches of the United Nations Association inviting support for the petition and claiming that it could be supported by all who wanted peace regardless of their political views. The Hull branch of the U.N.A. replied pointing out that a number of articles in the Soviet press had claimed that those who signed the petition were thereby expressing their support for the foreign policy of the Soviet government. They asked "(1) Does the British Peace Committee consider that the signing of the petition commits those who sign it to the support of anything beyond the specific proposals contained in the petition? In particular, does the British Peace Committee consider that the signing of the Peace Petition can correctly be taken as an expression of approval or disapproval for the general policies of either the Soviet Union or the United States? (2) If the answer to both sections of the first question is negative, has the British Peace Committee taken, or does it propose to take, any steps to dissociate itself from the incorrect interpretations which have been placed on the signing of the Petition?" The first question received a perfectly clear negative answer but it proved impossible to obtain an answer to the second question from the British Peace Committee. The Committee first said that it could not interfere in the affairs of other countries but that it would dissociate itself from incorrect interpretations made in Great Britain. When it was pointed out that the quotations from the Soviet press had been taken from *Soviet News,* which was published in London by the Soviet embassy, the Committee retreated into still further evasions.

If the British Peace Committee had been acting in good faith it should have had no objection to dissociating itself from interpretations of the Petition which it agreed were incorrect. In fact, it refused to defend its claim to be acting in good faith when this would have implied criticism of the Soviet government, although it had no hesitation about denouncing in the most violent terms those who expressed suspicions that it was acting as a Soviet propaganda agency. This provided fairly strong evidence that the leaders of the British Peace Committee gave a higher priority to avoiding the slightest criticism of the Soviet government than to securing co-operation for peace.

A study of the material issued by the World Council of Peace provides evidence for a similar conclusion. For example, the World Council of Peace has committed itself to completely uncritical support for the Communist line on every issue connected with the Korean war—the origins of the war, germ warfare, voluntary repatriation, etc. It might have been possible to respect the good faith of the World Council of Peace if it had supported the Communist view while admitting that the issues were controversial and had taken a stand for the type of investigation and discussion which would have provided more definite evidence about disputed matters of fact. Actually the Communist case was always stated in a question-begging form which assumed that it was not only correct but also obviously correct. On the germ warfare issue the Council claimed that the Communist case had been proved by the International Scientific Commission, and said "The objectivity of this report, the competence of the scientists who drew it up, their indisputable impartiality leave no room for doubt."[1] Whatever the merits of the case, the impartiality of the president of the Communist controlled Britain-China Friendship Association was certainly not "indisputable".

Again, in July, 1952, a Resolution on the Cessation of the Korean War refers to "the illegal intervention of the United Nations into the internal conflict in Korea . . ." and ". . . calls on all peoples to demand . . . the American delegation to abandon its unjust demands concerning the repatriation of prisoners-of-war."[2] In both instances the Communist case is introduced as a question-begging assumption.

A still more curious resolution was passed at the session of the World Council of Peace at Berlin (21-26 February, 1951) saying "The World Council of Peace recalls the definition of aggression adopted by the Second World Peace Congress: 'That State commits the crime of aggression which first employs armed force under any pretext whatever against another State' and it declares unjust and illegal the resolution adopted by the General Assembly of the United Nations naming the Chinese People's Republic an 'aggressor' in Korea. This decision constitutes a serious obstacle to the peaceful solution of the Korean question; it threatens extension of the War in the Far East and, consequently, threatens the outbreak of a new world war. The World Council of Peace demands that the United Nations rescind this resolution."[3] In fact, the definition of aggression adopted by the Second Congress (Warsaw, 16-22 November, 1950) would actually justify the U.N. resolution. Chinese armed forces entered Korea, including South Korea, while no foreign forces entered China. And the original definition has another paragraph. "(2) No political, economic or strategic consideration, no pretext based on the internal situation of a state, can justify armed intervention."[4] This would explicitly rule out the strongest argument justifying Chinese intervention in Korea— that the presence of U.N. forces on the Korean border would have been a strategic threat which China could not tolerate. It appears that the World Council of Peace is not even prepared to abide by its own definitions when they have implications which could condemn a Communist government.*

The same refusal to accept any implications which would involve criticism of Communist governments is shown in the record of the World Council of Peace on European questions. It denounces German rearmament, but says nothing about the East German "*Bereitschaften*"; it denounces American military bases in foreign countries, but says nothing about Soviet bases in Finland or the countries of Eastern Europe; and so on.

The record of the Communist peace movement in China is similar, though perhaps slightly better than that of the World Council of Peace. The handling of the Peking Peace Conference was a good illustration. The original invitation to the Conference contained several question-begging assertions of the Communist case, and the signatures of Kuo Mo-jo and Ch'en Shu-tung as Chairman and Vice-chairman of the "Chinese People's Committee in defence of World Peace and against American (*sic!*) aggression" were not calculated to inspire confidence that the Conference would be ready to discuss all threats to peace. The Australian delegates to the Preliminary Conference claimed that

---

* It is possible to think of arguments through which the World Council of Peace might try to evade this conclusion. It might, for example, be argued that the United States had first committed aggression against China by the neutralization of Formosa and by bombing in Manchuria. But this argument would not be very convincing. The United States government had expressed its regret for one admitted case of bombing on Chinese territory and had offered to pay compensation for all cases in which the Chinese charges of such bombing could be substantiated by a neutral Indian-Swedish commission. U.S. action on Formosa did not involve any attack on territory controlled by the Peking government and both official Chinese statements and the time sequence of events linked Chinese intervention in Korea with the U.N. advance to the Chinese border and not with U.S. action in Formosa.

If the definition of aggression adopted by the Warsaw Congress is combined with the Communist claim that the Korean war was originally purely a civil war it would imply that both the United Nations and China were aggressors. To arrive at the conclusion that the former was an aggressor while the latter was not it would be necessary to add the principle that two blacks make a white, that only the first act of military intervention constitutes aggression and justifies all subsequent interventions.

there was a genuine readiness to discuss peace which seemed to be markedly different from the situation at conferences in Europe sponsored by the World Council of Peace. But the Chinese sponsors of the Conference were curiously reluctant to provide any definite evidence of this difference. The decision of an Australian delegation to attend the Preliminary Conference had caused considerable public controversy in Australia which had been increased by the cables which one delegate had sent from Peking. It was putting the delegates in an intolerable position to expect them to convince Australian opinion of the good faith of the Conference simply by their reports of freedom of discussion without a single bit of documentary evidence to support them. It was said that Australian representations had produced a considerable modification of the statement issued by the Preliminary Conference, but the delegates could not support this claim by producing a copy of the original draft statement which had been modified. All the duplicated reports of speeches followed the regular Communist or Fellow Traveller line. The delegates may well have been right in saying that this duplicated material did not give a fair picture of discussion at the Conference but they would have been in a far stronger position if they had been able to produce some documentary evidence showing that the Conference had allowed statements of non-Communist views.

The main Conference provided examples of the technique of stating excellent general principles and refusing to draw any implications from them which would have involved criticisms of Communist governments. The item on the agenda calling for the prohibition of propaganda for racial hatred was never applied to the "Hate America" campaign in China. In his address to the Conference, Kuo Mo-jo proposed a demand "that the people of all countries should have the freedom to choose the political system and way of life they prefer . . ."[5] As a general principle this would be highly desirable and would do much to ensure world peace. But no one at the Conference seems to have suggested that it would probably imply a change of government in most if not all Communist-ruled countries. The evidence as to the good or bad faith of the Conference is not conclusive because delegates who might have asked appropriate questions were kept out by non-Communist action. But there is nothing in any of Kuo Mo-jo's speeches or writings to suggest that he would have been willing to allow his principles to be applied to Communist-ruled countries.

This complete onesidedness and lack of objectivity makes it impossible for the Communist peace movement to make the relevant distinctions within non-Communist countries between the people who might reasonably be denounced as "warmongers" and those who oppose Communism and support military preparations against it because they are genuinely afraid of Communist aggression and have some rational grounds for this fear. By vastly exaggerating the hostility to peace in non-Communist countries the Communist peace movement helps to produce the situation which was excellently described by Mr. George Kennan. "It is the undeniable privilege of every man to prove himself right in the thesis that the world is his enemy; for if he reiterates it frequently enough and makes it the background of his conduct he is bound eventually to be right."[6]

There is a great deal of evidence that many of the supporters of the Communist inspired peace movement are quite sincere in wanting peace. To people who are not inclined to make a critical examination of its claims the movement must appear quite impressive, especially since it meets so little effective competition. However, the total effect of the movement is probably to endanger rather than to promote peace. By providing a great deal of evidence to support the hypothesis that the movement gives first priority to Communist power and very little evidence against it, the Communist inspired peace movement inevitably discredits not only itself but peace movements in general. When one highly publicized peace movement shows that in many instances it gives a lower priority to peace than to the interests of a particular political group and when it takes a great deal of trouble to deny that it is doing this and to claim that it is trying to secure the co-operation of all who want peace regardless of their political views, it becomes very difficult for the ordinary public to distinguish between the false claims of the Communist peace movement and the true claims of other peace movements. This directly helps the people in non-Communist countries who oppose all forms of peace movement and who are able to make very effective use of the confusion caused by the Communist peace movement to obtain support for their position.

It has already been argued that a Communist peace campaign which gave first priority to peace and was conducted with functional rationality would have a much easier task than a non-Communist peace campaign, because it would not face the same problem of establishing communication with the people it needed to influence. But if Communists ever did decide to conduct a genuine peace campaign they would probably find that their greatest obstacle was the reputation acquired by the present Communist peace movement. People interested in international affairs, who have found over a period of years that every Communist claim of readiness to co-operate in good faith for peace has had some trick in it, would be hard to convince that a new Communist peace campaign was really different and did imply a readiness to accept the objective standards essential for genuine co-operation for peace.

11

Why is there no effective peace movement?

It is fairly easy to give an explanation for the ineffectiveness of the Communist inspired peace movement. In order to conduct a genuine peace campaign the Communists would have to modify important parts of their system of faith. They would have to give up their belief in the infallibility of the Communist Party of the Soviet Union and become ready to judge Soviet policies by empirical scientific standards. They would have to give up their belief in the Marxian theory of the causes of war and become ready to admit that Communist governments might behave in ways that threatened peace and that capitalist governments might really be willing to co-operate for peace. And such modifications in practical beliefs would involve modifications in basic philosophical assumptions.

The reasons for the failure of non-Communist governments to attempt an effective peace campaign are less obvious, mainly because the non-Communist position is less homogeneous and less clearly formulated. Mistaken theoretical beliefs have almost certainly been an important factor, especially belief in power-politics theory and in the "essentialist" view of Communism. For example, the current American theory of "massive retaliation" is a logical deduction from these beliefs. If world Communism is a homogeneous and completely unified organisation acting with functional rationality for the extension of its power, then the only possibility of maintaining peace is through a balance of power situation. The way to keep the risk of war to a minimum will be to make clear that any act of Communist aggression will lead to a general war which the Communists will probably lose. But the assumptions which would justify this strategy are by no means certain and by accepting the strategy before making an adequate experimental investigation of its basic assumptions the American government has debarred itself from exploiting the much more favourable situation which may exist if these assumptions are not true. The kind of discriminating peace campaign suggested in the previous chapter might end by showing that the strategy of "massive retaliation" was the only possible one for the non-Communist world. But the strategy would then be based on assumptions for which the evidence was practically conclusive. On the other hand such a peace campaign might show that world Communism is not homogeneous and that elements in Communism are not irrevocably committed to the extension of Communist power as a basic objective, and if this were so then some form of peaceful co-existence would be possible which would be far preferable to peace dependent simply on a balance of power.

There is a very marked positive feed back between power politics strategies in different countries. The Soviet policies of the immediate post-war period seem to have been based on similar assumptions about the capitalist world. The strategy of consolidating Soviet power in all the countries of Eastern Europe was an equally logical deduction from the assumption that capitalism was irrevocably committed to the extension of its power and that it was not worth making any serious investigation of the possibility that elements in capitalist governments who preferred peaceful co-existence to power-politics strategy might be strong enough to make peaceful agreement possible. To anyone living in Western countries it has been fairly obvious that the resulting Soviet policy very greatly weakened the forces in favour of "peaceful co-existence" and has consolidated a great deal of support behind the people in favour of a pure power-politics strategy towards the Communist powers. This creates a presumption that similar non-Communist strategy exerts a similar influence on Communism. In so far as Western strategy concentrates on building up power positions which would make "massive retaliation" possible and neglects to make clear its preference for "peaceful co-existence" it must tend to unify and strengthen Communist support for power-politics strategies. In the case of non-Communist countries there is enough evidence to say with considerable assurance that the situation was sufficiently unstable for a different Soviet strategy between 1944 and 1946 to have produced a completely different non-Communist response. The evidence about the degree of stability behind Communist power-politics strategy is much less satisfactory and it is possible that the influence which could be exerted by a change in non-Communist strategy would be insufficient to change the Communist position. But the Western powers are behaving just as irrationally as the Communists if they refuse to make experiments to determine whether their basic assumptions are correct.

Power politics theory appears in a much less explicit form in the attitude of the very influential group who might be described as "respectable conservatives". Such people quite sincerely want peace and would agree that international co-operation would be much more desirable than a struggle for power but assume that this is inherently impossible, without ever formulating the reasons for this assumption. A good illustration was the view ascribed by Stresemann to Hindenburg: "He was not in principle against a policy of understanding but as an old soldier did not believe that there was any practicable substitute for war." The arbitrary basis of this belief showed even more clearly in the reaction of a Reichswehr officer of the same period to a lecture on international co-operation: "Gentlemen, this simply won't do. After all, *somebody's* got to be our enemy." ("*So geht das doch nicht, meine Herren, einen Feind muss man doch haben.*")[1] The same general pessimism about the possibility of any substitute for war seemed to be behind a great deal of foreign policy in other countries during the inter-war period and has continued since 1945. It explains some of the reluctance of the Western powers to produce any imaginative proposals for peaceful co-operation. People who are inclined from the beginning to think that the chances of peaceful international co-operation are very small are easily discouraged. Instead of taking Communist unreasonableness as a challenge, they accept it as a confirmation of their original prejudice that genuine peaceful co-existence is unattainable and that attempts to work out any alternative to preparations for war are simply a waste of time. For example, it may be true that there has been no practicable alternative to Japanese and German rearmament but this attitude of general pessimism has certainly hindered the full investigation of possible alternatives.

A very similar attitude among people of left-wing sympathies is produced by a partial acceptance of Marx-Leninism. In discussing political questions one frequently meets people who accept the usual Marx-Leninist arguments that beliefs are all expressions of various interests and cannot be distinguished as objectively true or false, but who are not Communists because they do not accept the view that beliefs produced by one particular interest are "historically correct" and should, therefore, be treated as absolutely certain truth. People who hold such views tend to be sceptical about the possibility of any real settlement of international disputes. They argue that no one can be expected to distinguish what is true from what is expedient for their interests, which implies that people with differing interests can never be expected to agree.

This general view provides a logical justification for the type of diplomacy which concentrates on evading or postponing every issue. If no objective standards exist no dispute can really be settled and peace can only be preserved if people can be prevented from feeling sufficiently strongly about any dispute to be willing to fight about it. On these assumptions attempts to produce a settlement of any dispute are not only futile but also dangerous. A clarification of the issues will only make clear that the conflict is irreconcilable and the more clearly people see that a conflict is irreconcilable the more inclined they will be to resort to force if the opportunity seems favourable for making their view prevail by force. Furthermore, attempts to produce a definite settlement are likely to commit the parties to definite conflicting claims which they cannot abandon without loss of prestige. On the other hand, if some conflict can be postponed, or if a power-politics compromise can be expressed in a form of words acceptable to both parties, then feelings are less likely to be roused. At the worst, the use of force can be postponed; at the best, a dispute which has been evaded for long enough may lose its practical importance and never produce a resort to force. The basic assumption, that nearly all disputes are insoluble to begin with, rules out the obvious argument against this type of diplomacy—that disputes which might be settled in their early stages through a little courage and initiative may become steadily harder to solve through evasion and postponement.

The "respectable conservative" and the well-meaning but woolly minded left-wing sympathiser are very common types in non-Communist societies. (While the respectable conservative might accept this name the people whom I have described as "woolly minded" would often claim that their partial acceptance of Marx-Leninism entitles them to be called "realistic".) Though such people are no particular danger to peace by themselves they are quite incapable of competing with people who do have fanatical beliefs and they are a serious hindrance to any effective action to meet the threat to peace produced by fanatical beliefs.

There are also cases in which rational action for peace is hindered by determination to maintain some indefensible position. And these indefensible positions are often the results of prejudices which can be explained in psychological terms but which do not form part of any coherent system of theory. An especially good illustration of this is the White Australia Policy, because the people who are most determined to maintain the policy unchanged also demonstrate their belief that it could not be defended by rational arguments, and because comparatively slight modifications would produce a policy that could be defended. On a whole series of questions connected with international relations the Australian government has been unwilling to consider any scheme on its merits because of preoccupation with the question "Would this make possible any international discussion of the White Australia Policy?" And this extreme fear of allowing the policy even to be discussed is evidence of a belief that the policy could not be defended in any discussion.

At the expense of a slight digression it is worth pointing out that quite small changes would produce a policy that could very effectively be defended in international discussions. There is a great deal of evidence that unassimilable groups in any country create serious social problems, especially when their traditional standard of living is widely different from the rest of the community. There is, therefore, a very strong case for holding that immigration policy should avoid the creation of such groups. This is not only a strong argument but also one which would be easily understood by several of Australia's Northern neighbours which have practical experience of the difficulties caused by unassimilable minorities. The Australian government would have an entirely defensible case if it maintained that it was not prepared to allow immigration which might destroy the general homogeneity of Australian society and might cause economic complications, especially since even completely unrestricted immigration would not provide more than very temporary relief for the population problem of any of the major Asian countries. And it could very well be argued that differences in cultural traditions and economic standards justified a distinction between European and non-European immigrants, that the latter were much more likely than the former to form unassimilable groups.

The indefensible aspect of the present policy is its refusal to take account of this genuine criterion of assimilability. To give extreme examples, an Asian national with a British or American education is likely to be much more easily assimilated in Australian society than someone who does not speak English from a European peasant background, and Asians married to Australians of European descent have given the most direct evidence of readiness to become assimilated, evidence which is much weaker in the case of some non-British European groups. All that would be needed to make the White Australia policy defensible would be to replace the present entirely arbitrary ban on racial grounds, which can only be defended in terms of something like Nazi race theory, with a policy which took account of the fact that small numbers of Asian immigrants with suitable qualifications would not in any way endanger the general homogeneity of Australian society. While a quota system might not be the best solution in Australia the Canadian quota of one hundred Indian immigrants a year is extremely unlikely to cause any social or economic complications in Canada and it does produce a considerable difference in the feelings of many Indians towards Canada as compared with Australia. And the abandonment of an indefensible and irrational position would considerably increase Australia's freedom of action in international affairs.

Many Australians will admit the force of such arguments and agree that the goodwill of Asian countries which are highly sensitive to claims of racial superiority is very important to Australia, but say that it would be very difficult to oppose the fanatical minority who would oppose any change in existing policy. But it is precisely this weakness in resisting fanatical and irresponsible minorities that constitutes the main threat to peace in democratic countries. A desire for peace is of little practical value so long as it is qualified by a refusal to resist the minorities whose prejudices endanger peace, and this applies to other democratic countries even more than to Australia. Communist propaganda is certainly wrong in accusing the governments of democratic countries of not wanting peace, but it would have a much stronger case if it accused them of lacking the courage to do what they know to be necessary to promote peace.

More important than prejudices about particular policies has been the pure conservatism which is reluctant to make any changes in conventional procedures and traditional ways of behaviour. It has been argued that an essential part of any effective non-Communist peace campaign would be the use of publicity aimed at discrediting the aspects of orthodox Communism incompatible with peace and at winning the support of all opinion in Communist ruled countries which would give peace a higher priority than the extension of Communist power. But the whole tradition of Western diplomacy has been against the use of publicity and especially against trying to change the policy of some government by appealing directly to the people. And the discrimination necessary for a selective attack on the aspects of Communism incompatible with peace would conflict with the dislike of ideological issues and the preference for evading clear contradictions between rival views which also form part of Western diplomatic tradition.

It is possible to give various explanations of the origins of this tradition. One is in Marxian terms. Western diplomacy remained under fairly exclusive upper class control even longer than other branches of government; the ruling classes in different Western countries had a community of interest against revolution; and, until fairly recently, the view that government should be responsible to popular opinion was revolutionary. At the beginning of this century many political leaders even in England did not accept democracy as a desirable principle.* And the distrust of popular power was much stronger in Central and Eastern Europe. In such a situation it was natural for those in control of foreign affairs to be very reluctant to use the strategy of appeal to public opinion, especially to public opinion in other countries. Common class interest could explain the acceptance of a convention to pursue international disputes without calling in the forces of revolution which might lead to general catastrophe. It was expedient to accept at their face

---

* Cf. R. C. K. Ensor's discussion of the attitude of the Conservatives after the 1906 election. "In the light of post-war democracy no student can avoid asking, how practical men like Balfour and Lansdowne . . . could be so short sighted. The psychology of it was that both were aristocrats . . . passionately devoted to the greatness of England, these men were convinced that she owed it to patrician rule. In their view her nineteenth-century parliamentarianism had worked successfully, because the personnel of parliaments and cabinets was still (with a few much-resented exceptions like Bright) upper-class, and the function of the lower orders was limited to giving the system a popular *imprimatur* by helping to choose which of two aristocratic parties should hold office." (R. C. K. Ensor, *England, 1870-1914*. Oxford University Press, 1936. Page 387.)

value the claims of every government to represent the people of its country because of the practice of challenging such claims would discredit nearly every government.

Traditional diplomacy is also defended with arguments that international disputes can be settled more easily if publicity and ideological issues are avoided. Secret diplomacy, it is claimed, can reach peaceful compromises which would be° impossible if popular feelings became roused or if practical problems became entangled with questions of principle. And these arguments have some real force even though they could also be rationalisations for the Marxian explanation.

However, whatever its origins and whatever its advantages in the past, traditional diplomacy does not make sense in the modern world. Even if it were true that foreign policy was better managed when the public was content to entrust its conduct to experts and leave them a free hand, this is no longer a possible alternative. People in democratic countries realise that their fate depends on the handling of international relations and consider that they have a right to be informed and to discuss the policies of their governments. A democratic government which does not take the trouble to ensure support from an informed public opinion will soon find its freedom of action restricted by the influence of an uninformed public opinion. Even if it were true that peaceful compromises could be reached more easily if all governments accepted a convention to avoid psychological warfare against one another, this convention is one which totalitarian governments do not observe and are not likely to observe. It may well have been easier to maintain peace when the great powers quarrelled over conflicts of interest rather than over differences in ideology, but it is no use trying to evade the fact that most major disputes in the modern world have a large ideological component.

But though the tradition no longer makes sense many of the people responsible for the handling of international affairs still have a deep attachment to it. And attachment to precedents and conventional forms of behaviour can be an extremely powerful motivation. During the war there were many instances of officials and officers behaving in a way which showed that they attached greater importance to conventional correctness than to doing what was most likely to promote victory. For example, in 1940 the official in charge of the British Embassy at Shanghai refused to have official relations with the local leader of the Free French movement on the ground that he was the representative of a rebel government.* And any study of accounts of war experiences will show numerous cases in which the action necessary for effective conduct of the war was obstructed by officials or officers with a horror of anything unconventional. (Sir Winston Churchill's *Second World War* gives many examples which indicate that an important part of his qualifications as war leader was a refusal to tolerate this preference for conventional defeat over unconventional victory.)

In the post-war period a hypothesis which would explain some important aspects of British policy is that the Foreign Office has seldom thought in terms of the question "What course of action is most likely to produce the results we desire?" but has more often thought in terms of the question "How far can the results we desire be attained without doing anything unconventional?"

The attachment to conventional diplomatic correctness was an important contributory cause of the American failure in China. The U.S. government repeatedly failed to use its real power to secure its objectives. For example, General Hsueh Yo was one of the ablest commanders in the National Army and held a front which defended some of the most important American air bases against the Japanese offensive of 1944. But, according to General Chennault, he received no supplies between May, 1944, and the end of February, 1945, because he was not on good terms with the dominant clique in Chungking.[2] The Americans preferred to lose their bases rather than to act against diplomatic convention by over-ruling the men in the Chinese government who were using American supplies for their political intrigues rather than the common war effort. A similar episode occurred in 1948 over supplies to General Fu Tso-yi. These examples involve a very simple technical issue. It is not controversial that supplies should be given to the most competent commanders in the most important sections of the front. But the same inhibition was important in the failure of the U.S. government to attain its more controversial political objectives. (For a discussion of this see an article by the author, *Post-mortem on American Mediation in China* in the *International Journal*. Summer, 1947.)

This article produced an interesting illustration of a similar

---

* I was able to confirm this in 1949 from a conversation with M. Egal's son.

attitude in Australia. It contained a passage saying "The moral of all this is obvious. Assistance to a country where there is a violent political struggle must be, in effect, assistance to the group that controls the recognised government so long as the forms of non-intervention and diplomatic correctness are preserved. There is no choice between supporting this group and discontinuing all assistance." The conclusion drawn from this was that, in the modern world, a government which wishes to attain its objectives must be prepared to abandon traditional diplomatic correctness. An Australian with a distinguished diplomatic career to whom the article was shown underlined this passage but drew the opposite conclusion, that the U.S. government could not have acted more effectively in China because this would have involved departing from traditional diplomatic correctness.

This attachment to tradition is very important in producing a pessimistic and defeatist attitude among people responsible for Western foreign policy. Instead of the new situation being taken as providing opportunities for trying new strategies it is resented as an obstacle hampering the continued use of old strategies. Thus, a government which could base its foreign policy on support from an informed public opinion would be in an extremely strong position. And the increasing public interest in international affairs provides an opportunity for creating an informed public opinion. To exploit this opportunity would need some initiative, imagination and courage. It might be necessary to form some special organisation which would collect all the information that it was not genuinely essential to restrict for reasons of security and would present it in ways that would be intelligible to the ordinary citizen interested in international affairs but without a background of expert knowledge. This would involve some expenditure and would involve a struggle both against officials who like to operate with the greatest possible secrecy and against the people who want democratic countries to follow totalitarian propaganda techniques—to give the public, not accurate information, but a distorted picture of the world in black and white calculated to make them believe what their rulers consider expedient. However, the advantages of an informed public opinion would almost certainly be far greater than the costs required to produce it.

In fact the reaction of many Western governments to public

desire for information is one of scarcely disguised annoyance. They seem to show by many of their actions and statements that their ideal is the totalitarian situation in which the people have "learned to obey their rulers" (to use Mr. Vyshinski's phrase) and are content with whatever information their rulers choose to give them. An informed public opinion would be largely immune to orthodox Communist propaganda because people would see for themselves the contradictions and false-hoods on which most of it is based. But Communist attempts to influence public opinion, as through the Communist inspired peace campaign, are met with obstruction and attempts at repression and very seldom with competition or public challenge to indefensible Communist claims. (It is interesting that in the published accounts of Communist inspired peace conferences or interviews at which Communist leaders proclaim their good intentions to visitors from democratic countries one never finds a case in which the non-Communist representatives have been sufficiently well briefed to ask the obvious questions which would challenge Communist "doublethink" positions. For a government which was interested in presenting an accurate picture to its own public or in obtaining evidence about Communist intentions such briefing would be an obvious step.)

Again, the whole field of psychological warfare is very largely unexplored by the democratic powers. In cases where some country has come under the control of an irrational or fanatical minority psychological warfare may be the only possible alternative to actual warfare. (It might have prevented both World Wars.) The diversion into psychological warfare of a few per cent of the effort and money now devoted to rearmament would almost certainly prove an extremely good investment for any democratic country. But the attitude of many people responsible for Western foreign policy is to look on psychological warfare as an unsavoury business in which a democratic country should only enter with great reluctance when forced to by totalitarian competition. And psychological warfare conducted by people who do not really believe in it is not likely to be effective. As a result the most effective non-Communist psychological warfare at present is probably that conducted by private organisations such as Radio Free Europe or the Investigating Committee of Free Lawyers (*Untersuchungsausschuss Freiheitlicher Juristen der Sowjetzone*).

The dynamism of totalitarian societies is often contrasted

with the feebleness of democratic societies. In so far as the contrast exists it is largely the result of democratic countries allowing their policies to be determined, not by democratic principles, but by bureaucratic timidity and conservatism. Under the stress of war democratic societies have shown themselves to be more efficient than totalitarian societies, because the stimulus has been sufficient to overcome this timidity and blind conservatism. What is neded to compete with totalitarianism in peace time is not any lessening of democracy but readiness to over-rule the widespread preference among officials and politicians for drifting into war according to traditional rules and precedents rather than keeping out of it by breaking them.

12

One-dimensional politics

PERHAPS the most important inhibition on clear thinking about international problems is the assumption that the only relevant variable is the range from political right to political left. And the assumption is more confusing because it is seldom clearly and explicitly formulated. Consider the implications of Mao Tse-tung's statement "Not only in China but also in the world, without exception, one either leans to the side of imperialism or to the side of socialism. Neutrality is a camouflage and a third road does not exist."[1] It is assumed that an adequate analogy for the world political situation is a model with one dimension, towards imperialism or towards socialism. (The "road" metaphor implies a two-dimensional surface but one dimension of this is time, so that politics is still one-dimensional.) The same type of metaphor with the same implications can be found in numerous statements from both Communists and non-Communists. The extreme anti-Communists would agree with Mao Tse-tung that middle positions are untenable though they would disagree about the right names for the two directions. Others argue that the forces working for peace can be found in some middle range. But the assumption common to all these arguments is that political differences can be adequately described in terms of a one-dimensional analogy.

The same assumption is also expressed without spacial analogies. For example, people argue that Asia is almost certain to become Communist in the long run because there is little chance of solving its social and economic problems except by measures which would include radical land reforms with development of collective farming, state control of industry and so on. The implicit assumption behind such arguments is that a society which adopts some parts of the orthodox Communist programme must adopt the rest. But the interdependence of different parts of the orthodox Communist programme is something which would need to be proved. Some of the measures adopted by orthodox Communist regimes can only be justified in terms of Marx-Leninist theory, others can be justified without any reference whatever to Marx-Leninism. There is nothing obviously impossible about rejecting the former and adopting the latter. It is possible that some Asian societies can only solve their economic and social problems through measures that are considerably more collectivist than the policies of most Western countries. But societies which were Communist in this sense could still be very different from societies organised according to orthodox Marx-Leninism. There is nothing obviously impossible about a largely collectivist society without a highly privileged ruling group maintaining its power by police state methods. For example, Israel provides practical illustrations of collective farming on a democratic and equalitarian basis. The difficulty some people find in admitting such possible differences comes from the assumption that the differences between different types of society must depend on a single variable—towards individualism or towards collectivism.

By giving up the assumption of one-dimensional politics it becomes possible to give a much more satisfactory description of the situation. Variation in the range towards individualism or towards collectivism is different from variation in the range of more or less democracy. How far the two variables are actually related in existing human societies is a highly controversial question. The Marxian analysis claims that modern societies can only move towards greater democracy by moving very far towards collectivism and that a society which tries to retain individualist economic organisation must lose democracy through the development of monopoly capitalism. Economists such as Mises, Hayek or Colin Clark claim that democracy is only possible with individualist economic organisation and that a move towards collectivism must involve degeneration into totalitarianism. Each analysis makes out quite a strong case on the dangers to democracy involved in the type of economic organisation which it opposes but almost completely ignores the dangers involved in the type of economic organisation which it favours. And both analyses may be partially correct. There is nothing impossible about loss of democracy being caused by different forms of social development. The weakness of both analyses lies in the same implicit assumption restricting the number of variables in terms of which the problem is considered. It is assumed that if people realise that socialism may involve dangers to democracy their only possible course of action is to move towards capitalism, and vice versa, because capitalism and collectivism are systems within which no important variation is possible. The inevitability implied by either analysis disappears in a theory which is prepared to consider at least three dimensions, towards individualism or towards collectivism, towards more or less democracy, and towards different forms of capitalism or socialism. The world implied by such a theory is not one in which anything is possible but it does offer more alternative possibilities, especially if it is admitted that the realisation of various social objectives in different types of society may be more or less difficult and not simply possible or impossible. In terms of such a general view both socialist and capitalist societies may face difficulties in moving towards greater democracy. It is possible that, for a given society, any progress in this direction must involve some change in the individualist-collectivist dimension and that progress will be easiest at some particular position. But this does not rule out the possibility that widely different positions in the individualist-collectivist dimension may be compatible with the same degree of democracy.

To put it in more concrete terms: there is a very strong case for believing that both socialism, as understood by Stalin, and capitalism, as understood by Herbert Hoover, impose fairly low though necessarily equal limits on development towards democracy. It is also fairly clear that these are not the only possible forms of socialism and capitalism and that suitable modifications in either would make more democracy possible, and the boundary between socialism and capitalism may not be equally sharp in all their forms. The question of whether the difficulties in the way of attaining democratic socialism are greater or less than the difficulties in attaining democratic capitalism is an important practical problem which can only really be decided by experiment. And, in the present state of knowledge, reasonable men may honestly hold differing views about the point in the individualist-collectivist dimension at which progress towards greater democracy is least difficult.

The important implication of one-dimensional politics which is continually drawn by those who see the world in this way is that the only political decision an individual can make is to choose sides. Having once chosen a side the individual is then bound to accept its policies whatever they may happen to be and has no right to use any further discrimination. Any disagreement with the policies of one side can only imply a movement towards the other side and is, therefore, an act of treachery.

For example, Communist publicity will never allow the possibility of disagreements within Communism. Those Communists who disagree with the orthodox view are almost always presented as deviating towards capitalism. The extreme anti-Communists make an exactly similar claim that those who disagree with them are deviating towards Communism. In both cases the claim is entirely logical on the assumption that politics is one-dimensional.

This view that everyone must choose a side and then un-critically accept its leadership is often reinforced by considerations based on the irrationalism which forms part of totalitarian philosophies. And the issue involved is so important for practical problems of international co-operation that it demands at least a short discussion here.

If it is assumed that there is some sort of objective real world about which human minds can obtain some sort of true knowledge by thinking, observation and experiment then it follows that people who share some common general aim can co-operate while retaining freedom of judgment, because they will tend to agree about what is the right thing to do to attain this aim. This does not imply that anarchism would be a workable system. There must be some authority or some accepted convention, such as majority rule, to decide which course of action to follow in the many cases where the available evidence is not sufficient to show clearly which of several possible courses of action would be the best. And where rapid and decisive action is important, as in military operations, a great deal of subordination to authority may be necessary. But rational independent judgment would recognise this necessity for authority and the acceptance of authority will never be unqualified. In the last resort there will always be the right to defy authority if authority tries to prescribe action clearly incompatible with the objective for which people are co-operating.* Mr. R. H. Tawney once said "England has always been saved by its traitors", that is by the people who have been prepared to take a stand for what they believed to be right even when this involved being denounced as traitors to their country or to their class. And societies which do not produce such traitors are likely to become involved in fatal mistakes.

* The plot of Herman Wouk's *The Caine Mutiny* turns on paragraph 184 of the U.S. Naval Regulations which officially recognises this right. It would be interesting to know if the corresponding regulations of totalitarian states have similar paragraphs.

On the other hand, in terms of a philosophy which rejects objectivity the exercise of independent individual judgment will be incompatible with co-operation. It will be meaningless to talk of "the right thing to do" as an objective concept about which people will tend to agree in so far as they use rational judgment. People will only agree if they start with the same class status, racial origin or whatever other factor is accepted as the determinant of human thought. This means that human action can only be co-ordinated by the acceptance of authority and no standards exist in terms of which it would be possible to criticize the decisions of this authority. In practice totalitarians are not consistently irrationalist and recognise that in some fields, especially technical fields, people can co-operate without the uncritical acceptance of authority. But their general view that highly authoritarian organisation is essential for effective action and their distrust of all discussion and criticism above the purely technical level are logical consequences of their basic beliefs.

All this is trying to compress into a few hundred words the discussion of a subject which would really need a complete book. I have made the attempt because the confusion caused by trying to consider political problems in terms of too few variables and by accepting the totalitarian theory of co-operation almost certainly exerts an important influence on both Communist and non-Communist policies.

The real world

Giving up the assumptions of one-dimensional politics, it is fairly clear that the division between influences working for and against peace cuts right across the division between political right and political left. Fanaticism and irrationality can be found on both sides of the division between Communist and non-Communist, even though the distribution is uneven. And the Stalinist left and the extreme anti-Communist right are very largely in agreement over many of the main issues relevant to world peace.

On basic philosophical assumptions, both reject objectivity and maintain more or less explicitly that truth, or justice, is that which serves the interest of one side. And any form of these beliefs, if consistently maintained, must make peaceful settlement of any dispute almost impossible.

215

Both want the same general type of social structure—strongly authoritarian, with the dominant minority enjoying a high degree of power and privilege, and with social stability secured by the inculcation of an official ideology and the suppression or criticism and discussion. And this is a type of social structure which is almost always dangerous for world peace. A totalitarian state under peace loving leadership may not be theoretically impossible but it is very unlikely to be stable. The institutions of totalitarian society favour the rise to power of unscrupulous intriguers and fanatical megalomaniacs. Even within a single generation of leadership the corrupting effects of arbitrary power are likely to weaken any original desire for peace. A totalitarian ruling group which maintains its power by rousing hatred against other nations or by alleging the danger of foreign attack is especially dangerous because it will acquire a strong vested interest in the continuance of international tension and is very likely to come to believe its own propaganda.

An amusing illustration of the similarity between the extreme right and the extreme left was a controversy in the Australian Communist press which showed that Communist sympathizers could not distinguish whether the imaginary totalitarian state depicted in Menotti's opera *The Consul* was Fascist or Communist. On the one hand it was denounced as "dirty American hate propaganda against the countries of socialism"; on the other hand it was defended on the grounds that "there is far more to show in that striking work that Menotti's attacks were against Fascism and Nazism."[2]

In the case of Germany these similarities exerted a real power of attraction and made important elements in the German army leadership pro-Soviet. "But Russia also provided the example of a unitary political party which educated the masses in discipline and stimulated their military zeal. It is true enough that Schleicher, Blomberg, Haase and the other generals who went to Russia had little use for Bolshevik ideology. Yet Blomberg once admitted in a conversation with Rauschning that the example of mass discipline which he had got to know in Russia had nearly made a Bolshevik out of him and had certainly turned him into a National Socialist."[3] The similarities were also commented on by German visitors to Russia in the period of the Nazi-Soviet Pact and, at lower levels, there were considerable interchanges of membership between the Communist and National Socialist Parties.

216

In America the extreme right has been anti-Soviet but what its representatives denounce as "communism" has often very little relation to the practices of contemporary Communist ruled societies. For example, General MacArthur (in a speech before the Mississippi Legislature on 23 March, 1952) declared that "American fiscal policy is being brought into line with the Karl Marx Communist theory . . ." because it was trying to reduce inequality of wealth and incomes. This would have made some sense in the early 1920's but when the speech was made the inequality in real incomes was probably at least as great in the U.S.S.R. as in the U.S.A. (While General MacArthur's pay as General of the Army was fifteen times that of an American private, the pay of a Soviet Marshal was 114 times that of a Soviet private.) If United States-Soviet relations ever improve to a point which makes more direct acquaintance possible it is quite likely that the next crop of Fellow Travellers in America will come from the extreme right. The Fellow Travellers of the 1930's were attracted by an earlier Soviet society which, though they failed to realise it, was already disappearing. The Texas millionaires who now support Senator McCarthy, if they knew anything about existing Soviet society, would find much in it to attract them—great opportunities for anyone with energy, ambition and lack of scruples to get to the top; no interference with management by independent trade unions; no Bill of Rights or independent judiciary to restrict the operations of Senator McCarthy's opposite numbers; and so on.*

The similarities between the Stalinist left and the extreme anti-Communist right do not imply that the struggle between them is an unreal one. There have been a number of cases

* Compare George Orwell's analysis of the pro-Soviet group in England in his essay on James Burnham. "If one examines the people who, having some idea of what the Russian regime is like, are strongly Russophile, one finds that, on the whole, they belong to the 'managerial' class of which Burnham writes . . . middling people who feel themselves cramped by a system that is still partly aristocratic, and are hungry for more power and more prestige. These people look towards the U.S.S.R. and see in it, or think they see, a system which eliminates the upper class, keeps the working class in its place, and hands unlimited power to people very similar to themselves. It was only *after* the Soviet regime become unmistakably totalitarian the English intellectuals, in large numbers, began to show an interest in it. Burnham, though the English Russophile intelligentsia would repudiate him, is really voicing their secret wish: the wish to destroy the old, equalitarian version of socialism and usher in a heirarchical society where the intellectual can at last get his hands on the whip." (George Orwell, *Shooting an Elephant and Other Essays*. Secker & Warburg, London, 1950. Page 160.)

of definite co-operation between the two extremes,* but all these cases can be explained as the result of pure expediency through which each party expected to get the better of the other when the temporary co-operation was over. The real question which is raised by these similarities is this "What are they fighting about?" The answer is fairly obvious. The Stalinist left and the extreme anti-Communist right are fighting about the qualifications for belonging to the privileged group and about the type of ideology which this privileged group should enforce. Both agree that there should be a high concentration of power and real income in the hands of a small privileged group and that society should enforce an official ideology and not allow it to be discussed or criticized. And it is this agreement which makes the struggle so bitter because it implies that a defeated group can expect no mercy from its opponents. However, for people who prefer a society without sharp class distinctions and who hold the scientific view about the nature of human knowledge, the points of agreement are more important than the points of disagreement. The points of disagreement are of secondary interest because they presuppose the destruction of free and democratic society and the suppression of its supporters. (It could be argued that Buchenwald, as described by Eugen Kogon[4] was slightly more unpleasant than Kargopol, as described by Gustav Herling.[5] But the distinctions are of very minor importance to anyone who prefers a society in which he can express his opinions and work for what he believes to be just without the risk of ending in a concentration camp.)

This means that anyone who wishes to defend peace, freedom or democracy cannot operate effectively in terms of one-dimensional politics. Anyone who ignores the dangers of Stalinism in order to concentrate on fighting the dangers of McCarthyism, or vice versa, is bound to become involved in a situation which can be described by the Chinese proverb "Front

* For example, there has been recurrent co-operation between Communists and Nazis; in 1931-2 against the Social Democrats, in 1939-41 in the Nazi-Soviet Pact, and more recently in Communist support for the neo-Nazi movement in West Germany. In America the right-wing Republicans co-operated with the American Communist Party to oppose Roosevelt in the 1940 elections. (Robert E. Sherwood. *The White House Papers of Harry I. Hopkins.* Eyre & Spottiswoode, London, 1948. Vol I, Pp. 193-4.) And at present Communists support right-wing police states in Argentina, Peru and Venezuela. (See articles by Victor Alba and Robert J. Alexander in *The New Leader* of 21 September, 1953, and 14 December, 1953.)

door out tiger, back door in wolf." (*Ch'ien men ch'u hu, hou men chin lang.*)

In so far as actual power is in the hands of the extreme right and the extreme left the world situation is similar to that of China in the warlord period. At one time almost all effective power in China was in the hands of warlords and it was possible for people to argue that the only practicable choice in Chinese politics was to choose which warlord to support. Distinctions could be drawn between different warlords. Wu P'ei-fu offered warlordism combined with social conservatism, Feng Yü-hsiang offered a combination of warlordism with social revolution, Chang Tso-lin offered a combination of warlordism with railway building and industrialisation; the comparatively respectable warlords could be distinguished from the pure gangster types like Chang Tsung-chang, and so on. But any form of warlordism was incompatible with the development of China into a state capable of acting effectively for either nationalism or social reform. People working for nationalist or social objectives faced a very complicated problem. On the one hand they had to take account of actual warlord power. It was impossible to get results without some co-operation with warlords; and limited co-operation was possible because some warlords had some genuine patriotism. On the other hand, anyone who became too deeply involved in warlord politics would find that, instead of inducing some warlords to co-operate in a programme which involved the destruction of warlordism, their patriotic or social enthusiasm was being used as an instrument of some warlord's ambitions.

Similarly, in world politics it is necessary to take account of the power-politics situation. People working for peace and democracy who set too rigorous standards for co-operation and refuse to participate in power politics thereby condemn themselves to ineffectiveness. Actual power is in the hands of governments and political parties which all include some groups primarily concerned with power, either for its own sake or for their personal advantage; and to get things done it is necessary to co-operate with such people. On the other hand people who become too deeply involved in power politics are likely to find themselves acting in ways directly contrary to their basic objectives.

The situation can be described in terms of the "road" analogy, provided its two dimensions are both used for politics (as against the "road" analogy which uses one dimension for time). It will normally be true that we are restricted to a limited choice of roads, in the sense of the policies of existing organisations with power, and that progress in any direction will become much more difficult if we try to go off a road. It will also normally be true, if we are interested in some definite objective such as peace, that no road will lead in the exact direction we want to go. We will have to choose the road we consider most likely to lead towards our objective, and to make the choice without a reliable map and with signposts that are often deliberately misleading. We may find that the road we have chosen starts to turn away from our objective and we will then face a difficult choice as to whether to continue along it in the hope that it will curve back, or whether to retrace our steps or try a difficult short-cut across country.

The analogy cannot be carried too far because it is only in the short run that the roads are determinate. We can exert some influence on the policies of organisations to which we belong, which would imply that by travelling along a road we can do something to make it curve in the direction we want, though it may often be true that the natural features of the country which we cannot alter greatly limit the possible changes in direction. Nevertheless, the analogy does illustrate some of the important features of political choice. People continually face problems analogous to the problem of whether or not to continue along a road when they begin to suspect that they have made a mistake about where it will lead. That is, how far should they continue to work with an organisation when its policies seem to be leading away from the objective for which they originally supported it. The simple idealist views, such as pure pacifism, are analogous to proposals to take a straight line towards an objective ignoring the difficulties of moving off a road and the possibility of meeting insuperable natural obstacles on the direct course. The attitude of people with doctrinaire beliefs is analogous to an uncritical faith in maps and signposts. The Communists say in effect "We know from the maps prepared by Marx and Lenin and from the signposts put up by Stalin that the road of the Soviet Union must lead to peace and democracy even if it sometimes makes detours which take it directly away from these objectives. We know from our maps that other roads which may seem better are actually dead ends." Finally, the real complications of political choice correspond to a situation in which our range of vision is limited and in which any maps can only be based on speculations about the way in which the imperfectly known features of the country we have already traversed will continue into completely unexplored country. Even in unexplored country with limited visibility someone who observes the countryside and tries to work out the best route and who is ready to admit if necessary that what seemed a promising route has actually turned out to be a mistake is more likely to make progress than someone who tries to go blindly across country or someone who blindly follows a map even after he has found that it is not accurate. But though this is the most effective way of reaching our objective it will involve the continual use of judgment and decision. And a further point where the analogy applies to the real world is that people who are faced with an urgent necessity for making progress under such conditions are liable to panic and to walk in circles or behave in other ways that actually lessen their chances of reaching their objective.

13

Psychological influences

THERE is abundant empirical evidence that psychological discomfort is produced by a situation in which it is necessary to make a decision but extremely hard to make a rational choice between different possibilities. And this discomfort can explain the powerful attractions of some one-dimensional view of politics in which only one decision is really fundamental and all others basically technical. There is also abundant evidence that frustration and disappointment of expectations can produce definite mental illness.

Some interesting work has been done on the reaction of animals to this type of situation. In one set of experiments rats were made to jump from a small platform towards two doors. Each door could either be firmly shut causing the rat to fall to the ground or else could be left loose so that it would fall open and normally reveal food behind it. In a situation which followed simple definite rules, those rats soon learned to behave rationally. The rats would always jump towards the door with the marking or the position which indicated that it would fall open and lead to food. They could even learn to adjust themselves to a change in the rules. But if rats so trained experienced a period in which no rules applied, in which the right side or the right marking was continually changed at random, they soon developed symptoms of mental illness. The actual situation was no worse than that which they had experienced at the beginning of the experiment when they had no means of knowing that there were any rules according to which they could make a successful choice but their reaction was very different. They were far more reluctant to choose and could often only be induced to jump by the stimulus of electric shocks if they refused. In many cases they developed a stereotyped response and always jumped towards one particular side or one particular marking without ever trying the other alternative and would continue to do so even when the other door was left open with food visible behind it. It was only after a long period of retraining that such rats could be restored to

222

the rational type of behaviour they had shown at the beginning of the experiment.

Though analogies between animal and human behaviour must be treated with caution there are obvious similarities between the behaviour of Maier's rats and certain types of human behaviour. It is notorious that people become demoralised in a situation in which the rules according to which they have been conducting their lives have become incapable of dealing with the problems which they face, unless they are able to discover and adjust themselves to some new system of rules which do work in the new situation. And in such human situations there is often the extreme dislike of making any choice and completely irrational obsessive behaviour. The officials and politicians in Western countries who produce every possible excuse for postponing or evading action even when it is obvious that postponement or evasion only makes the situation still more difficult are behaving very like the rats which refused to jump unless compelled to by electric shocks. The Communist leaders who persist in threats and abusive denunciations even in situations where it is obvious that they are much more likely to get what they want by a little reasonableness and good manners are behaving like the rats which continued to jump at the closed door even when they could see that the other door was open with food behind it.

Of course human behaviour is more complex than that of rats. All the same an important factor in complicating the difficulties of the international situation is the tendency of people to take refuge in irrational obsessions or an equally irrational scepticism when faced with problems which they do not feel capable of solving. And such reactions show a marked positive feed-back effect by making all problems still more difficult to solve.

David Hume some two centuries ago gave a very good description of the people with whom rational discussion is impossible. "Disputes with men pertinaciously obstinate in their principles, are, of all others, the most irksome; except, perhaps, those with persons entirely disingenuous, who really do not believe the opinion they defend, but engage in the controversy from affectation, from a spirit of opposition, or from a desire of showing wit and ingenuity superior to the rest of mankind. The same blind adherence to their own arguments is to be found in both; the same contempt of their antagonists; and the same passionate vehemence in enforcing sophistry and falsehood. And as reasoning is not the source whence either disputant derives his tenets, it is vain to expect that any logic, which speaks not to the affections, will ever engage him to embrace sounder principles."[2] If one group whose co-operation is essential for the solution of some urgent problem has become demoralised and can contribute nothing but "passionate vehemence in enforcing sophistry and falsehood" then the rest of the community face a vastly more difficult problem and are likely to become demoralised in their turn. (As will be argued below we have not yet developed a "logic which speaks to the affections", that is, a psychological technique for curing mental illness with political symptoms.) When the demoralization has become general and the community has become polarized in groups with obsessive reactions, usually of hatred, all social problems have become almost insoluble. There are many cases which illustrate this feed-back process through which demoralization in one party or one country induces demoralization in others and ends by producing a situation in which every group has lost the power of rational response. The development of relations between the United States government and the Chinese Communist Party is quite a good illustration of this feed-back process.

Different groups vary considerably in the point at which they lose their nerve and become demoralized and incapable of rational behaviour, but the difference is one of degree. G. F. Kennan was almost certainly right in saying that "Totalitarianism is not a national phenomenon; it is a disease to which all humanity is in some degree vulnerable . . ."[3*]

If we accept this kind of disastrous feed-back process as something inevitable and unchangeable there is obviously nothing we can do about it. But it is equally futile to ignore the problem, because we cannot take steps to deal with a danger if we refuse to recognise its existence. We cannot take rational

* It is possible to analyse some of the factors which make some national groups more vulnerable than others. For example, Trevor-Roper (in the Epilogue to his The Last Days of Hitler) suggests that political failure tends to be self-perpetuating and explains the rise to power of the Nazis in terms of the historical tradition which had made most Germans regard politics as an insoluble mystery and concentrate their rational intelligence on industrial or military problems. Others have explained Japanese developments in terms of the educational system which subjected male children to the shock of sudden transition from being badly spoilt to severe discipline; and so on. There is no reason to reject such theories because they do not give a complete explanation. In the corresponding case of vulnerability to physical illness several independent factors such as heredity, nutrition, etc., all play a part.

action to deal with the world political situation unless our nerves are strong enough to face the possibility that some countries may be "experimenting in government by the insane." (This phrase was used to describe the pre-war Axis powers and there is a great deal of evidence to show that it was apposite. But it may still be a correct description for some countries.)

Many people are reluctant to admit the importance of psychological influences in world politics, sometimes because they feel that such an admission would make the situation too frightening to contemplate and sometimes for the better reason that explanations in terms of psychology often belong to the pseudo-science which dismisses a problem by classifying it without giving any theory capable of yielding verifiable predictions. But, in the present world, the evidence for the importance of mental illness as a factor in politics is too strong to ignore. A recent article by an American psychologist discussing the probable American reaction to atomic warfare[4] declares that ". . . our public is already exhibiting on a massive scale a vast variety of 'symptoms' which, in clinical psychology, are known to be the results of deeply repressed fear, and these symptoms, classical in nature, are called 'hysterias'." He instances the widespread belief in "flying saucers" as vehicles in which "higher beings", who have become aware of atomic experiments, are coming to rescue humanity from itself, and the hysterical blindness which has made many people fail to see the air raid shelter signs in their own city though they would talk about the air raid shelter signs in other cities as evidence of "atomic jitters". "The mechanism which substitutes for a fear repressed as unbearable, a target for aggression, a 'whipping boy', is equally noticeable today." He points out that the elimination of Communist agents from government service is, in itself, a desirable objective. But even if all Communists in America were eliminated it would do very little to reduce the real danger from Communist-ruled states possessing atomic weapons. And the means employed and recommended to deal with the minor problem of Communists in America "degrade America before the world as the chief protagonist of liberty, outrage the sovereignty and freedom of our allies, and throw suspicion and fear in the hearts of all true American patriots. Such dire and immensely stupid results are exactly those toward which the Soviet propaganda machine has been striving for decades!" "To feel that the whole 'fight' against communism is the *relatively minor* and *wholly local* problem of 'spies' is to be very hysterical indeed. But the emotion does serve to drain away a gigantic amount of hysterical energy in a seemingly effective effort— which actually merely *deludes* millions. Because it is a kind of unreason and not a logical or systematic phenomenon, I suggest the name 'McCarthyism' be withdrawn and a suitable, pathological term be used such as 'McCarthy-itis'.

"Closely associated with McCarthy-itis is an allied manifestation common among hysterics and typical of those truly insane persons who suffer from paranoia. To maintain an unreal expression of a real fear that has been repressed requires the individual to establish a false sense of *reality itself* . . . Wherever it is necessary to defend one's false position, principle and truth must either be sacrificed or warped to match the obsessive escape concept. This leads to rigidity of the personality. It causes an absolute antagonism to controversial or disagreeing opinion . . . Among the sufferers of McCarthy-itis, needless to say, those pathological symptoms are constantly exhibited . . . Neither ill-will nor deliberate bad citizenship motivates them; but only the automatic pattern of a mental sickness."[*]

While a repressed fear of atomic warfare may be the main source of political hysteria in present day America it is certainly not the only possible source of political hysteria. Even more marked symptoms of hysteria have existed for much longer in the Soviet Union. As far back as 1927 there was a violent war scare. Louis Fischer reporting this states "But no one who lived in Russia at the time will be shaken in his conviction that the majority of Bolsheviks were thoroughly and sincerely frightened by the prospect of immediate hostilities."[5] Though this fear proved to be unfounded, within a few years conspiracy delusions had become much stronger than in present day America. No doubt there were some real conspiracies and some real foreign

---

[*] The diagnosis of widespread hysteria in America was confirmed by Dr. Charles W. Mayo. (*The Superpatriot—Menace to American Freedom. The New Leader.* 24 May, 1954.)

Good illustrations of the tendency to delusions of conspiracy can be found in recent issues of *The American Mercury.* For example, an editorial by Russell Maguire in the issue of February, 1954, includes the following as alleged conspiracies against the United States: "The United Nations with its sinister plan to ensnare and destroy the United States" and the "two diabolical instruments, the Geneva Genocide Covenant and the Covenant of Human Rights"; "the Nürnberg trials, which gained us the hatred of the Germans"; "the graduated income tax to weaken us so that our people would depend upon an ever-growing Government bureaucracy"; and "the campaign to condition and sell us the unsound Keynesian theory of manipulated currency."

agents engaged in espionage or sabotage, just as there have been some real Soviet agents in the American government organisation. But the actual allegations of conspiracy had an even larger element of delusion than current McCarthy-itis in America. The Ramzin case of 1930, in which the defendants were convicted for conspiring with Russian émigrés who had actually been dead for several years before the alleged contacts, would be hard to match outside the allegations of the completely lunatic fringe in American politics.* And the great purges of 1937 showed a degree of hysteria which could only be matched in the West in some of the local witchcraft scares several centuries earlier.† The present mental climate of the Soviet Union seems less hysterical than in 1937 but there is little reason to suppose that delusions of conspiracy have become unimportant.

American policy in China gave the Chinese Communist Party a perfectly real basis for suspicion of American intentions. But even in 1949 the Chinese Communist attitude towards America had a strong element of hysterical exaggeration in it and the later allegations that almost all Americans for the past century have been plotting against China show a degree of delusion coming near definite persecution mania.

Again, the "absolute antagonism to controversial or disagreeing opinion" is a very marked feature of the mental climate of Communism.‡ And there are many examples of hysterical

* There are people who defend the hysteria in either case with the argument that some real dangers were exposed. The reply to this argument was excellently stated by Mr. Elmer Davies: "Archbishop Richard J. Cushing of Boston has said that 'despite any extremes, or mistakes that might have been made, I don't believe anything has brought the evils and methods of Communism more to the attention of the American people than his (McCarthy's) investigations.' This amounts to saying that nothing brings the danger of fire more to the attention of the public than turning in false alarms all over town." (From review in *The New Leader* of 1 March, 1954, of *But We Were Born Free*. By Elmer Davies. Bobbs Merrill. New York. 1954.)

† There is some controversy as to how far the top Soviet leadership really believed its own allegations of conspiracy. Weissberg, who had fairly good opportunities for observation, considered that the conspiracy charges were a deliberate manoeuvre by Stalin to eliminate all potential opposition to his absolute power. (Alex Weissberg. *The Conspiracy of Silence*. Hamish Hamilton. London. 1952.) But this would only show that Stalin's mental illness took the form of delusions of omnipotence rather than delusions of conspiracy. And at any rate the conspiracy charges were believed by many Communists.

‡ A good illustration was the argument, used by the management of the Britain-China Friendship Association, that it would have been insulting to expect the Chinese "friendship" delegation to join in any discussions where their views might be criticized. (See page 16.)

blindness to any evidence incompatible with Communist claims. To give an example from my personal experience. In 1949 a Chinese Communist representative at Hongkong argued that the Communist authorities were showing their genuine goodwill to England by allowing British ships the special privilege of entering Chinese ports while flying the British flag. He had only to look at Hongkong harbour to see that it was the normal practice for ships of all countries to enter foreign ports flying their national flags. And the man concerned was one of the more reasonable and mentally balanced members of the Chinese Communist Party. For Russia, official Soviet publications provide many illustrations of refusal to admit unwelcome evidence.*

What causes hysteria?

It is possible to give fairly satisfactory hypotheses to explain the development of political hysteria. In general the repressed fear which causes hysteria has comparatively little relation to any actuarial measure of danger. The danger from atomic warfare is certainly greater for England than for America but the British public does not show hysterical symptoms to anything like the same extent as the American and in either country the actuarial risk of death from atomic warfare is probably smaller than the risk of death from famine or disease which the Chinese peasant has accepted as a normal part of his life. A danger which is accepted as normal and inevitable seems to have little effect in producing hysteria nor does a danger which people feel they understand and can take steps to reduce. In fact, an element of danger reducible by skill is an attraction in many sports. What produces hysteria is a fear which leads to a refusal to face some aspect of empirical reality and this is usually the result of frustration or the disappointment of expectations. People become hysterical in a situation in which they feel that they should act but cannot see how to act, or in which their expectations have failed to materialise and they cannot understand what is happening.

The article quoted above attributes a large part of American hysteria to the policies of the American authorities. "Finally, the

* For example, some Soviet economists got into serious trouble for publishing in technical works figures showing that U.S. production had risen during and after the war. (See article *Economic Thought in the Soviet Union.* By A. Zauberman in *The Review of Economic Studies.* Vol. XVI (3), No. 41. 1949-50. Page 196.)

general population has been subjected, for nearly nine years, to a 'war of nerves' unwittingly waged against it by its own leaders. There has been no coherent plan for atomic information, for public education, or even for presenting simple fact. Secrecy has built up potential psychological catastrophe to a degree so great that secrecy *alone* (in a nation unused to it) explains much of the 'repressed fear' discussed here. *Hysteria and panic arise from the unknown and the misunderstood, the withheld, the hinted, the suspected, the ignored, and from the repressed dread that materialises unexpectedly.*

"In addition to making the average citizen feel he is not allowed to understand atomic weapons—the leaders and spokesmen of the government—along with a multitude of military men —have produced a nine-year torrent of *contradictions*.

"If an enemy had wanted to achieve the utmost in the sabotage of American morale in the Atomic Age, he could have found no better method than to let American 'spokesmen', officials, soldiers, airmen, sailors, and other 'experts' blow their atomically empty tops on T.V., radio, and in the press, for nine shameful years. This amounts to an inadvertent, nationwide use of the psychology lab. method of driving test animals crazy! Yet this is what *has happened!* In addition, Russia has, from time to time, calculatingly augmented the confusion and horror by making reports of its progress at moments psychologically effective—for Russia."

Other aspects of American hysteria, such as the emotionally charged delusions about China policy, can be explained in terms of the disappointment of expectations. American opinion started with quite exaggerated hopes about China.* Starting with these high expectations, most sections of the American public are conscious of having acted with genuine goodwill towards China and find that their expectations have been completely disappointed for reasons which they do not understand or which it would be emotionally disturbing to admit. A flight from reality into mental illness is a natural reaction.

The comparative absence of hysteria in British countries can be

* Compare Churchill's comments at the beginning of 1942. "At Washington I had found the extraordinary significance of China in American minds, even at the top, strangely out of proportion. I was conscious of a standard of values which accorded China almost an equal fighting power with the British Empire, and rated the Chinese armies as a factor to be mentioned in the same breath as the armies of Russia." (Winston Churchill. *The Second World War.* Cassell. London. Vol. IV. Page 119.)

attributed partly to their having started with less definite and less optimistic expectations. The war of 1914-18 did involve a disappointment of general expectations and British opinion became markedly hysterical. But the war of 1939-45 had been expected by large sections of British opinion and, compared with America, opinion was always less optimistic about the post-war world.

The disappointment of expectations may also explain the development of hysteria among Communists. The Bolsheviks of 1917 were men who had devoted their lives to the revolution. They believed in a theory according to which all that was really essential for the transformation of society was a transfer of power and the reorganisation of property relations. At the time this belief was not really a delusion even though it was mistaken because there had been extremely little serious discussion of the problems of running a socialist system. The views on socialist administration which Lenin expressed in *The State and Revolution* were not very different from those held at the time by many other socialists. There was a general assumption among socialists that it would be difficult to overthrow the forces of capitalism but that the running of a socialist system would present no specially difficult problems. Marx had made a few general statements about the organisation of a socialist economy in the *Critique of the Gotha Programme*, but Marxian economists had concentrated on analysing capitalist economy rather than discussing the problems likely to arise in a future socialist economy. Among non-Marxists, even the Webbs who were specially interested in problems of organisation say almost nothing, writing in 1920, about the basic problem of how to replace the automatic regulation of the economic system provided, however imperfectly, by the operation of competitive markets under capitalism.[6] There is, therefore, no need to bring in any psychological influences to explain the failure of the Bolshevik leaders of 1917 to consider problems of which almost the only serious discussion had been in a largely mathematical article by E. Barone on *The Ministry of Production in the Collectivist State* in the *Giornale degli Economisti* in 1908.

However, having seized power, the Bolsheviks found that the organisation of a new society was vastly more complicated than they had expected and presented them with problems for which their theories were useless or positively misleading.[*]

* A good illustration of the complete gulf between theory and practice in the early years of the Soviet system can be found by comparing Krassin's

A rational response to the situation would have involved the rethinking of a good deal of current Marxian theory and would probably have led to something like the position stated in 1935 by Lange: "Clearly the relative merits of Marxian economics and modern 'bourgeois' economics belong to different 'ranges' . . . This difference is connected, of course, with the respective social functions of 'bourgeois' and Marxian economics. The first has to provide a scientific basis for rational measures to be taken in the current administration of the capitalist economy . . . the social function of the latter has been to provide a scientific basis for long term anticipations guiding the rational activity of a revolutionary movement directed against the very institutional foundations of the capitalist system. But in providing a scientific basis for the current administration of the capitalist economy 'bourgeois' economics has developed a theory of equilibrium which can also serve as a basis for the current administration of a socialist economy. It is obvious that Marshallian economics offers more for the current administration of Soviet Russia than Marxian economics does, though the latter is surely the more effective basis for predicting the future of Capitalism."[7] By taking up this sort of position the Bolsheviks could have preserved most of their faith in Marxism while taking full account of the empirical evidence about the difficulties of setting up a satisfactory socialist economy.

However, given their state of mind immediately after the revolution this would have been a difficult response to make. It was psychologically easier to repress the fear that the establishment of socialism might be much more difficult than they had anticipated, and this repression would explain hysterical symptoms. In practice adjustments to reality were made, though it needed the authority of Lenin to secure the acceptance of N.E.P. But, because there was never an adequate revision of theory, the psychological tension remained. After the Kronstadt revolt there was always the glaring contrast between the claims of the Soviet government to represent the masses and to base its power on popular support, and the actual reliance of the Soviet government on the techniques through which dominant minorities are able to suppress and exploit subject populations.

---

glowing account of how "moneyless economy" was supposed to work with the accounts of the complete chaos it actually produced. (For Krassin's lecture, see Sydney and Beatrice Webb. *Soviet Communism*. Longmans. London. 1944. Page 506. For an account of the reality see Maurice Dobb. *Russian Economic Development Since the Revolution*. Routledge. London. 1928. Chapters 4 and 5.)

Delusions of conspiracy and sabotage served to conceal the fear that Marx-Leninist theory did not offer an adequate foundation for the construction of a socialist system.*

In the international field the failure of the revolution in every country outside Russia was another serious disappointment to Bolshevik expectations which must also have produced considerable psychological tension.

I would not claim that this analysis is anything more than a speculative hypothesis to explain the original development of hysteria among Communists.† But there are many aspects of Communist behaviour which are easily explained as symptoms of mental illness and are very hard to explain on any other hypothesis and it is possible to suggest with considerably more confidence a number of processes which could account for the continuance and spread of mental illness.

* A great deal of progress was made in economic planning on a trial and error basis but, as late as 1935, a Soviet economist could discuss the optimum organisation of the brick-making industry in terms which completely ignored transport costs. (A. Leontiev. *Political Economy*. Moscow. 1935. Page 101.) This would seem to show that there had been little progress in any general theory of economic planning. Even in the post-war period Soviet economists seem to have considerable difficulty in developing satisfactory theories within the limits imposed by Marxian orthodoxy. (See articles on *Economic Thought in the Soviet Union* by A. Zauberman in *Review of Economic Studies*. Vol. XVI, Nos. 39-41.) While the Soviet system has produced impressive results in heavy industry and military production its performance in serving the economic interests of the ordinary citizen has been comparatively poor. (See, for example, S. W. Schwarz. *Labor in the Soviet Union*. Praeger. New York. 1951.)

† It is interesting that twenty years ago Palme Dutt, the British Communist theorist, made a slightly similar analysis of Social Democratic parties. (R. Palme Dutt. *Fascism and Social Revolution*. Lawrence. London. 1934.) He attributed the cowardice and ineffectiveness of Social Democratic parties in resisting the growth of fascism to the demoralisation caused by their failure to use opportunities to seize power. And this hypothesis does provide at least a partial explanation for demoralisation among people who accepted the Marxian theory, according to which it was the duty of a working class party to seize power, but who had failed to use opportunities for fear of the responsibilities in which it would have involved them.

The weakness of Palme Dutt's analysis was the assumption that Communist action had been successful. In fact, neither wing of Marxism had made plans for the establishment of a socialist system and this meant that both responses to an opportunity to seize power were failures. While the Social Democratic response may have produced a psychological tension which weakened the courage necessary to meet the external challenge of fascism, the Communist response produced a tension which destroyed the ability to prevent internal degeneration into a system which was much nearer to fascism than to anything which Marx or even Lenin would have recognised as socialism. It could be argued that the basic weakness of socialist parties is still the failure to think out the problems involved in establishing a democratic socialist system.

The strong emotional attachment of many Communists to their system of faith, which implies an equally strong force for the suppression of fears that this faith may be mistaken, offers a continuing explanation for hysteria among Communists. A good illustration of the strength of this faith is its persistence even among Communists in Soviet concentration camps. Herling describes two cases among the men he knew in the Kargopol forced labour camp, one an Old Bolshevik and the other a product of the revolution. "Sadovski despite everything had remained a Communist . . . 'If I ceased to believe in that,' he would often say, 'I would have nothing left to live for.' 'That' meant in practice a deep attachment to the tradition of the 'old guard', chiefly Lenin and Dierzhynski . . . Sadovski was completely in the power of the demon of logical reasoning—all that could be logically proved became automatically just and true for him. Sometimes, in a kind of somnambulistic trance, his own reasoning would lead him to the conclusion that the Great Purges, of which he himself was a victim, were the logical outcome of certain unquestionable dialectic premises of the October Revolution." The other man, Gorcev, had been an examining judge responsible for the torture of suspects and was finally slowly done to death by his fellow prisoners, with the tolerance of the camp authorities, after some of his former victims had discovered him. "But for the Gorcevs the breakdown of their faith in Communism, the only faith which has directed their lives, would mean the loss of the five basic senses, which recognise, define and appraise the surrounding reality. Even imprisonment cannot goad them into breaking their priestly vows, for they treat it as temporary isolation for a breach of monastic discipline, and wait for the day of release with even greater acquiescence and humility in their hearts."[8] For people with this kind of faith in Communism the fear that their Communist doctrine might be wrong would be a fear they would almost certainly repress, which means that contact with an empirical reality which does not fit the implications of Communist theory is almost certain to produce mental illness. And so long as the system of education and indoctrination in Communist ruled states continues to turn out people with such blind uncritical faith in Communism a continuance of widespread mental illness is almost certain.

Again, the zig-zag Party Line is a very good example of the "psychology lab. method of driving test animals crazy". Successful adjustment to a Communist environment depends on close adherence to the pattern of thinking and action prescribed by the official Party Line. But the rules for thinking and acting successfully are subject to sudden changes which it is almost impossible for the ordinary Party member to anticipate. And sudden and arbitrary changes in the rules for successful conduct are just what produced mental illness in Maier's rats.

Yet again, a great deal of Communist publicity seems to be aimed at producing obsessions rather than rational convictions. If one looks, for example, at the series of "movements" sponsored in recent years by the Chinese Communist Party they nearly all seem to be aimed at producing a hysterical response, diverting a vast amount of emotional energy into some relatively minor problem, just as McCarthy-itis diverts emotional energy into the relatively minor problem of Communist agents in America.

Totalitarian techniques

Generalizing further, a great deal of totalitarian action makes sense in terms of psychological theory as designed firstly to produce hysteria and then to stabilize some particular system of hysterical delusions. Towards societies not under totalitarian control, totalitarian propaganda and activity concentrates on producing confusion and frustration by distorted or misleading statements or forms of sabotage. And this tends to produce a reaction which will make people likely to accept totalitarian leadership as an escape from the complexities of a situation which they feel unable to face. A good illustration of a technique apparently designed to produce frustration is the combination of the Communist inspired peace campaign, rousing hopes of peace, with the behaviour of Communist governments, blocking almost every practical move towards peace. And it is interesting that Hitler used a very similar technique. "Hitler summed up his attitude with the words: 'Not a single German for a new war; every German for the defence of the Fatherland' . . . It will at once be seen that it was profoundly difficult to counter the German 'peace offensive'. If Germany's neighbours rejected her advances, they laid themselves open to the charge of sabotaging the peace of Europe by refusing to enter into *bona fide* negotiations for a settlement. If, on the other hand, they accepted the German proposals, they placed themselves in a position of disadvantage in the event of Germany's bad faith, which they more than suspected."[9]

Once totalitarian leadership has been accepted the efforts of totalitarian publicity are concentrated on stabilizing compensatory hysterical delusions into one particular pattern with one particular parent substitute—the Party or the Leader—and one particular target for aggression—the Jews or the Americans, or the Communists. In terms of this hypothesis other features of totalitarian rule such as terrorism, purges and sudden shifts in the Party Line serve a definite function by maintaining the insecurity and frustration without which the original mental illness might gradually diminish.

What is uncertain is how far such totalitarian action is deliberate. Are totalitarian leaders people who are acting with functional rationality for a system of ends in which the "fantasy of total power" plays a dominant part, or is their behaviour determined by the "automatic pattern of a mental sickness"? It is likely that there is no simple answer to this question. How far, for example, is the desire for power in itself a symptom of mental illness and can it exist in an extreme form without other symptoms? Is it not possible that the mentality of totalitarian leaders can only be described in terms of something like Klaus Fuchs's concept of "controlled schizophrenia" with one personality accepting hysterical delusions while another personality uses them? Consider the following passage from a description of intellectual life under Communist rule. "After long acquaintance with his role, a man grows into it so closely that he can no longer differentiate his true self from the self he simulates, so that even the most intimate of individuals speak to each other in Party slogans."[10] We may be dealing with individuals for whom different roles have become something like different personalities and what may be true for one personality may be false for another.

The complexity of totalitarian motivation can be seen very clearly in the system about which we have most information. Hitler was obviously a psychopath, as shown by such symptoms as emotionally charged delusions (on racial questions), megalomania, obsessive attraction to bloodshed and destruction, fits of rage and so on and, towards the end of his career, he lost the power to take account of empirical reality. But it was also true that "Hitler himself, in one sense, was not a Nazi, for the doctrines of Nazism, that great system of teutonic nonsense, were to him only a weapon of politics; 'he criticized and ridiculed the ideology of the S.S.' . . ."[11] At the time when Hitler was carrying on his peace campaign he was explaining to the army leaders his determination to wage war.[12] But even here his success in deceiving Neville Chamberlain or George Lansbury may have depended on his ability to identify himself temporarily with the ideas he sometimes expressed of retiring to a life of culture at Linz. It is also clear that there was a wide variation in motivation within the Nazi leadership. For Göring even anti-Semitism was only a political device which he was prepared to ignore when expedient,[13] while Himmler appeared to take seriously a large part of Nazi doctrine.

Far less information is available about the motivation of Communist leadership. It is certain that there are important differences between Communist motivation and Nazi motivation but there may well be a similar complexity. The question "Was the Communist inspired peace campaign planned as a device to weaken opposition to the spread of Communist power?" is very likely a question which could not be correctly answered by either "yes" or "no".

I have not got the qualifications to answer the questions I have raised here but I would suggest that the psychology of political extremism is a subject of very great practical importance on which comparatively little work has been done.

The Chinese Communist Party

Some evidence to confirm these hypotheses can be obtained from the Chinese Communist Party. In the early 1940's it was noticeable that the people who had a reasonable attitude, markedly different from that of most Western Communists, were people who seemed to treat their Marx-Leninism as a scientific hypothesis and not as a quasi-religious dogma. And people, for whom the empirical disproof of parts of Marx-Leninist theory would not be a blow to their whole system of faith, would obviously be free from the fear which I have suggested may be the origin of hysterical symptoms among Communists.

The existence in the Chinese Communist Party of an abnormal proportion of people with a reasonable scientific attitude can be explained in terms of the history of the Party. Every other Communist Party now in power, with the partial exception of the Yugoslav Communist Party, has changed within a few months from a revolutionary party with no responsibilities for administration to a party in power able to act with comparatively little

236

regard for the actual wishes of the masses because of its control of the apparatus of government. The Chinese Communist Party, on the other hand, had responsibilities for administration of its own areas from 1927 on under conditions which compelled them to take account of the wishes of the masses. Up till 1946 at least, the inhabitants of most Communist areas could exchange Communist administration for Kuomintang or Japanese administration, not by opposing the Communists, but simply by ceasing to give them active support. And the continuous military struggle against much better equipped enemies made any kind of doctrinaire policy disastrous. In the history of the Party as told to Anna Louise Strong at Yenan in 1946 this was officially admitted. "From January 1931 onward, a group now known as the dogmatists gained intermittent control of high party policy. Many of them had studied abroad, especially in Moscow; they could quote Marxist theory in overpowering detail. Their ignorance of China's practical conditions was catastrophic. Under their leadership the Communists finally lost their Kiangsi base."[14] The result was a strong selective influence in favour of the least doctrinaire elements in the Party leadership.

Even at the lower levels of the Party it was noticeable that the scientific attitude towards Marx-Leninism was much more common among people with practical experience in the front line areas. A Communist official, especially in the guerilla areas, could only survive if the local population was prepared to take considerable risks in order to protect him. The doctrinaire type who persisted in believing that his knowledge of Marx-Leninism enabled him to know the interests of the masses better than they did themselves was likely to have a comparatively short expectation of life. The really doctrinaire type of Communist was much more common among those members of the Party who had spent their career at headquarters organisations and the general atmosphere of Yenan was much more doctrinaire than that of Shansi-Chahar-Hopei. This discouragement of dogmatism by the environment was reinforced, in the period from 1937 to 1946, by the reformist policies to which the Party was committed by its acceptance of the united front. This eliminated the psychological tension produced by an attempt to deal with empirical reality in terms of policies based on theories whose implications were incompatible with empirical evidence. The Party was able to a large extent to give the peasants what they actually wanted and not simply what Marx-Leninist theory said they ought to want and could accept such obvious empirical distinctions as that between good and bad landlords instead of a rigid classification by class status.

There are, therefore, influences which can explain the exceptional position of the Chinese Communist Party in the period from 1937 to 1946. And it is also possible to suggest reasons for the spread of hysterical symptoms since that time.

To begin with the more scientific attitude towards Marx-Leninism was never given a firm theoretical basis. As has been pointed out in chapter 6 the *"cheng feng"* movement contained contradictory elements which were never reconciled. A possible exception was Mao Tse-tung's lectures on dialectical materialism, but the book reproducing them did not have a wide circulation and was only in circulation for a limited period.* The result was that the training of new cadres produced people with a predominantly doctrinaire attitude certain to produce the confusion and suffer from the frustration which such an attitude implies. Thus, the mere expansion of the Party tended to increase doctrinaire influence and many of the new recruits were all the more doctrinaire because they had a bourgeois background to live down. It was noticeable that veteran Communists were much more ready to use their own critical judgment than new recruits, who were inclined to feel that any weak points they saw in the orthodox doctrinaire position were merely the result of their non-proletarian background.

The failure of the negotiations in 1945 and 1946 certainly had an important influence on developments within the Party. On the doctrinaire Marxist view it was theoretically impossible to reactionaries to yield except to force and for capitalist America to act as an honest mediator between Communists and non-Communists. By behaving very much as orthodox Communist

---

* I say "possible exception" because I am not completely confident about a judgment based on reading a book eleven years ago. The book was lent to me at a local headquarters in Shansi-Chahar-Hopei at the beginning of 1943. It must have been very largely unorthodox because it struck me as being much more sensible than any other Communist book I had read on dialectical materialism and as reaching conclusions very similar to those of non-Marxian theorists of scientific method.

Unfortunately I did not obtain a copy at the time and, in 1949, even friends in the Party were unable to find one for me. It is possible that the book was a product of the period when the Chinese Communist Party was largely cut off from contact with Stalin's writings (see the article by Chen Po-ta to commemorate Stalin's seventieth birthday, *Stalin and the Chinese Revolution*), and that it was no longer issued when Mao found how seriously unorthodox his common-sense interpretation of Marxism had been.

theory said that they were bound to behave the Kuomintang and the Western powers discredited the elements in the Communist Party who had been ready to accept American mediation in the hopes of sparing the Chinese people the horrors of civil war and the frustration of the failure was, in itself, an influence producing extremism.

The original shift to a more radical land policy in 1946 may have coincided with popular pressure. Even during the war the peasants had been inclined to ask "If we can reduce rents to 37·5 per cent, why cannot we reduce them to zero?" and Communist handbooks had instructed Party organisers to reply to this by stressing the importance of maintaining a united front against the Japanese. In 1946, when landlords tended to be Kuomintang supporters and when the hopes of avoiding civil war disappeared, the reasons for restraining peasant demands also disappeared. But by 1947 the new land policy had become, in many areas, a doctrinaire policy which actually alienated peasant support and serious mistakes were admitted by official Communist announcements in 1948.*

The mistakes of this period were quite probably the reason for a certain weakening of extremist influence from 1948 to 1950, but it was obvious in 1949 that the scientific attitude among the Chinese Communists was weaker than it had been in 1945.†
From 1950 on, the Korean war stimulated the growth of hysteria (one British observer sympathetic to the regime compared the atmosphere of China to that of England during the 1914-18 war), and the resort to widespread terrorism must have started the vicious circle of insecurity producing hysteria producing further insecurity. By proclaiming, and to a large extent practising,

* There is evidence to show that the working of the new policies varied very greatly according to the interpretation placed by local Communist authorities on directives from the Central Committee. In extreme cases this produced something like a Communist version of the Nuremburg laws according to which anyone with a landlord grandparent was classified as a landlord. (This case was described in a manuscript by two British anthropologists, David and Isabel Crook, who worked in a North Honan village for a period in 1947-8.)

† For a discussion of the conflicting tendencies in the Chinese Communist Party in 1949, see the author's contribution to *The New China. Three Views.* (Turnstile Press. London. 1950.) Subsequent developments have shown that I was then too optimistic and underestimated the strength of the doctrinaire, hysterical tendencies in the Party. On the other hand, the development of the Party along "doctrinaire" rather than along "scientific" lines is confirmed by the criteria I suggested in 1949—the Communist policy over the collectivization of agriculture, the attitude to the population problem and the use of terrorism as evidence of inability to retain popular support.

its determination to follow Soviet methods and to channel Chinese developments along Soviet lines, the Chinese Communist Party has become involved in the same frustrations, contradictions and psychological tensions as other Communist Parties in power, with similar results in producing mental illness.

The two aspects of irrationality

This hypothesis of mental illness as the source of irrational political behaviour is not incompatible with the hypothesis suggested in earlier chapters which explained irrational behaviour as the result of belief in unsatisfactory theories. The two can be combined as describing interacting aspects of the same process. On the one hand unsatisfactory theories make people incapable of dealing with practical problems, thereby producing the frustration and disappointment which tend to cause a flight from reality into mental illness. On the other hand, mental illness can take the form of emotional attachment to some unsatisfactory theory which substitutes a simplified mental world for the real world whose complications the mentally ill are unable to face.

In particular cases it may be possible to select one aspect as dominant. At one extreme are people whose psychological condition determines their belief in some form of extremist theory. The cases in which this causation is clear are those in which a cure of the mental illness by the treatment of repressions quite unconnected with politics produces a shift to rational political beliefs.[15] It is probable that most of the people who change round between different forms of extremism belong to the same class; they may become disillusioned with one system of extremist beliefs but something in their character seems to impel them towards some other system of equally extremist beliefs.[16] At the other extreme are people who start by being, to all appearances, reasonable and well balanced individuals who gradually become more hysterical as they become involved in the consequences of mistaken political theories. And either way round the process is only a tendency and not an inevitable development. Many cases of mental illness do not take political forms and many cases of confusion in political theory do not lead to mental illness.

As a further hypothesis I would suggest that people are more likely to take flight from reality when their intellectual environment offers them apparently easy ways of escape. The frustrations and disappointments involved in facing reality will normally produce a certain amount of fear and consequent emotional energy tending to produce a flight into delusions. But a great deal of emotional energy is needed to produce a flight into the delusions characteristic of definite insanity which cut off the people who hold them from normal human society. On the other hand, it is very easy to evade the problems presented by empirical reality by accepting some comparatively plausible, over-simplified theory or some system of delusions which is already widely held and can therefore be shared with possibly an actual gain in the satisfactions of social relations. Psychologically, a refusal to accept responsibility is a symptom of regression towards infantilism, and the outward manifestation of some forms of this regression are opposed by the super-ego; that is, people are ashamed of behaving in a way which would be recognised as running away from their adult responsibilities. But, in many cases, people are not ashamed of handing over responsibility for their actions to some totalitarian leader or some allegedly infallible organisation because they can do this without admitting that their motive is a fear of facing the world without some human parent substitute.

More generally, a flight from reality into delusions will meet less resistance in an environment where various forms of irrationalist philosophy are widely held. Someone who believes in objective standards for judging truth or falsehood will be reluctant to believe obvious nonsense. On the other hand, someone who starts from something like Ludwig Wittgenstein's position according to which almost all beliefs are nonsense, though often "deeply significant nonsense",* will have few scruples about believing whatever form of nonsense he finds emotionally satisfying. And it is noticeable that many people sympathetic towards totalitarianism defend their position with arguments which imply that truth or falsehood are simply matters of personal taste.

To summarize what I discuss in more detail in an appendix, scientific knowledge, though objective, is always uncertain and

---

*For a discussion of this point, see note 51 to chapter 11 of Professor Popper's *Open Society*. It is also worth noting that Wittgenstein starts his *Tractatus Logico-philosophicus* (Kegan Paul. London. 1922) by saying "What can be said at all can be said clearly . . ." His system could be taken as an instance of a generalisation that impossibly high standards of clarity and certainty lead in practice to complete confusion and uncertainty.

the use of scientific reasoning implies faith. Totalitarian philosophers are attractive to people who want certainty or who want to manage without faith. The same general idea was expressed by Milosz in his *The Captive Mind.* "Today man believes there is *nothing* in him, so he accepts *anything,* even if he knows it to be bad, in order to find himself at one with others, in order not to be alone. As long as he believes this, there is little one can reproach in his behaviour. Perhaps it is better for him . . . to submit to pressure and thus feel that he *is,* than to take a chance on the wisdom of past ages which maintains that man is a creature of God."[17]

14

What should be done?

THE discussion of the last two chapters has very direct relevance for practical policy. If it is true that the division between the forces working for and against peace or other desirable objectives cuts across the division between political right and left and across existing power-politics alignments it follows that a strategy aimed at these objectives cannot take the simple course of choosing a side and supporting it. Co-operation must always have the qualification "in so far as our allies are following policies calculated to promote our common objectives." Co-operation given without this qualification involves a loss of power to influence policy. In the short run it may seem easiest to preserve unity by refusing to make an issue of points of disagreement. In the long run this involves a grave risk of increasing divergence of policy and objectives which makes continued co-operation harder to maintain.

Some illustrations

The war-time alliance between the Soviet Union and the Western powers provides a good example of contrast between discriminating and undiscriminating co-operation. The common state of war with Nazi Germany provided an obvious common objective. On the Soviet side, the record of Soviet policy seems to show that the Soviet government never allowed co-operation for this common objective to obscure its realisation that its other objectives were quite different from those of its allies. As soon as the most urgent danger from Germany was over it was even prepared to subordinate the war effort against Germany to considerations of post-war advantage. (The failure to support the Warsaw rising or to allow the Western air forces to support it by using Soviet bases was a good example of this.) On the other side, the Western governments showed much less discrimination in co-operation. Under the slogan of maintaining allied unity they consistently minimized or evaded their points of disagreement with the Soviet Union. By doing so they did

243

little to influence Soviet policy and a good deal to confuse themselves and still more to confuse public opinion. One need only look at the developments in Europe of 1945 and 1946 to see which strategy was the more successful. A more discriminating Western co-operation could almost certainly have restricted the growth of Soviet imperialism and might even have improved post-war relations with the Soviet Union.

Chinese Communist policy provides a whole series of examples to show the disastrous results of undiscriminating co-operation. There have been a number of periods in which there was a perfectly sound case for co-operation between China and the Soviet Union. In the early 1920's Sun Yat-sen turned to the Soviet Union for support after he had failed to get support from the Western democracies. It is possible to make excuses for Western policy.* But when these excuses have been made the fact remains that the Western powers were inclined to back the warlord regimes which obstructed any national development or social reforms while Russia was prepared to back the forces which, whatever their defects, did offer the best hope of making the changes essential for the Chinese nation and the Chinese people.

From 1937 to 1940 China got expressions of sympathy from the Western powers but got material help only from the Soviet Union. While the American government ordered General Chennault and other American airmen to leave China, Soviet air force units defended Hankow against a Japanese air force that had no difficulty in getting its supplies from American or British sources.[1]

In the 1940's the American actions which seemed to show that America would oppose the Chinese Communist Party whatever its policies gave the Chinese Communists good reasons for taking a pro-Soviet alignment.

In all these cases, however, the Chinese Communist Party

---

* Sun Yat-sen's requests for Western co-operation were often tactless. He approached the international banking consortium with a blunt request for a a loan of $50,000,000 in order to raise an army to make himself ruler of China, which was hardly the approach to impress commercially minded bankers. (This was told me by the late Mr. T. W. Lamont.) His *International Development of China* was in its basic ideas an anticipation of modern policies for the development of economically backward areas, but its detailed proposals were fantastic. Sun Yat-sen rightly saw that development of communications should have a high priority but his proposed railway network had large mileages serving the Gobi and Tarim deserts, five lines converging on Lhasa, and so on.

244

harmed both Chinese and its own interests by exaggerating co-operation with the Soviet Union into unconditional support for the Soviet Union. The disastrous results of Soviet directives in the 1920's have been described in a number of studies.* It cannot be proved that the Chinese Communists would have been successful or that they would have avoided the earlier civil war if they had taken an independent line, but they would almost certainly have avoided some of their worst blunders. And by refusing to allow the direction of the Chinese revolution to be subordinated to the Stalin versus Trotsky struggle in Russia they might have exerted an influence on developments in Russia.

By their completely uncritical support for the Nazi-Soviet Pact in 1939, the Chinese Communists contributed to the breakdown of the united front against Japan. By following every twist of the Soviet line on Europe in a way that could not be explained as the result of independent judgment, the Communists provided evidence to confirm the views of their bitterest enemies, who argued that the Communists must be opposed as an organisation whose loyalty was to Russia rather than to China. And by denouncing all who disagreed with them they were bound to antagonize the liberal elements in the Kuomintang who, on Chinese issues, would have been inclined to support them. It is hard to estimate the importance of this contribution because there were other important influences tending to make the Kuomintang take an anti-Communist line and these might have been decisive even if the Communists had acted differently. On the other hand, the Chinese Communist Party's support for the Nazi-Soviet Pact was followed by a shift in Kuomintang policy. The earlier Kuomintang-Communist clashes, such as the fighting with Chang Yin-wu in Central Hopei, were local affairs involving semi-independent Kuomintang commanders who were often fairly insubordinate even to their Kuomintang superiors.†

---

* For example: Harold R. Isaacs, *The Tragedy of the Chinese Revolution* (Stanford University Press. 1951). Benjamin Schwartz, *Chinese Communism and the Rise of Mao* (Harvard University Press. 1951). Robert C. North, *Moscow and the Chinese Communists* (Stanford University Press. 1954). All these support their argument with copious references to contemporary original sources, while the official Communist accounts of the period (such as Hu Chiao-mu's *Thirty Years of the Communist Party of China* in *People's China*, Vol. IV, Nos. 2 to 6. 1951), are extremely evasive or make demonstrably false statements.

† According to several informants, Chang Yin-wu appointed his own officials in the area he controlled who acted in rivalry with officials appointed by Lu Chung-lin, his nominal commander. In the 1940's the Communists

It was only towards the end of 1939, with the advance north-wards into Communist territory of Chu Huai-ping's 97th Army, that clashes started in which orders came from the higher levels of the Kuomintang command.

Finally, the uncritical pro-Soviet line after 1949 provided part of a vicious circle by increasing American popular support for the irreconcilable enemies of the Chinese Communists, thereby providing more reason for Chinese reliance on Russia. And, in so far as the uncritical pro-Soviet line has been responsible for the determination to copy Soviet methods in China, it has been responsible for the degeneration of the Chinese regime from a government depending on popular support towards a typical Stalinist police state.

The uncritical pro-Soviet line was not universal in the Chinese Communist Party even in 1949. I have already mentioned one case in which a Chinese Communist representative declared that Soviet behaviour in Germany was "theoretically impossible" (page 27). As against this, a high ranking Communist said that when the Chinese government was in a position to verify my accounts of Soviet behaviour in Europe they might have to denounce the Soviet Union for discrediting the good name of Communism. If this attitude ever became the official line of the Chinese Communist leadership the prospects for world peace would be vastly improved. It would then be possible for the supporters of peace in China and elsewhere to co-operate against the forces which threaten peace regardless of disagreements about the best form of economic and social organisation. It has already been argued that the main factor producing distrust of Chinese good faith in wanting peace has been the uncritical Chinese support for Soviet imperialism. If this support ceased, most reasonable people would concede that there was a real case for Chinese co-operation with the Soviet Union so long as present American policy towards China remained unchanged. But in this situation it is likely that American policy would change.

For the British Commonwealth, and indeed for most supporters of peace and democracy, there is an extremely strong case for a generally pro-American alignment. No doubt there are

---

would speak with respect of Lu Chung-lin as a genuine patriot even though they disliked his political views, while they claimed that Chang Yin-wu was the originator of the slogan "Crooked line save country" (*Ch'ü hsien chiou kuo*). That is "join the lesser enemy (the Japanese) in order to resist the main enemy (the Communists)."

supporters of peace and democracy in the Soviet Union but there is, at present, no way of making close enough contact with them for co-operation to be possible while the Soviet government seems to be firmly controlled by people who, whatever their motives, act primarily in terms of maintaining and extending their power. In America, on the other hand, the forces working for peace and democracy are large and active and have a dominant influence on policy. The totalitarians and dangerous psychopaths are a minority even though their influence, especially on China policy, has been important. Even though the division between the supporters and opponents of peace and democracy cuts across the division between Communist and non-Communist the distribution as between Russia and America is quite unsymmetrical and support for these objectives quite clearly implies support for America as against Russia.

However, co-operation with America for the objectives which the majority of the American people share with the majority of the people of the British Commonwealth can and should be combined with opposition to the minority in America who do not share these objectives and to America policies which hinder their attainment. And there is a very strong case for holding that opposition to America on issues where America is in the wrong is an essential condition for retaining public support for co-operation with America on the more important issues where America is in the right.

The point can be illustrated by an example from Korea. Consider the following passage from Reginald Thompson's *Cry Korea*[2] describing the reoccupation of Seoul in 1950. "Bravely Synghman Rhee took the stand. He promised justice, mercy and forgiveness to all who surrendered. It was a noble speech, holding all who heard it. '. . . Let the sons of our sons look backward to this day and remember it as the beginning of unity, understanding and forgiveness. And may it never be remembered as a day of oppression and revenge . . .'

"I am far from hard boiled. These words moved me deeply, as they did most of those who heard them. Even now it is as impossible to believe them to have been uttered in a spirit of the most appalling cynicism as it is equally impossible to believe that they were not. For it seemed to us that the mission of the United Nations was fulfilled . . . And if these promises of justice and mercy were true the promises of a new world might take root and, however haltingly, begin to flourish on this rim of Asia . . .

"I believe that here in the Council Chamber of the National Capitol of shattered Seoul was a crossroads in our story, not very difficult to recognise.

"But before the echo of these noble words of the South Korean President had died away the prisons had filled. Men, women and even children, suspect or guilty, were most brutally beaten up. Soon hundreds faced the firing squads, and, riddled with bullets, often slowly done to death, were heaped into common graves by their executioners.

". . . British troops, shocked by these massacres of peace as no horrors of war had moved them, forcibly prevented these shootings whenever they could and saved many from their executioners."

The United Nations had the power to compel Synghman Rhee to observe his promises. All that was needed was the courage higher up to generalize this spontaneous action by British troops and to insist that the United Nations forces, fighting to resist totalitarian aggression, must refuse to tolerate totalitarian atrocities. It could have been made clear to General MacArthur that refusal to carry out such a directive would be followed by immediate disciplinary action against him.

The failure to make a stand at this period made it impossible to co-operate with America on a later issue where the American military leaders were probably right. A strong case has been made out for believing that the Communist truce proposals of June, 1951, were made at a time when the Communist armies were in danger of a crushing defeat and that a continuance of full scale military operations until the Communists had agreed to a satisfactory general settlement in Korea would actually have shortened the war and produced a united Korea.[3] But the failure to restrain first Synghman Rhee and then General MacArthur had made it impossible to obtain support for such a policy. By allowing the justice of its cause to be discredited the United Nations made it impossible to refuse an offer to end the fighting even on unsatisfactory terms.

And this is only one instance of a general disagreement about policy. America's allies share the objective of preventing the expansion of Communist power. But this common objective is quite compatible with a belief that American policy thinks too much in purely military terms and that a tendency to support right-wing police state regimes simply because they are anti-Communist is short sighted and likely, in the long run, to be disastrous. If this issue about the best policy to secure the common objective had been argued openly, it is likely that several disputes could have been avoided.

The obvious weakness of both United Kingdom and Australian policy since the war has been a tendency to avoid any open disagreements with America for the sake of preserving the essential co-operation with America against the threat of Communist totalitarianism. This has almost certainly weakened the ability to influence American policy. An American official faces a strong temptation to prefer a quiet life if he knows that he will be publicly denounced by the right-wing press and politicians if he considers the views of America's allies, but will only have to read private protests from London, Canberra, or Ottawa if he ignores them.

More important, the appearance of unity has only been preserved at the expense of helping the growth of anti-American feeling. As the strongest partner in an alliance America is bound to face some suspicion and jealousy and if people find that their government appears to be unwilling to express disagreement with America they are bound to be more inclined to believe the charges of Communist propaganda that alliance with America involves acceptance of American domination. It is likely that America's allies would considerably strengthen co-operation with America if they were openly to demonstrate their hostility to the totalitarian and psychopathic groups in American politics. A government which had made clear to its public at home that it was prepared to oppose the totalitarian forces in America would be in a far stronger position to obtain popular support for co-operation with America for common objectives even when this involved sacrifices of material advantage or prestige in the common cause.

An obvious opportunity for doing this by perfectly discriminating retaliation is provided by the McCarran Act. As in the case of the White Australia policy it is necessary to make a clear distinction between objectives and methods. The objective of preventing the entry into America of Communist agents is quite as reasonable as the objective of preventing the entry into Australia of unassimilable migrants. But, just as the actual Australian laws only make sense in terms of something like Nazi race theory, so the McCarran Act only makes sense in

249

terms of an even more fantastic theory that Communism is some kind of contagious disease. And the law has often been administered in a way calculated to cause the maximum inconvenience. In many cases the American authorities have not definitely refused a visa but have kept the applicant in a state of uncertainty until it finally becomes impossible for him to get to America in time for his engagements. At least among intellectuals in countries allied with America, the McCarran Act has been a major influence in producing anti-American feeling and in discrediting American claims to be a democratic and not a totalitarian country.*

Within America there is widespread disapproval of the Act. It was only passed over a presidential veto and many Americans realise that it has seriously harmed American interests and assisted Communist propaganda. It has, for example, been attacked by the *Reader's Digest* which can hardly be suspected of any pro-Communist sympathies.[4]

It would be quite simple for the governments of America's allies to ask intending American visitors "Do you or do you not approve of the McCarran Act?" Those who answered that they did not would be given a visa in the normal way, unless their public record showed that this answer was false. Those who expressed their approval would be required to supply all the information required by the McCarran Act and would be subjected to similar delays and similar arbitrary refusals. Such action would not cause the slightest inconvenience to any American opposed to totalitarianism and favouring freedom and democracy. On the other hand, those Americans who agree with Stalinism on basic issues would find that any attempt to travel abroad involved them in serious inconvenience. And the inconvenience would be caused entirely by the application to them of the principles which they had supported.

This would offer the best chance of changing an American

---

* A good sample to illustrate the working of the law was given in the *Bulletin of the Atomic Scientists* for October, 1952. The clearest illustration of the "contagious disease" theory of Communism was the case of Professor Michael Polanyi. He had been consistently anti-Communist and even in the period of the war-time Soviet alliance he was strongly critical of the Soviet organisation of science and the Marxian theory of the social function of science. The American authorities refused to consider the evidence of his writings and refused to give him a visa because of his connection with two organisations, from one of which he had resigned as soon as it started to follow a pro-Communist line, and to the other of which he had given a strongly anti-Communist lecture.

policy which very seriously harms co-operation among the supporters of democracy. It would almost certainly raise the morale of those Americans who are fighting totalitarian tendencies at home and it would be much easier for an American government to change a law which was causing serious inconvenience to some American voters. More important, such action would provide an outlet for anti-American feeling. By allowing this feeling the outlet of action against the totalitarian minority in America, who have to be fought at some point if co-operation among the democratic powers is to continue, it would be possible very greatly to reduce the opposition to close co-operation with America on the issues where there is a genuine community of interest.

No doubt such suggestions will appear shocking to those who think in terms of conventional diplomatic behaviour. But, here again, I would maintain that people who restrict themselves to conventional behaviour have condemned themselves to futility. The logical conclusion of attachment to convention was summed up by Cornford. "Every public action which is not customary, either is wrong, or, if it is right, is a dangerous precedent. It follows that nothing should ever be done for the first time."[5] The growth of anti-American feeling among America's allies is a problem of which many thoughtful Americans are aware. In Australia, for example, American visitors are often shocked by the strength of anti-American feeling. The Australian authorities quite rightly consider that close co-operation with America is essential in Australia's interests and deplore and condemn anti-American feeling. But they seem to be powerless to do anything to prevent its growth or to secure a modification of American actions which strengthen it. When conventional action has led to a situation in which people deplore developments which they are unable to prevent there is a very strong case for trying unconventional action.

Of course a change from undiscriminating to discriminating co-operation would involve some risks. In the case of China these risks would be appreciable. The example of Yugoslavia indicated that the Soviet government is not satisfied with anything short of unconditional co-operation from other Communist ruled states. If China tried to change from unconditional to discriminating co-operation the Soviet government might react by refusing all forms of co-operation. For the British Commonwealth, co-operation with America is already partly discriminating and making it more so would only involve slight risks. The groups in America who would be antagonized are mostly anti-British in any case and their more active hostility would be at least partly compensated by support from American liberal opinion. In either case these immediate risks would almost certainly be worth accepting. In the long run the most danger-ous of all policies is to avoid taking any immediate risks.

The psychological problem

The relevance of the psychological factor for practical action is less obvious, not because it is unimportant but because we know too little about it. Techniques for curing mental illness are much less well understood than techniques for producing it. Even with patients who are consciously co-operating the cure of mental illness is an uncertain process, and totalitarians do not consciously want to be cured. In the future our knowledge of psychological techniques might improve to the point which would make it impossible for totalitarian beliefs to survive except in complete isolation. One could imagine a world in which it had become impossible for a totalitarian state to send any representatives outside its own borders because they would probably be cured of their delusions and become, from the totalitarian point of view, traitors. However, this is a speculation with little relevance to present practical action.

In dealing with the whole problems the standards relevant for politics are rather different from those relevant for psychology. The primary interest of the psychologist is in the mental illness and the precise symptoms in which the mental illness shows itself are mainly important in so far as they reveal the basis of the illness. For the politician, on the other hand, mental illness only becomes of major importance when it shows itself in particular symptoms. A change of symptoms may make some mental illness of very slight political importance. For example, if the Chinese Communists had delusions about fox-fairies instead of delusions about Americans or if Senator McCarthy's followers searched for witches' covens instead of for Communist cells a psychiatrist would almost certainly consider that their mental illness had become worse; from the political point of view they would have turned into comparatively harmless eccentrics. Or, to give a real though comparatively trivial example, the Dean of Canterbury was a harmless eccentric as an enthusiastic supporter of Major Douglas, but produced noticeable effects in causing international misunderstanding and ill-will as an enthusiastic supporter of Stalin.*

From the point of view of the psychologist the individual may make a fairly satisfactory adjustment through the "compensation" of some psychological disturbance, through devotion to some extremist political organisation. From the point of view of society the satisfied and energetic fanatic is a far greater danger than the individual with unsatisfactory "compensation" and a wide variety of symptoms of mental ill-health. The really dangerous form of mental illness is that which allows the practice of successful "doublethink"—"to deny the existence of objective reality and all the while to take account of the objective reality one denies." If people admit reality they are only a limited danger to the community because it is normally possible to reach a compromise with them even if their objectives are anti-social. If people are so deeply involved in a system of delusions that they cannot take account of objective reality, they are only a limited danger to the community because they cannot act effectively. The greatest danger comes from people who take sufficient account of reality to act effectively but who are too deluded to make it possible to reach agreement or compromise with them. It is people with this particular degree of mental ill-health who are likely to make war inevitable or pervert the social development of any society.

In the present state of knowledge there is no clear or complete solution for the problem of mental illness in politics. On the other hand, psychological considerations reinforce the case for trying the type of strategy suggested in earlier chapters, namely, to lose no opportunity of attacking and exposing "doublethink" positions while at the same time doing everything possible to decrease frustration by making it possible to solve urgent practical problems by rational behaviour.

There are considerable numbers of people who recover from political forms of hysteria, and the accounts they give of the

---

* The production of misunderstanding is fairly obvious. In England the Dean gives a grossly distorted account of conditions in Communist ruled countries and vice-versa. The production of ill-will is more disputable but I think it is a justifiable description for a process in which the people of Communist ruled countries are encouraged to show goodwill for what they are told is the majority of the British people but is actually a small minority and hatred for what they are told is a small minority but is actually a majority.

reasons which led them to desert totalitarian organisations seem to show that the decision was taken when the policies of the organisation they supported become too glaringly contrary to common sense rationality or elementary moral decency. Their evidence also shows that the decision to support a totalitarian party was usually the reaction to frustration in a situation where they could not see any rational course of action which would solve urgent problems. The suggested strategy would, therefore, weaken the forces which attach people to extremist political organisations.

Many political extremists are probably incurable by known techniques and in this case all that can be done is to try to divert their delusions into some less dangerous form. By making "doublethink" positions harder to maintain the suggested strategy would try to drive the incurable extremists into delusions further removed from reality which would make them less capable of acting effectively. This would involve some risk of upsetting a power-politics balance. As incurable extremists further lost touch with reality they would become more likely to start a war regardless of their chances of winning it.* But this risk must be compared with the risks involved in alternative strategies.

The alternative of refusing to challenge totalitarian "double-think" positions involves the maintaining of a power-politics balance until such time as psychopathic influences have spontaneously declined. And this is a strategy which is very unlikely to succeed. It is possible that a totalitarian society might finally recover from hysteria if left alone but, judging from known totalitarian societies, the process would probably take decades if not generations; while the inherent tendency of a power-politics balance to increasing instability is likely to cause a breakdown in a much shorter period. Except in terms of a very high rate of discount of the future, it is rational to prefer a strategy which offers a fair chance of greatly reducing the risk of war in a few years time at the expense of a slight increase in the present risk, as against a strategy which offers a probably increasing risk of war into the indefinite future.

* An illustration of this effect of a challenge to a totalitarian position was Hitler's reaction to the demonstration of solidarity in support of Czechoslovakia in May, 1938. He insisted that the Czech question must be settled in 1938 even at the risk of a war for which his military advisers did not consider themselves prepared. (*Munich. Prologue to Tragedy.* By J. W. Wheeler-Bennett. Macmillan, London, 1948. Pp. 54-62.)

Prophylaxis

While the cure of mental illness with political symptoms is an obscure and difficult problem, the means for preventing its development are much more obvious, and equally important. Mental illness is entirely a question of degree. Almost all human beings are subject to psychological influences which distort their powers of rational judgment to some extent. (I certainly would not claim to be exempt.) There is no sharp boundary between the day dreaming and wishful thinking in which almost everyone indulges on some questions and the definite delusions characteristic of totalitarianism. It is likely that a large proportion of almost any sample of humanity would develop symptoms of mental illness under conditions where the pressure of confusion and frustration was sufficiently strong. And this means that we can only act effectively against the dangers of totalitarianism to our continued existence if we take care to maintain an environment unfavourable to the development of mental illness.

This very strongly reinforces the case for action to produce an informed public opinion. The article I have quoted on hysteria in America states this conclusion very strongly. "What I have favoured, from the day the 'Enola Gray' returned with her bomb bay empty, was an *authoritative federal committee to present the facts and to suggest a constant, rational basis for atomic 'public relations'.* But, for nine years, with the exception of this *Bulletin* and the limits imposed on it, there has been no reliable information source and no responsible continuous discussion anywhere. Such a committee as I suggest should have had access to all facts and—among all the sciences—to the science of the unconscious mind, which I have made use of here." And the case for action is just as strong outside the field of atomic warfare. A public, which is confused by lack of reliable information and by conflicting reports which it has no means of testing, is extremely likely to react by refusing to face empirical reality and to take refuge in some plausible over-simplified fantasy. A government, which is not willing to take the public into its confidence, and which wishes to preserve the tradition that international relations is a field in which the public should trust the experts, may want to follow a rational policy but is very likely to find that public opinion develops in a way which makes this impossible.

As has been argued above, this implies that a democratic government should do far more than is now being done to give the public reliable information and should give this psychological defence against totalitarianism a priority comparable to that given to military defence. There is a case for some restriction on statements deliberately calculated to cause confusion, quite apart from the case for an international agreement to restrict "warmongering" which has been discussed above (page 185). If properly devised such restriction would not involve any real reduction of freedom. George Orwell argued that ". . . the controversy over freedom of speech and of the Press is at bottom a controversy over the desirability, or otherwise, of telling lies. What is really at issue is the right to report contemporary events truthfully, or as truthfully as is consistent with the ignorance, bias and self-deception from which every observer necessarily suffers."[6] Actual restrictions in the past have usually taken the form of restricting the publication of certain views or else of restricting the publication of what the authorities consider inexpedient for the public to know, which often means concealing official blunders and thereby preventing their correction. Such restrictions work directly against the objective of producing an informed public opinion and increase public suspicion and confusion. What is advocated here is some restriction on the publication of statements which those who make them know to be false or which are made without any reason for believing them to be true. Any satisfactory scheme would have to make clear that there would be no restriction on the publication of statements for which there was reasonable evidence (except, of course, for special cases involving military security, etc.).

Whatever their intentions or political affiliations, the people who publish statements on matters of urgent public interest with no evidence to support them are producing confusion tending to cause mental illness. If they could be restrained in some way that did not entail other dangers it would be in the public interest to do so.

Finally, totalitarianism can only be resisted by a government which has the courage to do whatever may be necessary to deal with urgent social problems. Totalitarian parties have usually become powerful only when existing governments have failed in their responsibilities; when the situation has called for action and the people in power have been unwilling to act, because of unwillingness to offend vested interests, because of attachment to. confusing theories, or simply because of bureaucratic timidity. Action may involve considerable risks in attacking powerful vested interests or in experimenting with new and untried policies and forms of organisation. But if reasonable people are too cautious and fail to change a situation which popular opinion feels to be intolerable they run the even greater risk of losing power to extremists.

Though this is one of the most important points in preventing the development of mental illness with political symptoms, and though it could be illustrated from almost every case in which totalitarian parties have become powerful I do not propose to discuss these illustrations because they do not indicate any specially new policies as desirable. They only illustrate the generalization that the political world is one in which the dangers of being too cautious are, in the long run, quite as great as the dangers of being too rash.

15

Conclusion

THE first part of this book considered a fairly definite and simple question: "Does the available evidence support the claims of the Chinese Government to be working rationally for peace?" The analysis of the record of Chinese policy and statements for the period up to the middle of 1954 gave a fairly definite answer to this question.

It was only possible to give a more speculative answer to the resulting question: "Are the Chinese Communists, and other Communists, acting rationally but not for peace, or for peace but not rationally?" (I hope soon to have the opportunity of making some of the experiments which could yield evidence relevant for this question.) It was suggested that a good deal of political behaviour could be explained as determined by the implications of faith in theories which were unsatisfactory by scientific standards and by psychological influences which could be explained in terms of empirically confirmed psychological principles.

Accepting this theory as a working hypothesis, the obvious question which it raises is: "What can be done about the situation?" And the answer to this question was bound to be still more speculative.

I certainly do not claim to have provided a definite answer to the major problem of international affairs: "How to remove the risk of another world war?" I would only claim to have suggested an approach to the problem, but I would maintain that this is important.

The crisis as challenge or as fate

Whether or not people succeed in preventing the collapse of our civilization through wars and militarism depends very largely on their attitude to this problem—whether they regard the present situation as a "challenge" or as "fate"—as a situation that has been produced by human action and is therefore, in principle, changeable by human action, or as a situation produced by impersonal forces beyond human control. If people regard

258

the situation as a challenge they will use their minds to solve a difficult and complicated but extremely interesting problem and are likely to succeed in controlling developments. If they regard the situation as fate they will use their minds to justify the acceptance of fate and developments will proceed uncontrolled largely because people are not really trying to control them. If people have a theory which seems capable of giving a satisfactory explanation of what is happening it will produce the feeling that what is happening presents an interesting and potentially soluble problem. And if they have this attitude they are likely to develop their theories to a point which makes effective control of the situation possible. Conversely, if people feel that they cannot really understand what is happening this will tend to produce the feeling that what is happening is a matter of uncontrollable fate. And if people have this attitude they are unlikely to develop any satisfactory theory.

One could draw an analogy with the economic problem. In the early 1930's it seemed as if Western civilization might collapse through failure to control the economic situation and existing economic theory did not offer any satisfactory explanation of what was happening. People faced an apparently irrational situation. The result of economic decisions turned out to be something which almost no one wanted or intended. People just did not know what kind of action could attain the simple and obvious objective of using idle labour, equipment and raw materials to produce the goods which people wanted. The reactions to this situation were similar to the reactions to the present international crisis. Some people just persisted in traditional policies even though the theories on which these policies were based had failed to explain the situation and the policies themselves had proved inffective. Others went in for all sorts of extremist and apocalyptic theories. Still others took the attitude of accepting the situation as inevitable fate.*

In fact, Western civilization did get through the Great Depression, largely by trial and error methods, and, by the late

---

* A very interesting example of this last attitude was Peter Drucker's *The End of Economic Man* (Heinemann, London, 1939). He talks about "the return of the Demons"—impersonal and irrational forces which made the economic system inherently irrational and economic crises uncontrollable and he compares the attempts of economists to find a satisfactory theory of the trade cycle to the attempts of the alchemists to find the philosopher's stone. Just because he had this attitude he failed to understand the significance of the developments in economic theory which were being worked out even before the publication of his book.

1930's the people who looked on economic crises as challenge and not as fate had developed economic theory to a point which makes it unlikely that the economic system will ever again get as far out of control as in the Great Depression. Most economists would admit that the control of depression or inflation presents very complicated problems and that control may fail in particular cases, but there is an understanding of the problems of general economic equilibrium which would prevent the feeling of helplessness that characterized the early 1930's. The apparent irrationality of the depression, when the result of economic decisions turned out to be quite different from what anyone wanted or expected, is now intelligible. Once it is realised that the automatic co-ordination of economic action provided by a market system does not extend to ensuring that the total of economic decisions shall add up to a possible result, we can both understand the sort of way in which an economic crisis can develop and also the sort of things which should be done to control it.

The crisis has now shifted from economics to international relations. As in the Great Depression, the obvious feature of the situation is its apparent irrationality. It is pretty certain that very few people in any country actually want a major war; it is equally certain that the actual results of human behaviour are producing a very serious risk of getting one.

What I have tried to suggest is that the equivalent of Say's law* in the theory of international relations is the assumption that most people are acting rationally, that is, that they are doing what, given their available knowledge, is something near what is most likely to promote their intentions. If this assumption is accepted then the drift of the world situation towards an outcome which almost no one wants and which might even involve the extinction of the human race can only be explained by some inherent irrationality in the whole system of international politics. As against this the system becomes intelligible on the assumption that a considerable proportion of political actions are irrational, though the causes which produce this irrational behaviour can be understood and explained through rational scientific investigation. I certainly do not claim to have

* Keynes points out that Say's law—that supply creates its own demand— "is equivalent to the proposition that there is no obstacle to full employment." And he argues that any economic theory which is based on this assumption is bound to fail in trying to give a satisfactory explanation of general unemployment.

produced the equivalent in international affairs of Keynes'
General Theory but I do hope that I may have suggested a
starting point from which other people may be able to work
out a body of theory in terms of which the international
situation would be controllable.

In the present situation it is very likely not possible to work
out any practicable scheme for reducing the risk of a general
war to zero in the foreseeable future. And attempts to do so
may merely be diverting human effort from the attainable
objective of decreasing the risks of war.

The survey of American opinion published last autumn[1]
showed that more than half the American public believed that
a major war was almost certain within the next twenty-five to
thirty years. "Almost certain" may be too pessimistic but the
odds may well be better than even in favour of a major war
within this period, if nothing is done about it and if existing
policies are continued. New policies based on a critical, scientific
examination of theories and assumptions might quite possibly
change the odds within a few years to, perhaps, four or five to
one against. I would suggest that this in itself is an objective
worth working for. And in what would then become the foreseeable future it might be practicable to work for some further
objective, such as a really effective world organisation, which
would make the risks of a general war extremely small.

Any continuing risk of war is certainly unpleasant but I do not
think that it offers us any real excuse for hysteria or panic.
Even at present the actuarial risk of death through a general
war is probably no greater than the risk of early death through
diseases or famine which almost all the human race faced till
quite recently and which a large part of it still faces. If a high
proportion of Chinese or Indian peasants remain calm and
reasonable under the appalling risks of their lives we have no
excuse for allowing the risks of atomic warfare to deflect us from
the rational behaviour which offers the only real hope of avoiding
it.

And there is no reason to suppose that rational political
behaviour must be confined to a ruling elite. Contempt for the
intelligence and the judgment of the ordinary citizen is yet
another point on which the extreme right and the extreme left
find themselves in complete agreement as against the supporters
of democracy. It may sound alarming to say that people should
learn to think in terms of functions of several variables or, as

Professor Wiener suggests, in terms of non-linear functions.[2] But these are things which most people can do without any difficulty in practice. Every housewife knows that cooking involves non-linear functions of time and temperature and any radio serviceman who adjusts the tracking of a broadcast receiver is dealing with a complicated function of three independent variables. It is not reasonable to expect that the ordinary citizen should be able to formulate policy. Democracy certainly needs leadership and certainly needs experts. But when the ordinary citizen is not deliberately confused and misinformed there is strong evidence for believing that he can form a fairly reliable judgment about how far his leaders and his experts deserve to be trusted.

APPENDIX

The standpoint of the author

A QUESTION which Communists ask about any book is "From what standpoint is it written?" By this they mean the class standpoint of the author and I would not admit that the question in this form is of fundamental importance. The Communists seem unable to distinguish between the theory that people's thinking is influenced by their class status, which is almost certainly true, and the theory that people's thinking is determined by their class status, which is almost certainly false. (This is another example of the refusal of orthodox Marx-Leninism to accept the concept of a function of several variables.) However, though I would not admit that class interests have played more than a quite subsidiary part in determining the argument of this book, I have no objection to giving information about my class status. My family background is almost pure intelligentsia. The great majority of my relations are or have been engaged in teaching, public service, professional or managerial jobs in which their incomes have depended on earnings and not on property. It is not until my great-grandparents' generation that a capitalist or a landlord could be found among my ancestors and the one landlord was a Liberal Member of Parliament who opposed the imperialist aspects of Palmerston's foreign policy.

On the other hand if the standpoint from which the book is written is taken to mean the basic philosophical assumptions of the author I would agree that the question is of considerable importance. Here I might quote the statement with which Czeslaw Milosz begins an article on modern totalitarian society. "It was only towards the middle of the twentieth century that the inhabitants of many European countries came, in general unpleasantly, to the realization that their fate could be influenced directly by intricate and abstruse books of philosophy. Their bread, their work, their private lives began to depend on this or that decision in disputes on principles to which, until then, they have never paid any attention."[1] It would not be a great exaggeration to say that all my criticisms of the orthodox

Communist position are implied by a disagreement about the nature of scientific knowledge.

This book has certainly been influenced by the fact that I specialized in science at a school in which science teaching was exceptionally good; that, in consequence, I found such books as J. M. Keynes' *Treatise on Probability* and Felix Kaufmann's *Methodenlehre der Sozialwissenschaften* more interesting than much of the philosophy I was taught at Oxford; and that I have kept up an interest in the work of those thinkers who have been trying, especially in the last thirty years, to clarify the philosophical assumptions behind scientific method. It will be obvious to anyone who has read Professor K. R. Popper's *The Open Society and its Enemies* that I have been considerably influenced by his attempt to work out the implications of these assumptions in the field of social science.

Professor Marcus Oliphant has defined science as follows: "Science is that body of knowledge which can be communicated to others and which can be verified by anyone willing to make the effort to do so. There are other kinds of knowledge, arising for instance from emotional or religious experiences, which are essentially personal and which cannot readily be communicated to others or be verified by them. Undoubtedly this personal knowledge plays an important part in the lives of individuals, but it can only affect the people as a whole if they are willing to accept the experience of others as an act of faith. There are fashions in science, just as there are fashions in art or literature, but there are never any dogmas and every part of the knowledge it represents is constantly sifted and checked; ideas which prove to be wrong are discarded ruthlessly."

Perhaps the easiest way to summarize the resulting position will be by an analogy. It seems to me that the most reliable kind of human knowledge is that obtained by a process like fitting together a jig-saw puzzle, in which the pieces are items of empirical evidence and the picture on the puzzle a theoretical system of the world. In the ordinary child's jig-saw puzzle the pieces have intricate shapes and it is usually possible to say of any two pieces taken together in isolation that they either do or do not belong together. The puzzle of this analogy is of the more difficult kind in which limited numbers of pieces can often be fitted together in several different ways and it is only in relation to the puzzle as a whole that any one can ultimately say which way is right. A further complication is that some pieces may turn out not to belong to the puzzle at all. What seems to be an item of empirical evidence may turn out to be an inaccurate observation or a deliberately false report.

Obviously, the analogy is not complete and cannot be extended too far. For the purposes of this book, however, I am not trying to give a general theory of scientific method even in a summarized form but only to indicate some of its main features. For this purpose an easily visualized analogy seems preferable to a more accurate but less easily understood abstract theory.

The analogy does show many of the important features of scientific knowledge. Without some idea of the picture to be produced it is almost impossible to select the right pieces to try. That is, the collection of empirical evidence is unlikely to yield any systematic knowledge unless it is guided by some theoretical hypothesis. There is a distinction between the cases where a set of pieces simply do not fit, or have only been made to fit by the fabrication of false pieces to fill the gaps, and the cases in which a number of pieces fit and appear to give part of a picture but in which it becomes more and more difficult to fit on extra pieces or to fit this collection of pieces into the rest of the puzzle. That is, there is a distinction between the cases in which it can be said that a generalisation is simply untrue or sustained by falsified evidence and the cases in which a generalization is not demonstrably false but is nevertheless unsatisfactory as a scientific theory. When a large number of pieces have been fitted together and produce a coherent picture we can feel almost certain that they have been fitted rightly and can predict with considerable confidence that the part of the picture thus obtained will be continued by new pieces which have not yet been fitted. But the prediction cannot be absolutely certain because we do not know the whole picture. It might be, for example, that the part of the puzzle we have solved shows a landscape, which leads us to expect that it will continue as a landscape; but in the puzzle as a whole this landscape might be a view out of a window so that new pieces correctly fitted would suddenly change to an indoor scene. That is, a theory confirmed by a great deal of empirical evidence is almost certainly correct and we can have considerable confidence in extending this theory to new data; but these extensions may prove wrong because the theory may have limitations of which we were not aware. For example, the theory of Newtonian mechanics in Euclidean space is almost certain to remain as a satisfactory theory for dealing with bodies within a certain range of magnitudes and velocities, but outside these limits it ceases to fit the evidence.*

Finally, because we do not know the whole picture or what it is going to be, we cannot prove that our pieces really belong to a single puzzle. If someone argues that the pieces really belong to several different puzzles and that we have merely been picking out those which give one of several possible pictures, or that the pieces do not belong to a puzzle at all so they need not be expected to fit properly, we cannot definitely prove him to be wrong. We can only say that we are acting on the assumption that the pieces belong to a single puzzle and that it is equally impossible to prove that this assumption is wrong. Many of the modern theorists of scientific method do come to this sort of conclusion; that the use of scientific method depends on ultimate assumptions which cannot in the last resort be proved, for instance, Keynes' assumption of "limited independent variety."[2]

Professor Popper argues that what he calls "uncritical rationalism" is an untenable position. The persons who says "I am not prepared to accept anything which cannot be defended by means of argument or experience" is maintaining a position which is paradoxical and leads to contradictions and confusion. He maintains that, on this level, "Irrationalism is logically superior to uncritical rationalism" and that the use of human reason can only be based on "an irrational *faith in reason.*" And he concludes that, so far as human reason goes, the choice is open between some form of irrational faith and what he calls "critical rationalism"—a use of reason which recognises its ultimate dependence on faith—a choice which is really a moral decision.[3]

As a personal opinion it seems to me that human reason is a rather unsatisfactory thing to have faith in. Faith in a God who largely transcends the world of our normal experience has the same implications as Professor Popper's "faith in reason"

---

* In one of J. B. S. Haldane's essays he suggests how we can visualize the universe by repeating the familiar process involved in representing the earth by a globe of five or six inches in diameter, a change of scale of about 100,000,000 to 1. He points out that this process can only be repeated twice at the most in the direction of smaller magnitudes and a limited number of times in the direction of larger magnitudes because, outside this range, space and matter would have completely different properties from those involved in the range within which we can represent the earth by a globe.

on all points which can be subjected to experimental test and is on other grounds more satisfactory.

These general views imply that scientific knowledge is both objective and uncertain. What we learn from science is not what is absolutely true but what is most reasonable to believe in the light of the evidence available to us, and these beliefs may have to be modified or restricted in the light of fresh evidence. On the one side it can often be said that some theory or generalization is untrue; on the other side the most that can be said is that some theory co-ordinates and explains all the known evidence and that it is very unlikely that fresh evidence will demand more than minor modifications of it in this field. But the most satisfactory theory may turn out to be a particular case of some wider generalization. For instance, on moving between the Northern and Southern hemispheres one finds that most generalizations about North and South have become reversed, but they can be restated in a form that is always true in terms of towards or away from the equator. The developments of the past fifty years in natural science have compelled similar restatements of many theories that were thought to be universally true.

In many cases scientific method does not even give a definite answer. It will often be true that scientific judgment can only say that, on the available evidence, several hypotheses are equally reasonable. And such cases are likely to be more frequent and the range of uncertainty is likely to be greater in the field of social science than in the field of natural science. This is because the number of relevant variables is usually larger, because the variables are often not susceptible of exact measurement and because it is seldom possible to make controlled experiments. There will often be a range within which entirely honest and reasonable people may reasonably differ in their analyses of some situation. And the range of disagreement will be even greater in the case of policy decisions because the relative importance of different objectives must be, to a considerable extent, a matter of opinion. To give a simple technical illustration, it is not possible to give a definite answer to the question "What is the best design for a motor car?" There would be almost universal agreement about what were desirable requirements; reliability, good performance, fuel economy, comfort, good road holding, low price and so on. But to a considerable extent any one of these objectives can only be pursued at the expense of others so that any actual design must be a compromise based on a weighting of their relative importance, which will be to a considerable extent a matter of personal taste. But this does not mean that objective standards cannot be applied. If one design is superior to another in some respects and inferior in none, the former is quite clearly better. And anyone who has some idea of the sort of car he requires will certainly be able to make a more rational choice through a study of the objective comparisons published in some periodicals.

Analytical deductive systems do, in some sense, give absolutely certain knowledge. But it is always knowledge with an "if" in it. *If* the axioms or assumptions of the system are true then its implications follow and this conditional clause introduces all the uncertainties of scientific judgments. Even in the case of mathematics Einstein once said that in so far as mathematics is absolutely true it does not apply to the real world and in so far as it applies to the real world it is not absolutely true. The following out of logical implications is a process of extrapolation and, even if the logic is quite correct, this will introduce uncertainty. A small and unnoticeable error in the premises may produce a glaring error in the conclusion. An illustration is Lewis Carroll's proof that an obtuse angle is sometimes equal to a right angle.[4] The proof is a strictly logical deduction from a figure which has been drawn slightly wrong. And generalizations which may appear self-evident and absolutely certain in some fields may break down when extended to others. For example, the following true anecdote provides a *reductio ad absurdum* of the generalization that the sum of two positive quantities is a greater positive quantity, a generalization that might appear at first sight as generally and self-evidently true. At the beginning of 1942 two allied citizens who had escaped from Japanese occupied Peking were given a welcoming banquet at General Hsiao K'e's headquarters. The dishes included fried eggs covered with sugar, both eggs and sugar being rare luxuries at the time. The next morning the cook asked Mrs. Lindsay "Did the foreign friends like my food?" "Very much indeed except for the eggs with sugar on them." "That's very strange. I knew that foreigners liked eggs and I knew that foreigners liked sugar so I was quite sure they would like it still more if I gave them eggs with sugar." The cook's reasoning was entirely logical on the assumption that liking for foods followed the rule that the sum of two positive quantities was a greater positive quantity.

Irrationalist philosophies reject the objectivity of scientific knowledge. And they often reach this conclusion by generalizing from the uncertainty of scientific knowledge. People point to the fact that theories which were at one time generally accepted have later been abandoned and to the fact that expert opinions differ on many problems at present, and argue that this shows that there are no real reasons for prefering one opinion to another. Having reached the conclusion that scientific judgments cannot be determined by the objective use of human reason they then proceed to explain human beliefs in terms of some factor such as race, class status, or cultural tradition. Such arguments are based on a complete misunderstanding of the nature of scientific knowledge, because the difference between reasonable judgments on any question is not indefinitely large. It may be admitted that such factors as race, class status or cultural tradition may influence the questions in which people are interested and may affect their preference within the range within which several alternative hypotheses are reasonable. But it will still be true that anyone who applies the standards of scientific method to a certain problem is bound to arrive at an answer within a certain range. Objective standards may not show unambiguously which of several views is the most reasonable, but they will usually imply quite unambiguously that other views are much less reasonable (on the available evidence) and that some are definitely false. For example, while I have tried to give what seems to me the most reasonable hypothesis to explain Chinese Communist policy I do not claim that the maximum is either sharp or obvious and would be quite ready to admit that other people might reasonably give alternative analyses whose results could be rather less or rather more favourable to the Chinese Communist Party. But I would maintain that my views are clearly more reasonable than those of Walter Judd on the one hand or of Rewi Alley on the other and that many of the arguments used by both Communist and anti-Communist propaganda are quite unambiguously false.

Other philosophies reject the uncertainty in scientific knowledge. A good short statement of one such view was given by Jacques Maritain in a recent book.[5] He says "and the truth of my mind lies in its conformity to *what is* outside it and independent of it. That is the fundamental realism and objectivism of Thomistic philosophy. St. Thomas teaches, moreover, that while the subjective inclinations of the appetite play an essential part in the practical knowledge which governs our behaviour, and while they can also intervene, either for good or evil, in our speculative knowledge, the latter, when it attains its natural perfection—that is, when it becomes *science*, and provides us with unshakable rational truths—is in itself absolutely pure and independent of all considerations of what is good or advantageous for the human subject (or the State, or the nation, or the social class or the spiritual family to which it belongs) . . . if, despite more than a century of sentimentalism, we still have some ideal of the adamantine objectivity of science, we owe it to the old Scholastic discipline." In this the acceptance of objectivity is quite unqualified and there is also the admission that thinking may be influenced by subjective factors. But the implied definition of science as something which can provide "unshakable rational truths" is one which few methodologically conscious scientists would accept. Many would, in fact, maintain that the spectacular development of natural science during the last three centuries has been the result of giving up the search for the unattainable objective of finding "unshakable rational truths" in favour of the limited but attainable objective of finding general principles which co-ordinate our experience.

This view of science as providing "unshakable rational truths" is hard to reconcile with the history of science. It is quite clear that scientists have not been able to distinguish between those parts of their theories which have, up to the present, remained unshaken and those parts which have now been disproved. Beliefs which were considered to be philosophically absurd in the seventeenth century were considered to be "unshakable rational truths" in the nineteenth century only to prove incompatible with new evidence in the twentieth century. And there are numerous cases in which the most eminent scientific opinion has committed itself to categorical statements which have later proved false.

The result is that this view of scientific knowledge is apt to be unstable. If the status of "unshakable rational truth" is only claimed for propositions which are outside the scope of scientific inquiry because they have no empirical implications which can be tested by scientific standards, or for propositions which, by scientific standards, are very unlikely to be shaken, then it approximates to the scientific position. Its main influence is then to produce a rather exaggerated confidence in the results of purely deductive reasoning.

On the other hand, if the belief in "unshakable rational truth" leads to a refusal to allow beliefs with empirically verifiable consequences to be shaken by scientific inquiry, it approximates to the totalitarian position. The totalitarian denies the existence of any objective standards which can be used to criticize the beliefs of human minds belonging to a certain group. Marx-Leninism, for example, accepts the view that science yields "unshakable rational truths" but goes on to claim that only people representing a certain class can think scientifically. Those who might be called religious totalitarians claim to believe in objective standards but refuse to allow any critical examination of their beliefs which they claim to represent the ultimate truth. One says "I recognise nothing higher than the beliefs of myself or the group to which I belong." The other says "There is an ultimate superhuman standard of truth which is exemplified only in the beliefs of myself or the group to which I belong." The practical implications of the two positions are nearly identical.

On the view which I have been maintaining the scientific use of reason does depend on an act of faith in God, or at least in the existence of impersonal objective standards which would be implied by a belief in God. But just because the standards for judging truth and falsehood are impersonal and objective no particular human belief can be exempted from possible modification by them.

(At the expense of a slight digression it might be suggested that George Orwell, whom I have often quoted, could be placed in Maritain's category of "pseudo-atheists, who believe that they do not believe in God but who in actual fact unconsciously believe in Him, because the God whose existence they deny is not God but something else."[6] Orwell clearly believed in most of the things which would be implied by a belief in God such as objective standards of truth and falsehood, justice and injustice. What he rejected was the view "that God exists and that the world of material objects is an illusion to be escaped from."[7] In fact the first statement does not, as he thought, imply the second.)

At the beginning of this appendix I quoted Czeslaw Milosz as saying that many people had come "to the realization that their fate could be influenced directly by intricate and abstruse books on philosophy." I have tried to argue that the basic dispute is about the nature of scientific knowledge, whether it is objective but uncertain, certain but not objective, both objective and certain, or neither objective nor certain. It would be easy to devote a complete book to discussing the political implications of these views and the reasons which lead people to hold them. (I would like, for example, to discuss the hypothesis that psychological influences producing a feeling of insecurity lead people to accept philosophies which promise certainty.) Obviously this treatment in a few pages has been extremely sketchy but I did wish to make clear that the basic assumption underlying all the argument of this book has been that scientific knowledge is objective but uncertain.

272

Postscript

In August, 1954, I had the opportunity of visiting China with the British Labour Party delegation. The point on which there seemed to have been an important change, as compared with the situation described in the main text of this book, was the general Chinese attitude towards the West. The attitude showing general hostility towards anyone who was not sympathetic to Communism had been replaced by an attitude showing a quite genuine desire for better relations with the non-Communist world and with Britain in particular. The Geneva Conference had obviously done a great deal to encourage this change by showing that the Chinese Government could get results by joining in negotiations and frank discussions with the governments of non-Communist powers and it seems to have been realized that France and the British Commonwealth did demonstrate a genuine desire for the peaceful settlement of disputes.

This change in attitude has made the general situation considerably more hopeful. The Chinese authorities are now at last willing to allow contacts and discussions with people able to explain the non-Communist point of view, which is the essential first step to better mutual understanding and peaceful co-existence. It is still suggested by some people that this change has been simply a tactical manoeuvre to split the Anglo-American alliance, but this hypothesis is hard to reconcile with the experience of the Labour Party delegates. Our contacts seemed to show very clearly the existence of a desire on the Chinese side for better and more friendly relations which was, at least subjectively, completely sincere and which could produce a great improvement in the international situation, if it is allowed to express itself in the necessary practical implications. The uncertainty about future developments lies in this conditional clause.

The evidence obtained during the visit seemed to confirm one of the main arguments of this book—that the Chinese Communists operate to a large extent in terms of the world as it should be according to their theories and not in terms of the empirically real world. There was considerable confirmation for the view suggested in Chapter III that the Chinese involvement in the Korean war was mainly the result of ignorance and confusion about the outside world. There seemed to be a universal conviction that United States forces would have invaded Manchuria if Chinese armies had not gone into Korea.

Mr. Attlee in a press conference at Hongkong referred to the "many delusions about the West" which were prevalent in China (*South China Morning Post*, 3 September, 1954). And the alarming feature of Chinese opinion was the extent to which intelligent and well-educated Chinese citizens held with firm conviction beliefs about the outside world so fantastic that they could only be called delusions. These delusions were the natural result of the information which has been available to the Chinese people during the past five years. Foreign opinion and foreign conditions had been reported in China almost exclusively from the Communist press or from non-Communist papers only when they happen to express agreement with some point in the general Communist position. It seemed that many of the previous foreign visitors to China had done a grave disservice to the cause of peace by reporting only what the Chinese authorities wanted to hear and thereby encouraging this belief in delusions. And increased contacts between China and the non-Communist world can only improve the international situation if they are allowed to produce mutual understanding.

This confusion about the outside world makes it uncertain how far the subjectively sincere Chinese desire for better relations will produce an actual improvement. People were inclined to believe that nothing more than nice-sounding expressions of goodwill and good intentions was required to improve relations with the West. There was little realization that the record of Chinese action had produced deep-seated suspicions which would take time and effort to remove and there was a reluctance to translate expressions of good intentions into practical action. For example, at the end of August, British firms in Shanghai complained that Chinese promises made at Geneva had still not been carried out by the local authorities and, while there had been an improvement over the completely unreasonable obstruction of exit permits, there had still been no change in the basic policy of holding British managers as hostages for the payment of demands on their firms, demands which in many cases still indicated a general policy of forcing British business into bankruptcy.

Chinese representatives would declare that the Communist

Party did not claim to be infallible and was ready to admit its mistakes. But in fact there was an almost complete unwillingness to admit any actual mistakes, for example in the handling of relations with Britain in 1950. One might have expected that the record of the Liu Ning-i "friendship delegation" (discussed in Chapter II) would at least have been allowed to remain in decent oblivion. On the contrary, the Labour Party delegates were presented with copies of *People's China* (Number 16, 1954), containing an article which cited the Liu Ning-i delegation as an instance of Chinese Communist policy which had consistently tried to promote Sino-British friendship, although the Labour Party had lodged a protest over the affair through the British Chargé d'Affaires and though several of the delegates had been present when Liu Ning-i made his insulting speech to the Labour Party executive.

All this means that, while the situation is considerably more hopeful than it was at the beginning of 1954, there are still serious difficulties to be overcome in order to produce a situation in which peaceful co-existence would be secure. A rational Western policy towards China will have to keep a very careful balance between two requirements. On the one hand it will need to show itself responsive to the Chinese desire for an improvement in relations. It is essential that the new Chinese desire for more friendly relations should not be discouraged. It must be clearly demonstrated that the Western powers would welcome genuine peaceful co-existence and would much prefer to have friendly rather than hostile relations with China. On the other hand, it must be made clear that peaceful co-existence can only be based on practical actions and not on mere words and that Chinese policy cannot act effectively to secure friendship and peaceful co-existence so long as it continues to maintain "doublethink" positions and to operate in terms of delusions about the outside world.

As a response to this problem present American policy is quite irrational. By continual demonstrations of hostility, by continued blocking of legitimate Chinese aspirations, such as the U.N. seat, and by continued support for pin-pricking military attacks from Formosa, American policy directly helps to maintain the atmosphere in which hysteria and delusions flourish. In so far as the embargo restricts exports to China more than exports to the Communist countries of Europe, its only effect is to increase Chinese economic dependence on the Soviet Union.

275

A rational policy would need considerable skill and, as suggested in earlier chapters, it might demand some modification of diplomatic conventionality. But, as I also suggested above, this is no reason for not trying it.

Internal conditions appeared to be better than I had judged from the evidence available outside China. There was very clear confirmation of the hypothesis that the Chinese Communist Party was doing an extremely good job in all the technical fields in which Marx-Leninist theory was irrelevant: public health, building construction, transportation, food distribution and so on. And the interference of Marx-Leninist faith with functionally rational action to benefit the Chinese people seemed to be less than I had judged from outside evidence. While talking about their determination to follow the Soviet Union the Chinese Communist leadership seems in practice to act with a great deal more intelligence and common sense.

Judged by the standards suggested in Chapter VI the system would be classified as undemocratic. Only the fourth condition is fulfilled to a considerable extent and a point on which Chinese Communism seems clearly superior to European Communism is that people connected with the former ruling classes are not made into outcasts but can obtain a satisfactory social position, provided that they fully accept the new system. The sample of Chinese opinion with which we had contact was not fully representative but it was wide enough to justify the generalization that very large sections of the Chinese population are strong supporters of the new regime even though, by Western standards, it is not democratic. After more than a generation of continued civil war and confusion the new regime has brought order, stability and security and its accomplishments have stimulated Chinese national pride. It seems quite likely that China would be an exception to the proposition that no orthodox Communist government could survive a free election.

It was clear that conditions in 1952 had been much worse than at present and that there had been a violent epidemic of Communist style McCarthy-itis. Though this had become much less virulent it was only after securing the universal acceptance of orthodox views; and a depressing feature of Chinese intellectual life was the complete absence of independent or critical thought, at least in the field of social science. I made inquiries both among university teachers and also among people in the Party as to whether there was any publication in China which would give articles on economic or social problems above the purely propaganda level and there was general agreement that no such material was now being produced in China. In the long run this destruction of independent thought may have serious social consequences but, at present, few Chinese intellectuals showed any signs of resenting it.

It is possible to suggest a number of developments which may produce serious difficulties in the future. A point at which Communist orthodoxy came into clear conflict with rational long term planning was the complete refusal to admit the possibility of a population problem. It also seemed fairly clear that the good features of the system depended on the altruism of most of the present leadership and the absence of democracy made it uncertain whether this would continue into the next generation. But these are long term problems, and it seemed almost certain that any estimate of the next decade at least must allow for the continuance and growing strength of the present regime.

Hongkong,
8 September, 1954.

References

INTRODUCTION

1. Orwell, George, *Nineteen Eighty-four* (Secker & Warburg, London, 1950), p. 213.

CHAPTER 1

1. *Hearings on the Institute of Pacific Relations before the Senate Committee.* Part 7A, Appendix II, page 2339.

CHAPTER 2

1. *People's China,* 1 June, 1951.
2. Chiang Kai-shek, *China's Destiny* (Roy Publishers, New York, 1946).
3. "The Scientific Outlook in 1851 and 1951." *British Journal for the Philosophy of Science,* August, 1951.
4. Russell, Bertrand, *The Theory and Practice of Bolshevism* (Allen & Unwin, London, 1921), p. 136.
5. Liu Shao-ch'i, *Internationalism and Nationalism* (Foreign Languages Press, Peking), pp. 18-19.
6. Popper, K. R., *The Open Society and its Enemies* (Routledge, London, 1945).
7. Paul, Elliot, *The Last Time I Saw Paris* (Bantam Books, New York, 1945), p. 204.

CHAPTER 3

1. Riley, John W., and Schramm, Wilbur, *The Reds Take a City. The Communist Occupation of Seoul* (Rutgers University Press, 1951).
2. Stone, I. F., *Hidden History of the Korean War* (Turnstile Press, London, 1952).
3. *Documents and Materials on the Korean Armistice Negotiations,* 2 vols. Chinese People's Committee for World Peace, Peking, 1952.
4. For an American view, see "What we should learn from Panmunjom," by V. Asparturian in *The Reporter,* 19 January, 1954.
5. For other illustrations see Dean Acheson's speech at the U.N. on 24 October, 1952 (Department of State Publication No. 4771).
6. *Report of the International Scientific Commission* (Peking, 1952), p. 2.
7. *The New Yorker,* 13 June, 1953. Article by E. J. Kahn, Jr., on an interview with Sgt. W. H. Treffery, a disabled prisoner exchanged in April, 1953.

CHAPTER 4

1. Harvard University Press, 1951.
2. *People's China,* vol. iv., nos. 2 to 26, 1951.
3. Strong, Anna Louise, *Dawn Out of China* (People's Publishing Company, Bombay, 1948), chap. 3.
4. See review by the author in *Virginia Quarterly Review,* vol. 23, no. 3, Summer, 1947.
5. Falconer, Alun, *New China: Friend or Foe?* (Naldrett Press, London, 1950). p. 51.
6. Shanghai *Ta Kung Pao,* 29 Sept., 1952.
7. One of the clearest expressions of this viewpoint was an article by Ai Ssu-ch'i in *Hsueh-hsi,* 16 March, 1952.

8. Cf. Tientsin *Chin Pu Jih Pao*, 17 March, 1952; and Hongkong *Ta Kung Pao*, 22 April, 1952.
9. See article by Desmond Donelly, M.P., in *Fabian International Review*, Jan., 1953.

CHAPTER 5

1. Prawdin, Michael, *The Mongol Empire* (Allen & Unwin, London, 1940), p. 60.
2. Orwell, George, *Nineteen Eighty-four*, p. 264.
3. Liu Shao-ch'i, *On the Party* (Foreign Languages Press, Peking, 1950), p. 55.
4. *Ibid.*, p. 147.
5. Kinglake, A. W., *Eothen* (Blackie & Sons, London), p. 17.
6. Williams, S. Wells, *The Middle Kingdom* (Charles Scribner's Sons, New York, 1907), 2nd ed., i., 411.
7. Caudwell, Christopher, *Studies in a Dying Culture* (Bodley Head, London, 1938), p. 14.
8. Quoted in Hsu Yung-ying, *A Survey of the Shansi-Kansu-Ninghsia Border Region* (I.P.R., New York, 1945), i., 77.
9. *Annals of the American Academy of Political and Social Science* (Sept., 1951), p. 22.
10. "The Soviet Union—Appearance and Reality." *Borba*, 19 and 20 Nov., 1950.
11. Liu Shao-ch'i, *On the Party*, p. 174.
12. Leites, Nathan: "Stalin as an Intellectual," *World Politics* (October, 1953).
13. *Kokutai no Hongi.* Japan Department of Education. Translated J. O. Gauntlett, with introduction by R. K. Hall. (Harvard University Press, 1949).
14. See Gollancz, Hermann, *Dodi ve-Vechdi* (Oxford University Press, 1920), p. 14.
15. Dedijir, Vladimir, *Tito Speaks* (Weidenfeld & Nicholson, London, 1953), p. 331.

CHAPTER 6

1. Rostow, W. W., *The Dynamics of Soviet Society* (W. W. Norton & Co. Inc., New York, 1953), p. 173.
2. *Ibid.*, p. 133.
3. Lippa, E. M., *I was a Surgeon for the Chinese Reds* (Harrap, London, 1953).
4. Hume, David, *A Treatise of Human Nature*, Book I, Part I, sect. 4.
5. Ulam, A. B., *Titoism and the Cominform* (Harvard University Press, 1952), p. 230.
6. Jonathan Cape, London, 1953.
7. U.S. White Paper on China, p. 93.
8. English version in Compton, Boyd, *Mao's China* (University of Washington Press, Seattle, 1952), p. 68. Chinese version in *Selected Works of Mao Tse-tung* (Peking, 1953), iii. 823.
9. English version, p. 57; Chinese version, p. 811.
10. English version, p. 57; Chinese version, p. 821.
    English version in Mao Tse-tung, *On Coalition Government* (New China News Agency, Yenan, 1945), p. 147. Chinese version, p. 1120.

CHAPTER 7

1. Macmillan, London, and St. Martin's Press, Inc., New York, 1939.
2. Linebarger, P. A. M., *The China of Chiang Kai-shek* (World Peace Foundation, Boston, 1941), p. 174.
3. Cf. Dr. Stuart's dispatches given in Annexes 156 (d) and 161 of the U.S. White Paper.

CHAPTER 8

1. Bloch, Marc, *Strange Defeat* (Oxford University Press, 1949), p. 145.
2. Trevor-Roper, H. R., *Last Days of Hitler* (Macmillan, London 1950), p. 255. (Also Macmillan Company, New York.)
3. *Chung Kung Wen-t'i T'i-yao Mu-lu* (Important points on the Chinese Communist question). Chungking, 1944.
4. Heinemann, London, 1946.
5. Committee on Foreign Affairs, Sub-Committee No. 5: Report on the Strategy and Tactics of World Communism, supplement III (U.S. Government Printing Office, 1948).
6. de Jaegher, R. J., and Kuhn, I. E., *The Enemy Within* (Doubleday & Co., New York, 1952).
7. *Problems of History.* January, 1950. Quoted by Edward Crankshaw in *Russia by Daylight* (Michael Joseph, London, 1951), p. 105.
8. Perkins, Frances, *The Roosevelt I Knew* (Hammond, London, 1947), p. 11.

CHAPTER 9

1. See article by John Hersey in the *New Yorker* in the spring of 1946.
2. For an account of this episode, see article in *The Times*, 20 September, 1947.
3. Cf. North, Robert, *Moscow and Chinese Communists* (Stanford University Press, 1954), p. 228.
4. *White Paper*, p. 688.
5. Utley, Freda, *Last Chance in China* (Bobbs Merrill Co., New York, 1947), pp. 79, 81.
6. Hudson, G. F., "The Anglo-American Quarrel," *The Twentieth Century*, October, 1953.
7. Millis, Walter (editor), *The Forrestal Diaries* (Viking Press, New York, 1951), p. 316.
8. Stettinius, E. R., Jr., *Roosevelt and the Russians* (Cape, London, 1950), p. 110.
9. *Public Opinion Quarterly*, September, 1953.

CHAPTER 10

1. Towards the People's Congress. No. 4, 12 October, 1952.
2. *Appeal and Resolutions of the Extraordinary Session of the World Peace Council.* Berlin, 1 to 6 July, 1952. World Peace Council (no date or place of publication).
3. *Acts and Resolutions. The World Peace Movement.* Published by the World Peace Council (no date or place of publication), p. 55.
4. *Ibid.*, p. 38.
5. *Important Documents of the Peace Conference of the Asian and Pacific Regions*, 2 to 12 October, 1952 (Peking), p. 39.
6. Kennan, George F., *American Diplomacy, 1900-1950* (Secker & Warburg, London, 1952), p. 111.

CHAPTER 11

1. Görlitz, Walter, *The German General Staff* (Hollis & Carter, London, 1953), p. 236.
2. Chennault, C. L., *The Way of a Fighter* (Putnam, New York, 1949), p. 334.

CHAPTER 12

1. *On People's Democratic Dictatorship* (New China News Agency, Peking, 1949), p. 7.
2. *The Tribune*, Sydney, 10 and 24 March, 1954.
3. Görlitz, Walter, *The German General Staff*, p. 233.
4. Kogon, Eugen, *The Theory and Practice of Hell* (Secker & Warburg, London, 1950).
5. Herling, Gustav, *A World Apart* (Heinemann, London, 1951).

CHAPTER 13

1. Described in *Frustration*, by N. R. F. Maier (McGraw Hill, New York, 1949).
2. *An Inquiry Concerning the Principles of Morals*, sect. I.
3. Kennan, G. J., "America and the Russian Future," *Foreign Affairs*, April, 1951.
4. Wylie, Philip, "Panic, Psychology and the Bomb," *Bulletin of the Atomic Scientists*, vol. x, no. 2, February, 1954.
5. Fischer, Louis, *The Soviets in World Affairs* (Cape, London, 1930), ii. 741.
6. Webb, Sydney and Beatrice, *A Constitution for the Socialist Commonwealth of Great Britain* (Fabian Society, London, 1920).
7. Lange, O., "Marxian Economics and Modern Economic Theory," *Review of Economic Studies*, June, 1935.
8. Herling, Gustav, *A World Apart*, pp. 185-6, 46.
9. Wheeler-Bennett, J. W., *Munich. Prologue to Tragedy* (Macmillan, London, 1948), p. 219. (Also Duell, Sloan and Pearce, Inc., New York.)
10. Milosz, Czeslaw, *The Captive Mind* (Secker & Warburg, London, 1953), p. 55.
11. Trevor-Roper, H. R., *The Last Days of Hitler*, p. 23.
12. Wheeler-Bennett, J. W., *The Nemesis of Power* (Macmillan, London, 1953), pp. 359-62.
13. *Ibid.*, p. 342.
14. Strong, Anna Louise, *Dawn Out of China*, p. 18.
15. Mayo, Elton, *The Social Problems of an Industrial Civilisation* (Routledge & Kegan Paul, London, 1949), pp. 23-4.
16. For a discussion of some American examples see Granville Hicks, "The Great Reversal," *The New Leader*, 29 March, 1954.
17. Milosz, Czeslaw, *The Captive Mind*, p. 81.

CHAPTER 14

1. Chennault, C. L., *The Way of a Fighter*, chap. 5.
2. Thompson, Reginald, *Cry Korea* (Macdonald, London, 1951), p. 88.
3. See, for example, articles by General Van Fleet in *Life*, 11 and 18 May, 1953.
4. Velie, Lester, "America's Shabby Welcome to Visitors," *Reader's Digest*, February, 1954.
5. Cornford, F. M., *Microcosmographia Academica* (Bowes and Bowes, Cambridge, 1933), p. 30.
6. Orwell, George, Essay on "The Prevention of Literature" in *Shooting an Elephant* (Secker & Warburg, London, 1950), p. 117.

CHAPTER 15

1. *Public Opinion Quarterly*, September, 1953.
2. Wiener, Norbert, *The Human Use of Human Beings* (Houghton Mifflin, Boston, 1950).

APPENDIX

1. Milosz, Czeslaw, "Murti-Bing," *The Twentieth Century*, July, 1951.
2. Keynes, J. M., *A Treatise on Probability* (Macmillan, London, 1921), chap. xxii.
3. Popper, K. R., *The Open Society and Its Enemies*. ii. 217-220.
4. Reproduced in Joseph, H. W. B., *Introduction to Logic* (Oxford University Press, 1916), p. 571.
5. Maritain, Jacques, *The Range of Reason* (Bles, London, 1953), p. 13.
6. *Ibid.*, p. 103.
7. Orwell, George, "Reflections on Gandhi" in *Shooting an Elephant*, p. 106.

Index

DATE DUE

OCT 5 1955	JUL 14 1966
JAN 7 1957	FEB 24 1967
MAR 21 1957	OCT 13 1967
OCT 29 1957	
MAY 19 1959	
DEC 3 1959	
JAN 5 1961	
APR 24 1961	
MAY 8 1961	
JAN 25 1962	
MAY 3 1964	
MAR 26 1965	
MAY 14 1965	
JAN 28 1966	
MAY 6 1966	

TERRITORIAL CHANGES
·IN·
EUROPE
SINCE 1937

SCALE
0   200
MILES

NORWAY

SWEDEN

FINLAND

PORKALA

DENMARK

U.S.S.R.

EIRE

UNITED KINGDOM

NDS

60°N

40°

30°

20°

10°E

0°

10°W

20°

10°W